Python Machine Learning Coo

100 recipes that teach you how to perform various
machine learning tasks in the real world

Prateek Joshi

[PACKT] open source *
PUBLISHING   community experience distilled

BIRMINGHAM - MUMBAI

Python Machine Learning Cookbook

First published: June 2016

Production reference: 1160616

Published by Packt Publishing Ltd.
Livery Place
35 Livery Street
Birmingham B3 2PB, UK.

ISBN 978-1-78646-447-7

www.packtpub.com

Credits

Author
Prateek Joshi

Reviewer
Dr. Vahid Mirjalili

Commissioning Editor
Veena Pagare

Acquisition Editor
Tushar Gupta

Content Development Editor
Nikhil Borkar

Technical Editor
Hussain Kanchwala

Copy Editor
Priyanka Ravi

Project Coordinator
Suzanne Coutinho

Proofreader
Safis Editing

Indexer
Hemangini Bari

Graphics
Jason Monteiro

Production Coordinator
Manu Joseph

Cover Work
Manu Joseph

About the Author

Prateek Joshi is an Artificial Intelligence researcher and a published author. He has over eight years of experience in this field with a primary focus on content-based analysis and deep learning. He has written two books on Computer Vision and Machine Learning. His work in this field has resulted in multiple patents, tech demos, and research papers at major IEEE conferences.

People from all over the world visit his blog, and he has received more than a million page views from over 200 countries. He has been featured as a guest author in prominent tech magazines. He enjoys blogging about topics, such as Artificial Intelligence, Python programming, abstract mathematics, and cryptography. You can visit his blog at www.prateekvjoshi.com.

He has won many hackathons utilizing a wide variety of technologies. He is an avid coder who is passionate about building game-changing products. He graduated from University of Southern California, and he has worked at companies such as Nvidia, Microsoft Research, Qualcomm, and a couple of early stage start-ups in Silicon Valley. You can learn more about him on his personal website at www.prateekj.com.

I would like to thank the reviewers of this book for their valuable comments and suggestions. I would also like to thank the wonderful team at Packt Publishing for publishing the book and helping me all along. Finally, I would like to thank my family for supporting me through everything.

About the Reviewer

Dr. Vahid Mirjalili is a software engineer and data scientist with a diverse background in engineering, mathematics, and computer science. Currently, he is working toward his graduate degree in Computer Science at Michigan State University. He teaches Python programming as well as computing concepts and the fundamentals of data analysis with Excel and databases using Microsoft Access. With his specialty in data mining, he is keenly interested in predictive modeling and getting insights from data. He is also a Python developer, and he likes to contribute to the open source community. Furthermore, he is also focused in making tutorials for different directions of data science and computer algorithms, which you can find at his GitHub repository, `http://github.com/mirjalil/DataScience`.

www.PacktPub.com

eBooks, discount offers, and more

Did you know that Packt offers eBook versions of every book published, with PDF and ePub files available? You can upgrade to the eBook version at www.PacktPub.com and as a print book customer, you are entitled to a discount on the eBook copy. Get in touch with us at customercare@packtpub.com for more details.

At www.PacktPub.com, you can also read a collection of free technical articles, sign up for a range of free newsletters and receive exclusive discounts and offers on Packt books and eBooks.

https://www2.packtpub.com/books/subscription/packtlib

Do you need instant solutions to your IT questions? PacktLib is Packt's online digital book library. Here, you can search, access, and read Packt's entire library of books.

Why Subscribe?

- ► Fully searchable across every book published by Packt
- ► Copy and paste, print, and bookmark content
- ► On demand and accessible via a web browser

Table of Contents

Preface   **v**

Chapter 1: The Realm of Supervised Learning   **1**

Introduction   1
Preprocessing data using different techniques   2
Label encoding   5
Building a linear regressor   7
Computing regression accuracy   11
Achieving model persistence   12
Building a ridge regressor   13
Building a polynomial regressor   15
Estimating housing prices   17
Computing the relative importance of features   20
Estimating bicycle demand distribution   22

Chapter 2: Constructing a Classifier   **27**

Introduction   27
Building a simple classifier   28
Building a logistic regression classifier   30
Building a Naive Bayes classifier   35
Splitting the dataset for training and testing   36
Evaluating the accuracy using cross-validation   38
Visualizing the confusion matrix   40
Extracting the performance report   42
Evaluating cars based on their characteristics   43
Extracting validation curves   46
Extracting learning curves   50
Estimating the income bracket   52

Chapter 3: Predictive Modeling — 55

Introduction	55
Building a linear classifier using Support Vector Machine (SVMs)	56
Building a nonlinear classifier using SVMs	61
Tackling class imbalance	64
Extracting confidence measurements	67
Finding optimal hyperparameters	69
Building an event predictor	71
Estimating traffic	74

Chapter 4: Clustering with Unsupervised Learning — 77

Introduction	77
Clustering data using the k-means algorithm	78
Compressing an image using vector quantization	81
Building a Mean Shift clustering model	85
Grouping data using agglomerative clustering	88
Evaluating the performance of clustering algorithms	91
Automatically estimating the number of clusters using DBSCAN algorithm	95
Finding patterns in stock market data	99
Building a customer segmentation model	102

Chapter 5: Building Recommendation Engines — 105

Introduction	106
Building function compositions for data processing	106
Building machine learning pipelines	108
Finding the nearest neighbors	110
Constructing a k-nearest neighbors classifier	113
Constructing a k-nearest neighbors regressor	119
Computing the Euclidean distance score	122
Computing the Pearson correlation score	123
Finding similar users in the dataset	125
Generating movie recommendations	127

Chapter 6: Analyzing Text Data — 131

Introduction	131
Preprocessing data using tokenization	132
Stemming text data	134
Converting text to its base form using lemmatization	135
Dividing text using chunking	137
Building a bag-of-words model	138
Building a text classifier	141
Identifying the gender	144

Analyzing the sentiment of a sentence	146
Identifying patterns in text using topic modeling	150

Chapter 7: Speech Recognition — 155

Introduction	155
Reading and plotting audio data	156
Transforming audio signals into the frequency domain	158
Generating audio signals with custom parameters	160
Synthesizing music	162
Extracting frequency domain features	164
Building Hidden Markov Models	167
Building a speech recognizer	168

Chapter 8: Dissecting Time Series and Sequential Data — 173

Introduction	173
Transforming data into the time series format	174
Slicing time series data	176
Operating on time series data	179
Extracting statistics from time series data	182
Building Hidden Markov Models for sequential data	185
Building Conditional Random Fields for sequential text data	189
Analyzing stock market data using Hidden Markov Models	192

Chapter 9: Image Content Analysis — 195

Introduction	195
Operating on images using OpenCV-Python	196
Detecting edges	200
Histogram equalization	204
Detecting corners	206
Detecting SIFT feature points	208
Building a Star feature detector	210
Creating features using visual codebook and vector quantization	211
Training an image classifier using Extremely Random Forests	214
Building an object recognizer	217

Chapter 10: Biometric Face Recognition — 219

Introduction	219
Capturing and processing video from a webcam	220
Building a face detector using Haar cascades	221
Building eye and nose detectors	224
Performing Principal Components Analysis	227
Performing Kernel Principal Components Analysis	228
Performing blind source separation	232
Building a face recognizer using Local Binary Patterns Histogram	236

Chapter 11: Deep Neural Networks — 243

Introduction — 243
Building a perceptron — 244
Building a single layer neural network — 247
Building a deep neural network — 250
Creating a vector quantizer — 254
Building a recurrent neural network for sequential data analysis — 256
Visualizing the characters in an optical character recognition database — 260
Building an optical character recognizer using neural networks — 262

Chapter 12: Visualizing Data — 265

Introduction — 265
Plotting 3D scatter plots — 266
Plotting bubble plots — 267
Animating bubble plots — 269
Drawing pie charts — 271
Plotting date-formatted time series data — 273
Plotting histograms — 275
Visualizing heat maps — 277
Animating dynamic signals — 278

Index — 281

Preface

Machine learning is becoming increasingly pervasive in the modern data-driven world. It is used extensively across many fields, such as search engines, robotics, self-driving cars, and so on. In this book, you will explore various real-life scenarios where you can use machine learning. You will understand what algorithms you should use in a given context using this exciting recipe-based guide.

This book starts by talking about various realms in machine learning followed by practical examples. We then move on to discuss more complex algorithms, such as Support Vector Machines, Extremely Random Forests, Hidden Markov Models, Conditional Random Fields, Deep Neural Networks, and so on. This book is for Python programmers looking to use machine learning algorithms to create real-world applications. This book is friendly to Python beginners but familiarity with Python programming will certainly be helpful to play around with the code. It is also useful to experienced Python programmers who are looking to implement machine learning techniques.

You will learn how to make informed decisions about the types of algorithm that you need to use and how to implement these algorithms to get the best possible results. If you get stuck while making sense of images, text, speech, or some other form of data, this guide on applying machine learning techniques to each of these will definitely come to your rescue!

What this book covers

Chapter 1, The Realm of Supervised Learning, covers various supervised-learning techniques for regression. We will learn how to analyze bike-sharing patterns and predict housing prices.

Chapter 2, Constructing a Classifier, covers various supervised-learning techniques for data classification. We will learn how to estimate the income brackets and evaluate a car based on its characteristics.

Chapter 3, Predictive Modeling, discusses predictive-modeling techniques using Support Vector Machines. We will learn how to apply these techniques to predict events occurring in buildings and traffic on the roads near sports stadiums.

Chapter 4, *Clustering with Unsupervised Learning*, explains unsupervised learning algorithms, including k-means and Mean Shift clustering. We will learn how to apply these algorithms to stock market data and customer segmentation.

Chapter 5, *Building Recommendation Engines*, teaches you about the algorithms that we use to build recommendation engines. We will learn how to apply these algorithms to collaborative filtering and movie recommendations.

Chapter 6, *Analyzing Text Data*, explains the techniques that we use to analyze text data, including tokenization, stemming, bag-of-words, and so on. We will learn how to use these techniques to perform sentiment analysis and topic modeling.

Chapter 7, *Speech Recognition*, covers the algorithms that we use to analyze speech data. We will learn how to build speech-recognition systems.

Chapter 8, *Dissecting Time Series and Sequential Data*, explains the techniques that we use to analyze time series and sequential data including Hidden Markov Models and Conditional Random Fields. We will learn how to apply these techniques to text sequence analysis and stock market predictions.

Chapter 9, *Image Content Analysis*, covers the algorithms that we use for image content analysis and object recognition. We will learn how to extract image features and build object-recognition systems.

Chapter 10, *Biometric Face Recognition*, explains the techniques that we use to detect and recognize faces in images and videos. We will learn about dimensionality reduction algorithms and build a face recognizer.

Chapter 11, *Deep Neural Networks*, covers the algorithms that we use to build deep neural networks. We will learn how to build an optical character recognition system using neural networks.

Chapter 12, *Visualizing Data*, explains the techniques that we use to visualize various types of data in machine learning. We will learn how to construct different types of graphs, charts, and plots.

What you need for this book

There is a lot of debate going on between Python 2.x and Python 3.x. While we believe that the world is moving forward with better versions coming out, a lot of developers still enjoy using Python 2.x. A lot of operating systems have Python 2.x built into them. This book is focused on machine learning in Python as opposed to Python itself. It also helps in maintaining compatibility with libraries that haven't been ported to Python 3.x. Hence the code in the book is oriented towards Python 2.x. In that spirit, we have tried to keep all the code as agnostic as possible to the Python versions. We feel that this will enable our readers to easily understand the code and readily use it in different scenarios.

Who this book is for

This book is for Python programmers who are looking to use machine learning algorithms to create real-world applications. This book is friendly to Python beginners, but familiarity with Python programming will certainly be useful to play around with the code.

Sections

In this book, you will find several headings that appear frequently (Getting ready, How to do it, How it works, There's more, and See also).

To give clear instructions on how to complete a recipe, we use these sections as follows:

Getting ready

This section tells you what to expect in the recipe, and describes how to set up any software or any preliminary settings required for the recipe.

How to do it...

This section contains the steps required to follow the recipe.

How it works...

This section usually consists of a detailed explanation of what happened in the previous section.

There's more...

This section consists of additional information about the recipe in order to make the reader more knowledgeable about the recipe.

See also

This section provides helpful links to other useful information for the recipe.

Conventions

In this book, you will find a number of text styles that distinguish between different kinds of information. Here are some examples of these styles and an explanation of their meaning.

Code words in text, database table names, folder names, filenames, file extensions, pathnames, dummy URLs, user input, and Twitter handles are shown as follows: "Here, we allocated 25% of the data for testing, as specified by the `test_size` parameter."

A block of code is set as follows:

```
import numpy as np
import matplotlib.pyplot as plt

import utilities

# Load input data
input_file = 'data_multivar.txt'
X, y = utilities.load_data(input_file)
```

Any command-line input or output is written as follows:

```
$ python object_recognizer.py --input-image imagefile.jpg --model-file
erf.pkl --codebook-file codebook.pkl
```

New terms and **important words** are shown in bold. Words that you see on the screen, for example, in menus or dialog boxes, appear in the text like this: "If you change the explode array to (0, 0.2, 0, 0, 0), then it will highlight the **Strawberry** section."

 Warnings or important notes appear in a box like this.

 Tips and tricks appear like this.

Reader feedback

Feedback from our readers is always welcome. Let us know what you think about this book—what you liked or disliked. Reader feedback is important for us as it helps us develop titles that you will really get the most out of.

To send us general feedback, simply e-mail `feedback@packtpub.com`, and mention the book's title in the subject of your message.

If there is a topic that you have expertise in and you are interested in either writing or contributing to a book, see our author guide at `www.packtpub.com/authors`.

Customer support

Now that you are the proud owner of a Packt book, we have a number of things to help you to get the most from your purchase.

Downloading the example code

You can download the example code files for this book from your account at `http://www.packtpub.com`. If you purchased this book elsewhere, you can visit `http://www.packtpub.com/support` and register to have the files e-mailed directly to you.

You can download the code files by following these steps:

1. Log in or register to our website using your e-mail address and password.
2. Hover the mouse pointer on the **SUPPORT** tab at the top.
3. Click on **Code Downloads & Errata**.
4. Enter the name of the book in the **Search** box.
5. Select the book for which you're looking to download the code files.
6. Choose from the drop-down menu where you purchased this book from.
7. Click on **Code Download**.

You can also download the code files by clicking on the **Code Files** button on the book's webpage at the Packt Publishing website. This page can be accessed by entering the book's name in the **Search** box. Please note that you need to be logged in to your Packt account.

Once the file is downloaded, please make sure that you unzip or extract the folder using the latest version of:

- WinRAR / 7-Zip for Windows
- Zipeg / iZip / UnRarX for Mac
- 7-Zip / PeaZip for Linux

The code bundle for the book is also hosted on GitHub at `https://github.com/PacktPublishing/Python-Machine-Learning-Cookbook`. We also have other code bundles from our rich catalog of books and videos available at `https://github.com/PacktPublishing/`. Check them out!

Downloading the color images of this book

We also provide you with a PDF file that has color images of the screenshots/diagrams used in this book. The color images will help you better understand the changes in the output. You can download this file from `https://www.packtpub.com/sites/default/files/downloads/PythonMachineLearningCookbook_ColorImages.pdf`.

Errata

Although we have taken every care to ensure the accuracy of our content, mistakes do happen. If you find a mistake in one of our books—maybe a mistake in the text or the code—we would be grateful if you could report this to us. By doing so, you can save other readers from frustration and help us improve subsequent versions of this book. If you find any errata, please report them by visiting `http://www.packtpub.com/submit-errata`, selecting your book, clicking on the **Errata Submission Form** link, and entering the details of your errata. Once your errata are verified, your submission will be accepted and the errata will be uploaded to our website or added to any list of existing errata under the Errata section of that title.

To view the previously submitted errata, go to `https://www.packtpub.com/books/content/support` and enter the name of the book in the search field. The required information will appear under the **Errata** section.

Piracy

Piracy of copyrighted material on the Internet is an ongoing problem across all media. At Packt, we take the protection of our copyright and licenses very seriously. If you come across any illegal copies of our works in any form on the Internet, please provide us with the location address or website name immediately so that we can pursue a remedy.

Please contact us at `copyright@packtpub.com` with a link to the suspected pirated material.

We appreciate your help in protecting our authors and our ability to bring you valuable content.

Questions

If you have a problem with any aspect of this book, you can contact us at `questions@packtpub.com`, and we will do our best to address the problem.

1
The Realm of Supervised Learning

In this chapter, we will cover the following recipes:

- ▶ Preprocessing data using different techniques
- ▶ Label encoding
- ▶ Building a linear regressor
- ▶ Computing regression accuracy
- ▶ Achieving model persistence
- ▶ Building a ridge regressor
- ▶ Building a polynomial regressor
- ▶ Estimating housing prices
- ▶ Computing the relative importance of features
- ▶ Estimating bicycle demand distribution

Introduction

If you are familiar with the basics of machine learning, you will certainly know what supervised learning is all about. To give you a quick refresher, supervised learning refers to building a machine learning model that is based on labeled samples. For example, if we build a system to estimate the price of a house based on various parameters, such as size, locality, and so on, we first need to create a database and label it. We need to tell our algorithm what parameters correspond to what prices. Based on this data, our algorithm will learn how to calculate the price of a house using the input parameters.

Unsupervised learning is the opposite of what we just discussed. There is no labeled data available here. Let's assume that we have a bunch of datapoints, and we just want to separate them into multiple groups. We don't exactly know what the criteria of separation would be. So, an unsupervised learning algorithm will try to separate the given dataset into a fixed number of groups in the best possible way. We will discuss unsupervised learning in the upcoming chapters.

We will use various Python packages, such as **NumPy**, **SciPy**, **scikit-learn**, and **matplotlib**, during the course of this book to build various things. If you use Windows, it is recommended that you use a SciPy-stack compatible version of Python. You can check the list of compatible versions at `http://www.scipy.org/install.html`. These distributions come with all the necessary packages already installed. If you use Mac OS X or Ubuntu, installing these packages is fairly straightforward. Here are some useful links for installation and documentation:

- **NumPy**: `http://docs.scipy.org/doc/numpy-1.10.1/user/install.html`
- **SciPy**: `http://www.scipy.org/install.html`
- **scikit-learn**: `http://scikit-learn.org/stable/install.html`
- **matplotlib**: `http://matplotlib.org/1.4.2/users/installing.html`

Make sure that you have these packages installed on your machine before you proceed.

Preprocessing data using different techniques

In the real world, we usually have to deal with a lot of raw data. This raw data is not readily ingestible by machine learning algorithms. To prepare the data for machine learning, we have to preprocess it before we feed it into various algorithms.

Getting ready

Let's see how to preprocess data in Python. To start off, open a file with a `.py` extension, for example, `preprocessor.py`, in your favorite text editor. Add the following lines to this file:

```
import numpy as np
from sklearn import preprocessing
```

We just imported a couple of necessary packages. Let's create some sample data. Add the following line to this file:

```
data = np.array([[3, -1.5,  2, -5.4], [0,  4,  -0.3, 2.1], [1,  3.3,
-1.9, -4.3]])
```

We are now ready to operate on this data.

How to do it...

Data can be preprocessed in many ways. We will discuss a few of the most commonly-used preprocessing techniques.

Mean removal

It's usually beneficial to remove the mean from each feature so that it's centered on zero. This helps us in removing any bias from the features. Add the following lines to the file that we opened earlier:

```
data_standardized = preprocessing.scale(data)
print "\nMean =", data_standardized.mean(axis=0)
print "Std deviation =", data_standardized.std(axis=0)
```

We are now ready to run the code. To do this, run the following command on your Terminal:

```
$ python preprocessor.py
```

You will see the following output on your Terminal:

```
Mean = [  5.55111512e-17  -1.11022302e-16  -7.40148683e-17  -7.40148683e-17]
Std deviation = [ 1.  1.  1.  1.]
```

You can see that the mean is almost 0 and the standard deviation is 1.

Scaling

The values of each feature in a datapoint can vary between random values. So, sometimes it is important to scale them so that this becomes a level playing field. Add the following lines to the file and run the code:

```
data_scaler = preprocessing.MinMaxScaler(feature_range=(0, 1))
data_scaled = data_scaler.fit_transform(data)
print "\nMin max scaled data =", data_scaled
```

After scaling, all the feature values range between the specified values. The output will be displayed, as follows:

```
Min max scaled data:
[[ 1.          0.          1.          0.        ]
 [ 0.          1.          0.41025641  1.        ]
 [ 0.33333333  0.87272727  0.          0.14666667]]
```

Normalization

Data normalization is used when you want to adjust the values in the feature vector so that they can be measured on a common scale. One of the most common forms of normalization that is used in machine learning adjusts the values of a feature vector so that they sum up to 1. Add the following lines to the previous file:

```
data_normalized = preprocessing.normalize(data, norm='l1')
print "\nL1 normalized data =", data_normalized
```

If you run the Python file, you will get the following output:

```
L1 normalized data:
[[ 0.25210084 -0.12605042  0.16806723 -0.45378151]
 [ 0.          0.625      -0.046875    0.328125  ]
 [ 0.0952381   0.31428571 -0.18095238 -0.40952381]]
```

This is used a lot to make sure that datapoints don't get boosted artificially due to the fundamental nature of their features.

Binarization

Binarization is used when you want to convert your numerical feature vector into a Boolean vector. Add the following lines to the Python file:

```
data_binarized = preprocessing.Binarizer(threshold=1.4).
transform(data)
print "\nBinarized data =", data_binarized
```

Run the code again, and you will see the following output:

```
Binarized data:
[[ 1.  0.  1.  0.]
 [ 0.  1.  0.  1.]
 [ 0.  1.  0.  0.]]
```

This is a very useful technique that's usually used when we have some prior knowledge of the data.

One Hot Encoding

A lot of times, we deal with numerical values that are sparse and scattered all over the place. We don't really need to store these big values. This is where One Hot Encoding comes into picture. We can think of One Hot Encoding as a tool to *tighten* the feature vector. It looks at each feature and identifies the total number of distinct values. It uses a *one-of-k* scheme to encode the values. Each feature in the feature vector is encoded based on this. This helps us be more efficient in terms of space. For example, let's say we are dealing with 4-dimensional feature vectors. To encode the *n*-th feature in a feature vector, the encoder will go through the *n*-th feature in each feature vector and count the number of distinct values. If the number of distinct values is *k*, it will transform the feature into a *k*-dimensional vector where only one value is *1* and all other values are *0*. Add the following lines to the Python file:

```
encoder = preprocessing.OneHotEncoder()
encoder.fit([[0, 2, 1, 12], [1, 3, 5, 3], [2, 3, 2, 12], [1, 2, 4,
3]])
encoded_vector = encoder.transform([[2, 3, 5, 3]]).toarray()
print "\nEncoded vector =", encoded_vector
```

This is the expected output:

```
Encoded vector:
[[ 0.   0.   1.   0.   1.   0.   0.   0.   1.   1.   0.]]
```

In the above example, let's consider the third feature in each feature vector. The values are 1, 5, 2, and 4. There are four distinct values here, which means the one-hot encoded vector will be of length 4. If you want to encode the value 5, it will be a vector [0, 1, 0, 0]. Only one value can be *1* in this vector. The second element is 1, which indicates that the value is 5.

Label encoding

In supervised learning, we usually deal with a variety of labels. These can be in the form of numbers or words. If they are numbers, then the algorithm can use them directly. However, a lot of times, labels need to be in human readable form. So, people usually label the training data with words. Label encoding refers to transforming the word labels into numerical form so that the algorithms can understand how to operate on them. Let's take a look at how to do this.

How to do it...

1. Create a new Python file, and import the preprocessing package:

```
from sklearn import preprocessing
```

2. This package contains various functions that are needed for data preprocessing. Let's define the label encoder, as follows:

```
label_encoder = preprocessing.LabelEncoder()
```

3. The `label_encoder` object knows how to understand word labels. Let's create some labels:

```
input_classes = ['audi', 'ford', 'audi', 'toyota', 'ford', 'bmw']
```

4. We are now ready to encode these labels:

```
label_encoder.fit(input_classes)
print "\nClass mapping:"
for i, item in enumerate(label_encoder.classes_):
    print item, '-->', i
```

5. Run the code, and you will see the following output on your Terminal:

```
Class mapping:
audi --> 0
bmw --> 1
ford --> 2
toyota --> 3
```

6. As shown in the preceding output, the words have been transformed into 0-indexed numbers. Now, when you encounter a set of labels, you can simply transform them, as follows:

```
labels = ['toyota', 'ford', 'audi']
encoded_labels = label_encoder.transform(labels)
print "\nLabels =", labels
print "Encoded labels =", list(encoded_labels)
```

Here is the output that you'll see on your Terminal:

```
Labels = ['toyota', 'ford', 'audi']
Encoded labels = [3, 2, 0]
```

7. This is way easier than manually maintaining mapping between words and numbers. You can check the correctness by transforming numbers back to word labels:

```
encoded_labels = [2, 1, 0, 3, 1]
decoded_labels = label_encoder.inverse_transform(encoded_labels)
print "\nEncoded labels =", encoded_labels
print "Decoded labels =", list(decoded_labels)
```

Here is the output:

```
Encoded labels = [2, 1, 0, 3, 1]
Decoded labels = ['ford', 'bmw', 'audi', 'toyota', 'bmw']
```

As you can see, the mapping is preserved perfectly.

Building a linear regressor

Regression is the process of estimating the relationship between input data and the continuous-valued output data. This data is usually in the form of real numbers, and our goal is to estimate the underlying function that governs the mapping from the input to the output. Let's start with a very simple example. Consider the following mapping between input and output:

1 --> 2

3 --> 6

4.3 --> 8.6

7.1 --> 14.2

If I ask you to estimate the relationship between the inputs and the outputs, you can easily do this by analyzing the pattern. We can see that the output is twice the input value in each case, so the transformation would be as follows:

$f(x) = 2x$

This is a simple function, relating the input values with the output values. However, in the real world, this is usually not the case. Functions in the real world are not so straightforward!

Getting ready

Linear regression refers to estimating the underlying function using a linear combination of input variables. The preceding example was an example that consisted of one input variable and one output variable.

Consider the following figure:

The goal of linear regression is to extract the underlying linear model that relates the input variable to the output variable. This aims to minimize the sum of squares of differences between the actual output and the predicted output using a linear function. This method is called **Ordinary least squares**.

You might say that there might be a curvy line out there that fits these points better, but linear regression doesn't allow this. The main advantage of linear regression is that it's not complex. If you go into nonlinear regression, you may get more accurate models, but they will be slower. As shown in the preceding figure, the model tries to approximate the input datapoints using a straight line. Let's see how to build a linear regression model in Python.

How to do it...

You have been provided with a data file, called `data_singlevar.txt`. This contains comma-separated lines where the first element is the input value and the second element is the output value that corresponds to this input value. You should use this as the input argument:

1. Create a file called `regressor.py`, and add the following lines:

```
import sys
import numpy as np
filename = sys.argv[1]
X = []
y = []
with open(filename, 'r') as f:
    for line in f.readlines():
```

```
xt, yt = [float(i) for i in line.split(',')]
X.append(xt)
y.append(yt)
```

We just loaded the input data into x and y, where x refers to data and y refers to labels. Inside the loop in the preceding code, we parse each line and split it based on the comma operator. We then convert it into floating point values and save it in X and y, respectively.

2. When we build a machine learning model, we need a way to validate our model and check whether the model is performing at a satisfactory level. To do this, we need to separate our data into two groups: a training dataset and a testing dataset. The training dataset will be used to build the model, and the testing dataset will be used to see how this trained model performs on unknown data. So, let's go ahead and split this data into training and testing datasets:

```
num_training = int(0.8 * len(X))
num_test = len(X) - num_training

# Training data
X_train = np.array(X[:num_training]).reshape((num_training,1))
y_train = np.array(y[:num_training])

# Test data
X_test = np.array(X[num_training:]).reshape((num_test,1))
y_test = np.array(y[num_training:])
```

Here, we will use 80% of the data for the training dataset and the remaining 20% for the testing dataset.

3. We are now ready to train the model. Let's create a regressor object, as follows:

```
from sklearn import linear_model

# Create linear regression object
linear_regressor = linear_model.LinearRegression()

# Train the model using the training sets
linear_regressor.fit(X_train, y_train)
```

4. We just trained the linear regressor, based on our training data. The fit method takes the input data and trains the model. Let's see how it fits:

```
import matplotlib.pyplot as plt

y_train_pred = linear_regressor.predict(X_train)
plt.figure()
plt.scatter(X_train, y_train, color='green')
```

```
plt.plot(X_train, y_train_pred, color='black', linewidth=4)
plt.title('Training data')
plt.show()
```

5. We are now ready to run the code using the following command:

    ```
    $ python regressor.py data_singlevar.txt
    ```

    You should see the following figure:

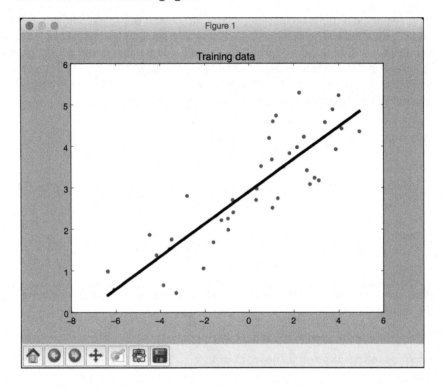

6. In the preceding code, we used the trained model to predict the output for our training data. This wouldn't tell us how the model performs on unknown data because we are running it on training data itself. This just gives us an idea of how the model fits on training data. Looks like it's doing okay as you can see in the preceding figure!

7. Let's predict the test dataset output based on this model and plot it, as follows:

    ```
    y_test_pred = linear_regressor.predict(X_test)

    plt.scatter(X_test, y_test, color='green')
    plt.plot(X_test, y_test_pred, color='black', linewidth=4)
    plt.title('Test data')
    plt.show()
    ```

If you run this code, you will see a graph like the following one:

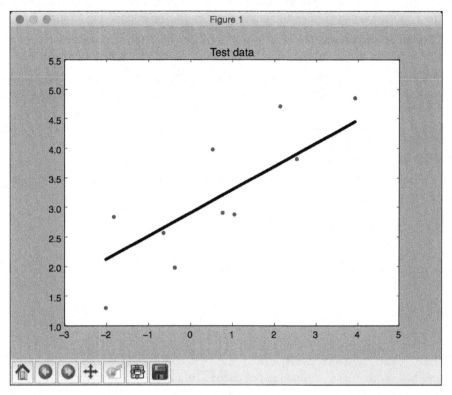

Computing regression accuracy

Now that we know how to build a regressor, it's important to understand how to evaluate the quality of a regressor as well. In this context, an error is defined as the difference between the actual value and the value that is predicted by the regressor.

Getting ready

Let's quickly understand what metrics can be used to measure the quality of a regressor. A regressor can be evaluated using many different metrics, such as the following:

▶ **Mean absolute error**: This is the average of absolute errors of all the datapoints in the given dataset.

▶ **Mean squared error**: This is the average of the squares of the errors of all the datapoints in the given dataset. It is one of the most popular metrics out there!

- ▸ **Median absolute error**: This is the median of all the errors in the given dataset. The main advantage of this metric is that it's robust to outliers. A single bad point in the test dataset wouldn't skew the entire error metric, as opposed to a mean error metric.

- ▸ **Explained variance score**: This score measures how well our model can account for the variation in our dataset. A score of 1.0 indicates that our model is perfect.

- ▸ **R2 score**: This is pronounced as R-squared, and this score refers to the coefficient of determination. This tells us how well the unknown samples will be predicted by our model. The best possible score is 1.0, and the values can be negative as well.

How to do it...

There is a module in scikit-learn that provides functionalities to compute all the following metrics. Open a new Python file and add the following lines:

```
import sklearn.metrics as sm

print "Mean absolute error =", round(sm.mean_absolute_error(y_test,
y_test_pred), 2)
print "Mean squared error =", round(sm.mean_squared_error(y_test, y_
test_pred), 2)
print "Median absolute error =", round(sm.median_absolute_error(y_
test, y_test_pred), 2)
print "Explained variance score =", round(sm.explained_variance_
score(y_test, y_test_pred), 2)
print "R2 score =", round(sm.r2_score(y_test, y_test_pred), 2)
```

Keeping track of every single metric can get tedious, so we pick one or two metrics to evaluate our model. A good practice is to make sure that the mean squared error is low and the explained variance score is high.

Achieving model persistence

When we train a model, it would be nice if we could save it as a file so that it can be used later by simply loading it again.

How to do it...

Let's see how to achieve model persistence programmatically:

1. Add the following lines to `regressor.py`:

```
import cPickle as pickle

output_model_file = 'saved_model.pkl'
```

```
with open(output_model_file, 'w') as f:
    pickle.dump(linear_regressor, f)
```

2. The regressor object will be saved in the `saved_model.pkl` file. Let's look at how to load it and use it, as follows:

```
with open(output_model_file, 'r') as f:
    model_linregr = pickle.load(f)

y_test_pred_new = model_linregr.predict(X_test)
print "\nNew mean absolute error =", round(sm.mean_absolute_
error(y_test, y_test_pred_new), 2)
```

3. Here, we just loaded the regressor from the file into the `model_linregr` variable. You can compare the preceding result with the earlier result to confirm that it's the same.

Building a ridge regressor

One of the main problems of linear regression is that it's sensitive to outliers. During data collection in the real world, it's quite common to wrongly measure the output. Linear regression uses ordinary least squares, which tries to minimize the squares of errors. The outliers tend to cause problems because they contribute a lot to the overall error. This tends to disrupt the entire model.

Getting ready

Let's consider the following figure:

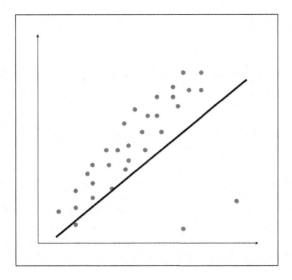

The two points on the bottom are clearly outliers, but this model is trying to fit all the points. Hence, the overall model tends to be inaccurate. By visual inspection, we can see that the following figure is a better model:

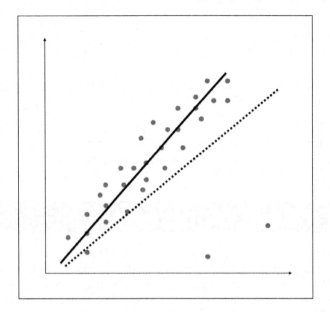

Ordinary least squares considers every single datapoint when it's building the model. Hence, the actual model ends up looking like the dotted line as shown in the preceding figure. We can clearly see that this model is suboptimal. To avoid this, we use **regularization** where a penalty is imposed on the size of the coefficients. This method is called **Ridge Regression**.

How to do it...

Let's see how to build a ridge regressor in Python:

1. You can load the data from the `data_multi_variable.txt` file. This file contains multiple values in each line. All the values except the last value form the input feature vector.

2. Add the following lines to `regressor.py`. Let's initialize a ridge regressor with some parameters:

    ```
    ridge_regressor = linear_model.Ridge(alpha=0.01, fit_
    intercept=True, max_iter=10000)
    ```

3. The `alpha` parameter controls the complexity. As `alpha` gets closer to 0, the ridge regressor tends to become more like a linear regressor with ordinary least squares. So, if you want to make it robust against outliers, you need to assign a higher value to `alpha`. We considered a value of `0.01`, which is moderate.

4. Let's train this regressor, as follows:

```
ridge_regressor.fit(X_train, y_train)
y_test_pred_ridge = ridge_regressor.predict(X_test)
print "Mean absolute error =", round(sm.mean_absolute_error(y_
test, y_test_pred_ridge), 2)
print "Mean squared error =", round(sm.mean_squared_error(y_test,
y_test_pred_ridge), 2)
print "Median absolute error =", round(sm.median_absolute_error(y_
test, y_test_pred_ridge), 2)
print "Explain variance score =", round(sm.explained_variance_
score(y_test, y_test_pred_ridge), 2)
print "R2 score =", round(sm.r2_score(y_test, y_test_pred_ridge),
2)
```

Run this code to view the error metrics. You can build a linear regressor to compare and contrast the results on the same data to see the effect of introducing regularization into the model.

Building a polynomial regressor

One of the main constraints of a linear regression model is the fact that it tries to fit a linear function to the input data. The polynomial regression model overcomes this issue by allowing the function to be a polynomial, thereby increasing the accuracy of the model.

Getting ready

Let's consider the following figure:

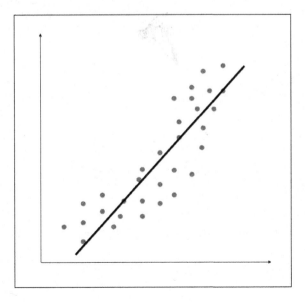

We can see that there is a natural curve to the pattern of datapoints. This linear model is unable to capture this. Let's see what a polynomial model would look like:

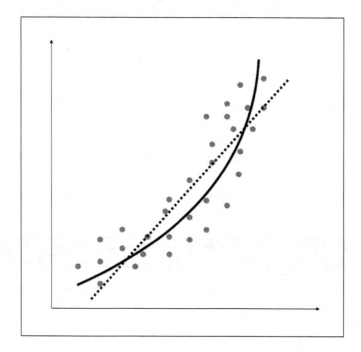

The dotted line represents the linear regression model, and the solid line represents the polynomial regression model. The curviness of this model is controlled by the degree of the polynomial. As the curviness of the model increases, it gets more accurate. However, curviness adds complexity to the model as well, hence, making it slower. This is a trade off where you have to decide between how accurate you want your model to be given the computational constraints.

How to do it...

1. Add the following lines to `regressor.py`:

   ```
   from sklearn.preprocessing import PolynomialFeatures

   polynomial = PolynomialFeatures(degree=3)
   ```

2. We initialized a polynomial of the degree 3 in the previous line. Now we have to represent the datapoints in terms of the coefficients of the polynomial:

   ```
   X_train_transformed = polynomial.fit_transform(X_train)
   ```

   Here, `X_train_transformed` represents the same input in the polynomial form.

3. Let's consider the first datapoint in our file and check whether it can predict the right output:

```
datapoint = [0.39,2.78,7.11]
poly_datapoint = polynomial.fit_transform(datapoint)

poly_linear_model = linear_model.LinearRegression()
poly_linear_model.fit(X_train_transformed, y_train)
print "\nLinear regression:", linear_regressor.predict(datapoint)
[0]
print "\nPolynomial regression:", poly_linear_model.predict(poly_
datapoint)[0]
```

The values in the variable datapoint are the values in the first line in the input data file. We are still fitting a linear regression model here. The only difference is in the way in which we represent the data. If you run this code, you will see the following output:

Linear regression: -11.0587294983

Polynomial regression: -10.9480782122

As you can see, this is close to the output value. If we want it to get closer, we need to increase the degree of the polynomial.

4. Let's make it 10 and see what happens:

```
polynomial = PolynomialFeatures(degree=10)
```

You should see something like the following:

Polynomial regression: -8.20472183853

Now, you can see that the predicted value is much closer to the actual output value.

Estimating housing prices

It's time to apply our knowledge to a real world problem. Let's apply all these principles to estimate the housing prices. This is one of the most popular examples that is used to understand regression, and it serves as a good entry point. This is intuitive and relatable, hence making it easier to understand concepts before we perform more complex things in machine learning. We will use a **decision tree regressor** with **AdaBoost** to solve this problem.

Getting ready

A decision tree is a tree where each node makes a simple decision that contributes to the final output. The leaf nodes represent the output values, and the branches represent the intermediate decisions that were made, based on input features. AdaBoost stands for Adaptive Boosting, and this is a technique that is used to boost the accuracy of the results from another system. This combines the outputs from different versions of the algorithms, called **weak learners**, using a weighted summation to get the final output. The information that's collected at each stage of the AdaBoost algorithm is fed back into the system so that the learners at the latter stages focus on training samples that are difficult to classify. This is the way it increases the accuracy of the system.

Using AdaBoost, we fit a regressor on the dataset. We compute the error and then fit the regressor on the same dataset again, based on this error estimate. We can think of this as fine-tuning of the regressor until the desired accuracy is achieved. You are given a dataset that contains various parameters that affect the price of a house. Our goal is to estimate the relationship between these parameters and the house price so that we can use this to estimate the price given unknown input parameters.

How to do it...

1. Create a new file called `housing.py`, and add the following lines:

```
import numpy as np
from sklearn.tree import DecisionTreeRegressor
from sklearn.ensemble import AdaBoostRegressor
from sklearn import datasets
from sklearn.metrics import mean_squared_error, explained_
variance_score
from sklearn.utils import shuffle
import matplotlib.pyplot as plt
```

2. There is a standard housing dataset that people tend to use to get started with machine learning. You can download it at `https://archive.ics.uci.edu/ml/datasets/Housing`. The good thing is that scikit-learn provides a function to directly load this dataset:

```
housing_data = datasets.load_boston()
```

Each datapoint has 13 input parameters that affect the price of the house. You can access the input data using `housing_data.data` and the corresponding price using `housing_data.target`.

3. Let's separate this into input and output. To make this independent of the ordering of the data, let's shuffle it as well:

```
X, y = shuffle(housing_data.data, housing_data.target, random_
state=7)
```

4. The `random_state` parameter controls how we shuffle the data so that we can have reproducible results. Let's divide the data into training and testing. We'll allocate 80% for training and 20% for testing:

```
num_training = int(0.8 * len(X))
X_train, y_train = X[:num_training], y[:num_training]
X_test, y_test = X[num_training:], y[num_training:]
```

5. We are now ready to fit a decision tree regression model. Let's pick a tree with a maximum depth of 4, which means that we are not letting the tree become arbitrarily deep:

```
dt_regressor = DecisionTreeRegressor(max_depth=4)
dt_regressor.fit(X_train, y_train)
```

6. Let's also fit decision tree regression model with AdaBoost:

```
ab_regressor = AdaBoostRegressor(DecisionTreeRegressor(max_
depth=4), n_estimators=400, random_state=7)
ab_regressor.fit(X_train, y_train)
```

This will help us compare the results and see how AdaBoost really boosts the performance of a decision tree regressor.

7. Let's evaluate the performance of decision tree regressor:

```
y_pred_dt = dt_regressor.predict(X_test)
mse = mean_squared_error(y_test, y_pred_dt)
evs = explained_variance_score(y_test, y_pred_dt)
print "\n#### Decision Tree performance ####"
print "Mean squared error =", round(mse, 2)
print "Explained variance score =", round(evs, 2)
```

8. Now, let's evaluate the performance of AdaBoost:

```
y_pred_ab = ab_regressor.predict(X_test)
mse = mean_squared_error(y_test, y_pred_ab)
evs = explained_variance_score(y_test, y_pred_ab)
print "\n#### AdaBoost performance ####"
print "Mean squared error =", round(mse, 2)
print "Explained variance score =", round(evs, 2)
```

Here is the output on the Terminal:

```
#### Decision Tree performance ####
Mean squared error = 14.79
Explained variance score = 0.82


#### AdaBoost performance ####
Mean squared error = 7.54
Explained variance score = 0.91
```

The error is lower and the variance score is closer to 1 when we use AdaBoost as shown in the preceding output.

Computing the relative importance of features

Are all the features equally important? In this case, we used 13 input features, and they all contributed to the model. However, an important question here is, "How do we know which features are more important?" Obviously, all the features don't contribute equally to the output. In case we want to discard some of them later, we need to know which features are less important. We have this functionality available in scikit-learn.

How to do it...

1. Let's plot the relative importance of the features. Add the following lines to housing.py:

```
plot_feature_importances(dt_regressor.feature_importances_,
        'Decision Tree regressor', housing_data.feature_names)
plot_feature_importances(ab_regressor.feature_importances_,
        'AdaBoost regressor', housing_data.feature_names)
```

The regressor object has a callable feature_importances_ method that gives us the relative importance of each feature.

2. We actually need to define our plot_feature_importances function to plot the bar graphs:

```
def plot_feature_importances(feature_importances, title, feature_
names):
    # Normalize the importance values
    feature_importances = 100.0 * (feature_importances /
max(feature_importances))
```

```
    # Sort the index values and flip them so that they are
arranged in decreasing order of importance
    index_sorted = np.flipud(np.argsort(feature_importances))

    # Center the location of the labels on the X-axis (for display
purposes only)
    pos = np.arange(index_sorted.shape[0]) + 0.5

    # Plot the bar graph
    plt.figure()
    plt.bar(pos, feature_importances[index_sorted],
align='center')
    plt.xticks(pos, feature_names[index_sorted])
    plt.ylabel('Relative Importance')
    plt.title(title)
    plt.show()
```

3. We just take the values from the `feature_importances_` method and scale it so that it ranges between 0 and 100. If you run the preceding code, you will see two figures. Let's see what we will get for a decision tree-based regressor in the following figure:

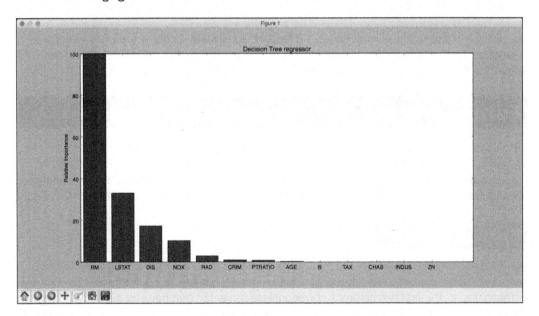

4. So, the decision tree regressor says that the most important feature is RM. Let's take a look at what AdaBoost has to say in the following figure:

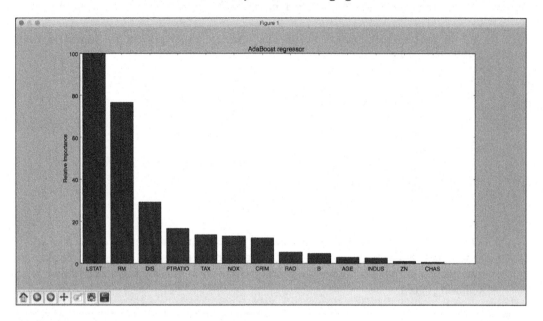

According to AdaBoost, the most important feature is LSTAT. In reality, if you build various regressors on this data, you will see that the most important feature is in fact LSTAT. This shows the advantage of using AdaBoost with a decision tree-based regressor.

Estimating bicycle demand distribution

Let's use a different regression method to solve the bicycle demand distribution problem. We will use the **random forest regressor** to estimate the output values. A random forest is a collection of decision trees. This basically uses a set of decision trees that are built using various subsets of the dataset, and then it uses averaging to improve the overall performance.

Getting ready

We will use the bike_day.csv file that is provided to you. This is also available at https://archive.ics.uci.edu/ml/datasets/Bike+Sharing+Dataset. There are 16 columns in this dataset. The first two columns correspond to the serial number and the actual date, so we won't use them for our analysis. The last three columns correspond to different types of outputs. The last column is just the sum of the values in the fourteenth and fifteenth columns, so we can leave these two out when we build our model.

How to do it...

Let's go ahead and see how to do this in Python. You have been provided with a file called `bike_sharing.py` that contains the full code. We will discuss the important parts of this, as follows:

1. We first need to import a couple of new packages, as follows:

```
import csv
from sklearn.ensemble import RandomForestRegressor
from housing import plot_feature_importances
```

2. We are processing a CSV file, so the CSV package is useful in handling these files. As it's a new dataset, we will have to define our own dataset loading function:

```
def load_dataset(filename):
    file_reader = csv.reader(open(filename, 'rb'), delimiter=',')
    X, y = [], []
    for row in file_reader:
        X.append(row[2:13])
        y.append(row[-1])

    # Extract feature names
    feature_names = np.array(X[0])

    # Remove the first row because they are feature names
    return np.array(X[1:]).astype(np.float32), np.array(y[1:]).astype(np.float32), feature_names
```

In this function, we just read all the data from the CSV file. The feature names are useful when we display it on a graph. We separate the data from the output values and return them.

3. Let's read the data and shuffle it to make it independent of the order in which the data is arranged in the file:

```
X, y, feature_names = load_dataset(sys.argv[1])
X, y = shuffle(X, y, random_state=7)
```

4. As we did earlier, we need to separate the data into training and testing. This time, let's use 90% of the data for training and the remaining 10% for testing:

```
num_training = int(0.9 * len(X))
X_train, y_train = X[:num_training], y[:num_training]
X_test, y_test = X[num_training:], y[num_training:]
```

5. Let's go ahead and train the regressor:

```
rf_regressor = RandomForestRegressor(n_estimators=1000, max_
depth=10, min_samples_split=1)
rf_regressor.fit(X_train, y_train)
```

Here, `n_estimators` refers to the number of estimators, which is the number of decision trees that we want to use in our random forest. The `max_depth` parameter refers to the maximum depth of each tree, and the `min_samples_split` parameter refers to the number of data samples that are needed to split a node in the tree.

6. Let's evaluate performance of the random forest regressor:

```
y_pred = rf_regressor.predict(X_test)
mse = mean_squared_error(y_test, y_pred)
evs = explained_variance_score(y_test, y_pred)
print "\n#### Random Forest regressor performance ####"
print "Mean squared error =", round(mse, 2)
print "Explained variance score =", round(evs, 2)
```

7. As we already have the function to plot the `importances` feature, let's just call it directly:

```
plot_feature_importances(rf_regressor.feature_importances_,
'Random Forest regressor', feature_names)
```

Once you run this code, you will see the following graph:

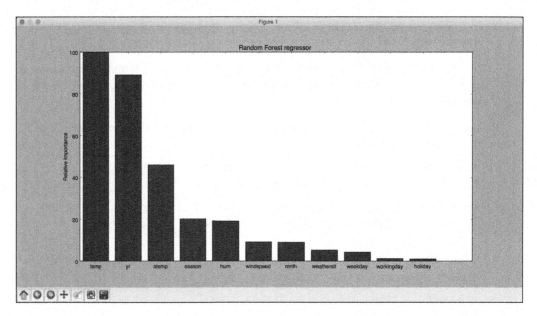

Looks like the temperature is the most important factor controlling the bicycle rentals.

There's more...

Let's see what happens when you include fourteenth and fifteenth columns in the dataset. In the feature importance graph, every feature other than these two has to go to zero. The reason is that the output can be obtained by simply summing up the fourteenth and fifteenth columns, so the algorithm doesn't need any other features to compute the output. In the `load_dataset` function, make the following change inside the for loop:

```
X.append(row[2:15])
```

If you plot the feature importance graph now, you will see the following:

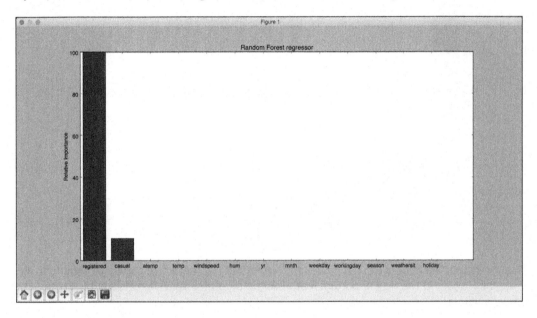

As expected, it says that only these two features are important. This makes sense intuitively because the final output is a simple summation of these two features. So, there is a direct relationship between these two variables and the output value. Hence, the regressor says that it doesn't need any other variable to predict the output. This is an extremely useful tool to eliminate redundant variables in your dataset.

There is another file called `bike_hour.csv` that contains data about how the bicycles are shared hourly. We need to consider columns 3 to 14, so let's make this change inside the `load_dataset` function:

```
X.append(row[2:14])
```

If you run this, you will see the performance of the regressor displayed, as follows:

```
#### Random Forest regressor performance ####
Mean squared error = 2619.87
Explained variance score = 0.92
```

The feature importance graph will look like the following:

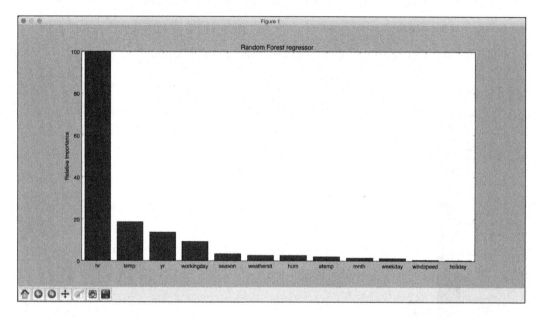

This shows that the hour of the day is the most important feature, which makes sense intuitively if you think about it! The next important feature is temperature, which is consistent with our earlier analysis.

2
Constructing a Classifier

In this chapter, we will cover the following recipes:

- ▶ Building a simple classifier
- ▶ Building a logistic regression classifier
- ▶ Building a Naïve Bayes classifier
- ▶ Splitting the dataset for training and testing
- ▶ Evaluating the accuracy using cross-validation
- ▶ Visualizing the confusion matrix
- ▶ Extracting the performance report
- ▶ Evaluating cars based on their characteristics
- ▶ Extracting validation curves
- ▶ Extracting learning curves
- ▶ Estimating the income bracket

Introduction

In the field of machine learning, classification refers to the process of using the characteristics of data to separate it into a certain number of classes. This is different from regression that we discussed in the previous chapter where the output is a real number. A supervised learning classifier builds a model using labeled training data and then uses this model to classify unknown data.

A classifier can be any algorithm that implements classification. In simple cases, this classifier can be a straightforward mathematical function. In more real-world cases, this classifier can take very complex forms. In the course of study, we will see that classification can be either binary, where we separate data into two classes, or it can be multiclass, where we separate data into more than two classes. The mathematical techniques that are devised to deal with the classification problem tend to deal with two classes, so we extend them in different ways to deal with the multiclass problem as well.

Evaluating the accuracy of a classifier is an important step in the world machine learning. We need to learn how to use the available data to get an idea as to how this model will perform in the real world. In this chapter, we will look at recipes that deal with all these things.

Building a simple classifier

Let's see how to build a simple classifier using some training data.

How to do it...

1. We will use the `simple_classifier.py` file that is already provided to you as reference. Assuming that you imported the `numpy` and `matplotlib.pyplot` packages like we did in the last chapter, let's create some sample data:

   ```
   X = np.array([[3,1], [2,5], [1,8], [6,4], [5,2], [3,5], [4,7],
   [4,-1]])
   ```

2. Let's assign some labels to these points:

   ```
   y = [0, 1, 1, 0, 0, 1, 1, 0]
   ```

3. As we have only two classes, the y list contains 0s and 1s. In general, if you have *N* classes, then the values in y will range from 0 to *N*-1. Let's separate the data into classes based on the labels:

   ```
   class_0 = np.array([X[i] for i in range(len(X)) if y[i]==0])
   class_1 = np.array([X[i] for i in range(len(X)) if y[i]==1])
   ```

4. To get an idea about our data, let's plot it, as follows:

   ```
   plt.figure()
   plt.scatter(class_0[:,0], class_0[:,1], color='black', marker='s')
   plt.scatter(class_1[:,0], class_1[:,1], color='black', marker='x')
   ```

This is a scatterplot, where we use squares and crosses to plot the points. In this context, the `marker` parameter specifies the shape you want to use. We use squares to denote points in `class_0` and crosses to denote points in `class_1`. If you run this code, you will see the following figure:

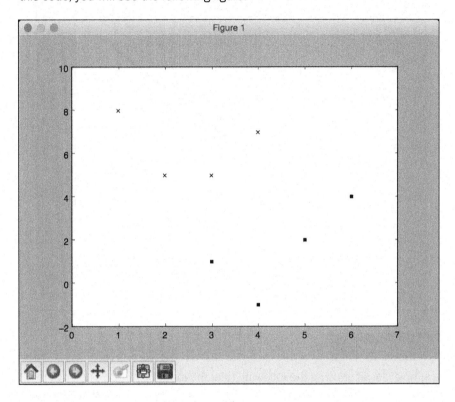

5. In the preceding two lines, we just use the mapping between x and y to create two lists. If you were asked to inspect the datapoints visually and draw a separating line, what would you do? You will simply draw a line in between them. Let's go ahead and do this:

```
line_x = range(10)
line_y = line_x
```

6. We just created a line with the mathematical equation $y = x$. Let's plot it, as follows:

```
plt.figure()
plt.scatter(class_0[:,0], class_0[:,1], color='black', marker='s')
plt.scatter(class_1[:,0], class_1[:,1], color='black', marker='x')
plt.plot(line_x, line_y, color='black', linewidth=3)
plt.show()
```

7. If you run this code, you should see the following figure:

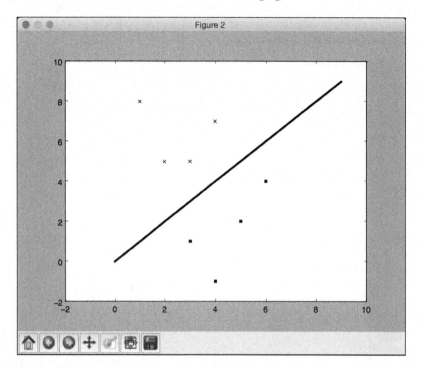

There's more...

We built a simple classifier using the following rule: the input point (a, b) belongs to `class_0` if a is greater than or equal to b; otherwise, it belongs to `class_1`. If you inspect the points one by one, you will see that this is, in fact, true. This is it! You just built a linear classifier that can classify unknown data. It's a linear classifier because the separating line is a straight line. If it's a curve, then it becomes a nonlinear classifier.

This formation worked fine because there were a limited number of points, and we could visually inspect them. What if there are thousands of points? How do we generalize this process? Let's discuss that in the next recipe.

Building a logistic regression classifier

Despite the word *regression* being present in the name, logistic regression is actually used for classification purposes. Given a set of datapoints, our goal is to build a model that can draw linear boundaries between our classes. It extracts these boundaries by solving a set of equations derived from the training data.

How to do it...

1. Let's see how to do this in Python. We will use the `logistic_regression.py` file that is provided to you as a reference. Assuming that you imported the necessary packages, let's create some sample data along with training labels:

```python
import numpy as np
from sklearn import linear_model
import matplotlib.pyplot as plt

X = np.array([[4, 7], [3.5, 8], [3.1, 6.2], [0.5, 1], [1, 2],
[1.2, 1.9], [6, 2], [5.7, 1.5], [5.4, 2.2]])
y = np.array([0, 0, 0, 1, 1, 1, 2, 2, 2])
```

    Here, we assume that we have three classes.

2. Let's initialize the logistic regression classifier:

```python
classifier = linear_model.LogisticRegression(solver='liblinear',
C=100)
```

    There are a number of input parameters that can be specified for the preceding function, but a couple of important ones are `solver` and C. The `solver` parameter specifies the type of solver that the algorithm will use to solve the system of equations. The C parameter controls the regularization strength. A lower value indicates higher regularization strength.

3. Let's train the classifier:

```python
classifier.fit(X, y)
```

4. Let's draw datapoints and boundaries:

```python
plot_classifier(classifier, X, y)
```

    We need to define this function, as follows:

```python
def plot_classifier(classifier, X, y):
    # define ranges to plot the figure
    x_min, x_max = min(X[:, 0]) - 1.0, max(X[:, 0]) + 1.0
    y_min, y_max = min(X[:, 1]) - 1.0, max(X[:, 1]) + 1.0
```

    The preceding values indicate the range of values that we want to use in our figure. The values usually range from the minimum value to the maximum value present in our data. We add some buffers, such as 1.0 in the preceding lines, for clarity.

5. In order to plot the boundaries, we need to evaluate the function across a grid of points and plot it. Let's go ahead and define the grid:

```
# denotes the step size that will be used in the mesh grid
step_size = 0.01

# define the mesh grid
x_values, y_values = np.meshgrid(np.arange(x_min, x_max, step_
size), np.arange(y_min, y_max, step_size))
```

The x_values and y_values variables contain the grid of points where the function will be evaluated.

6. Let's compute the output of the classifier for all these points:

```
# compute the classifier output
mesh_output = classifier.predict(np.c_[x_values.ravel(), y_
values.ravel()])

# reshape the array
mesh_output = mesh_output.reshape(x_values.shape)
```

7. Let's plot the boundaries using colored regions:

```
# Plot the output using a colored plot
plt.figure()

# choose a color scheme
plt.pcolormesh(x_values, y_values, mesh_output, cmap=plt.
cm.gray)
```

This is basically a 3D plotter that takes the 2D points and the associated values to draw different regions using a color scheme. You can find all the color scheme options at http://matplotlib.org/examples/color/colormaps_reference.html.

8. Let's overlay the training points on the plot:

```
plt.scatter(X[:, 0], X[:, 1], c=y, s=80, edgecolors='black',
linewidth=1, cmap=plt.cm.Paired)

# specify the boundaries of the figure
plt.xlim(x_values.min(), x_values.max())
plt.ylim(y_values.min(), y_values.max())

# specify the ticks on the X and Y axes
plt.xticks((np.arange(int(min(X[:, 0])-1), int(max(X[:,
0])+1), 1.0)))
```

```
    plt.yticks((np.arange(int(min(X[:, 1])-1), int(max(X[:,
1])+1), 1.0)))

    plt.show()
```

Here, `plt.scatter` plots the points on the 2D graph. `X[:, 0]` specifies that we should take all the values along axis 0 (X-axis in our case) and `X[:, 1]` specifies axis 1 (Y-axis). The `c=y` parameter indicates the color sequence. We use the target labels to map to colors using `cmap`. Basically, we want different colors that are based on the target labels. Hence, we use `y` as the mapping. The limits of the display figure are set using `plt.xlim` and `plt.ylim`. In order to mark the axes with values, we need to use `plt.xticks` and `plt.yticks`. These functions mark the axes with values so that it's easier for us to see where the points are located. In the preceding code, we want the ticks to lie between the minimum and maximum values with a buffer of one unit. Also, we want these ticks to be integers. So, we use `int()` function to round off the values.

9. If you run this code, you should see the following output:

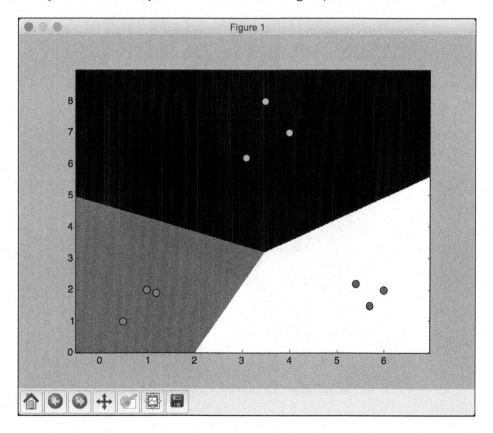

10. Let's see how the C parameter affects our model. The C parameter indicates the penalty for misclassification. If we set it to 1.0, we will get the following figure:

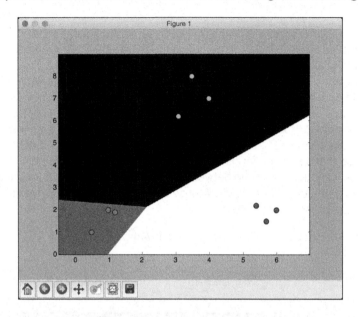

11. If we set C to 10000, we get the following figure:

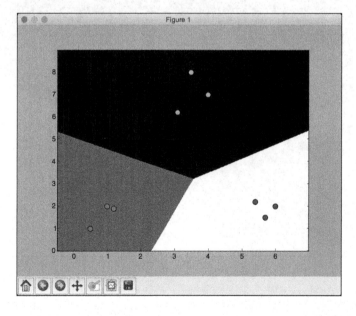

As we increase C, there is a higher penalty for misclassification. Hence, the boundaries get more optimal.

Building a Naive Bayes classifier

A Naive Bayes classifier is a supervised learning classifier that uses Bayes' theorem to build the model. Let's go ahead and build a Naïve Bayes classifier.

How to do it...

1. We will use `naive_bayes.py` that is provided to you as reference. Let's import a couple of things:

```
from sklearn.naive_bayes import GaussianNB
from logistic_regression import plot_classifier
```

2. You were provided with a `data_multivar.txt` file. This contains data that we will use here. This contains comma-separated numerical data in each line. Let's load the data from this file:

```
input_file = 'data_multivar.txt'

X = []
y = []
with open(input_file, 'r') as f:
    for line in f.readlines():
        data = [float(x) for x in line.split(',')]
        X.append(data[:-1])
        y.append(data[-1])

X = np.array(X)
y = np.array(y)
```

We have now loaded the input data into X and the labels into y.

3. Let's build the Naive Bayes classifier:

```
classifier_gaussiannb = GaussianNB()
classifier_gaussiannb.fit(X, y)
y_pred = classifier_gaussiannb.predict(X)
```

The `GaussianNB` function specifies Gaussian Naive Bayes model.

4. Let's compute the accuracy of the classifier:

```
accuracy = 100.0 * (y == y_pred).sum() / X.shape[0]
print "Accuracy of the classifier =", round(accuracy, 2), "%"
```

5. Let's plot the data and the boundaries:

```
plot_classifier(classifier_gaussiannb, X, y)
```

You should see the following figure:

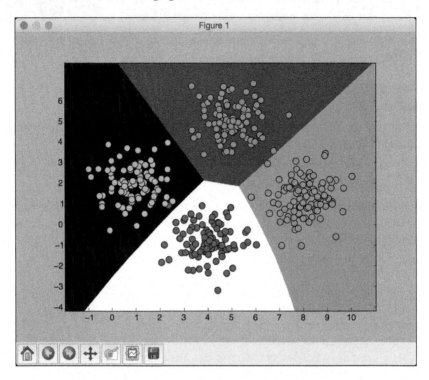

There is no restriction on the boundaries to be linear here. In the preceding example, we used up all the data for training. A good practice in machine learning is to have nonoverlapping data for training and testing. Ideally, we need some unused data for testing so that we can get an accurate estimate of how the model performs on unknown data. There is a provision in scikit-learn that handles this very well, as shown in the next recipe.

Splitting the dataset for training and testing

Let's see how to split our data properly into training and testing datasets.

How to do it...

1. Add the following code snippet into the same Python file as the previous recipe:

```
from sklearn import cross_validation

X_train, X_test, y_train, y_test = cross_validation.train_test_
split(X, y, test_size=0.25, random_state=5)
```

```
classifier_gaussiannb_new = GaussianNB()
classifier_gaussiannb_new.fit(X_train, y_train)
```

Here, we allocated 25% of the data for testing, as specified by the `test_size` parameter. The remaining 75% of the data will be used for training.

2. Let's evaluate the classifier on test data:

```
y_test_pred = classifier_gaussiannb_new.predict(X_test)
```

3. Let's compute the accuracy of the classifier:

```
accuracy = 100.0 * (y_test == y_test_pred).sum() / X_test.shape[0]
print "Accuracy of the classifier =", round(accuracy, 2), "%"
```

4. Let's plot the datapoints and the boundaries on test data:

```
plot_classifier(classifier_gaussiannb_new, X_test, y_test)
```

5. You should see the following figure:

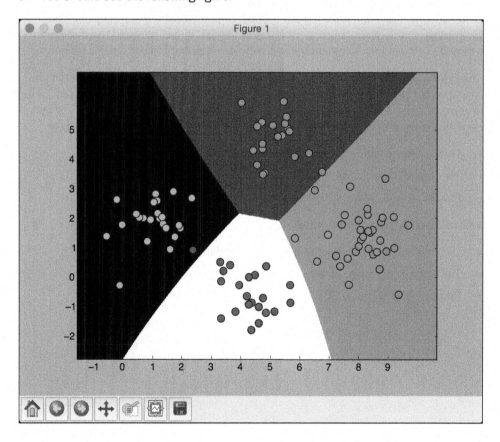

Evaluating the accuracy using cross-validation

The **cross-validation** is an important concept in machine learning. In the previous recipe, we split the data into training and testing datasets. However, in order to make it more robust, we need to repeat this process with different subsets. If we just fine-tune it for a particular subset, we may end up overfitting the model. Overfitting refers to a situation where we fine-tune a model too much to a dataset and it fails to perform well on unknown data. We want our machine learning model to perform well on unknown data.

Getting ready...

Before we discuss how to perform cross-validation, let's talk about performance metrics. When we are dealing with machine learning models, we usually care about three things: precision, recall, and F1 score. We can get the required performance metric using the parameter scoring. Precision refers to the number of items that are correctly classified as a percentage of the overall number of items in the list. Recall refers to the number of items that are retrieved as a percentage of the overall number of items in the training list.

Let's consider a test dataset containing 100 items, out of which 82 are of interest to us. Now, we want our classifier to identify these 82 items for us. Our classifier picks out 73 items as the items of interest. Out of these 73 items, only 65 are actually the items of interest and the remaining eight are misclassified. We can compute precision in the following way:

- ▶ The number of correct identifications = 65
- ▶ The total number of identifications = 73
- ▶ Precision = 65 / 73 = 89.04%

To compute recall, we use the following:

- ▶ The total number of interesting items in the dataset = 82
- ▶ The number of items retrieved correctly = 65
- ▶ Recall = 65 / 82 = 79.26%

A good machine learning model needs to have good precision and good recall simultaneously. It's easy to get one of them to 100%, but the other metric suffers! We need to keep both the metrics high at the same time. To quantify this, we use an F1 score, which is a combination of precision and recall. This is actually the harmonic mean of precision and recall:

*F1 score = 2 * precision * recall / (precision + recall)*

In the preceding case, the F1 score will be as follows:

*F1 score = 2 * 0.89 * 0.79 / (0.89 + 0.79) = 0.8370*

How to do it...

1. Let's see how to perform cross-validation and extract performance metrics. We will start with the accuracy:

```
num_validations = 5
accuracy = cross_validation.cross_val_score(classifier_gaussiannb,
        X, y, scoring='accuracy', cv=num_validations)
print "Accuracy: " + str(round(100*accuracy.mean(), 2)) + "%"
```

2. We will use the preceding function to compute precision, recall, and the F1 score as well:

```
f1 = cross_validation.cross_val_score(classifier_gaussiannb,
        X, y, scoring='f1_weighted', cv=num_validations)
print "F1: " + str(round(100*f1.mean(), 2)) + "%"

precision = cross_validation.cross_val_score(classifier_
gaussiannb,
        X, y, scoring='precision_weighted', cv=num_validations)
print "Precision: " + str(round(100*precision.mean(), 2)) + "%"

recall = cross_validation.cross_val_score(classifier_gaussiannb,
        X, y, scoring='recall_weighted', cv=num_validations)
print "Recall: " + str(round(100*recall.mean(), 2)) + "%"
```

Visualizing the confusion matrix

A confusion matrix is a table that we use to understand the performance of a classification model. This helps us understand how we classify testing data into different classes. When we want to fine-tune our algorithms, we need to understand how the data gets misclassified before we make these changes. Some classes are worse than others, and the confusion matrix will help us understand this. Let's look at the following figure:

	Predicted class 0	Predicted class 1	Predicted class 2
True class 0	45	4	3
True class 1	11	56	2
True class 2	5	6	49

In the preceding chart, we can see how we categorize data into different classes. Ideally, we want all the nondiagonal elements to be 0. This would indicate perfect classification! Let's consider **class 0**. Overall, 52 items actually belong to **class 0**. We get 52 if we sum up the numbers in the first row. Now, 45 of these items are being predicted correctly, but our classifier says that four of them belong to **class 1** and three of them belong to **class 2**. We can apply the same analysis to the remaining two rows as well. An interesting thing to note is that 11 items from **class 1** are misclassified as **class 0**. This constitutes around 16% of the datapoints in this class. This is an insight that we can use to optimize our model.

How to do it...

1. We will use the `confusion_matrix.py` file that we already provided to you as a reference. Let's see how to extract the confusion matrix from our data:

    ```
    from sklearn.metrics import confusion_matrix
    y_true = [1, 0, 0, 2, 1, 0, 3, 3, 3]
    y_pred = [1, 1, 0, 2, 1, 0, 1, 3, 3]
    confusion_mat = confusion_matrix(y_true, y_pred)
    plot_confusion_matrix(confusion_mat)
    ```

We use some sample data here. We have four classes with values ranging from 0 to 3. We have predicted labels as well. We use the `confusion_matrix` method to extract the confusion matrix and plot it.

2. Let's go ahead and define this function:

```
# Show confusion matrix
def plot_confusion_matrix(confusion_mat):
    plt.imshow(confusion_mat, interpolation='nearest', cmap=plt.
cm.Paired)
    plt.title('Confusion matrix')
    plt.colorbar()
    tick_marks = np.arange(4)
    plt.xticks(tick_marks, tick_marks)
    plt.yticks(tick_marks, tick_marks)
    plt.ylabel('True label')
    plt.xlabel('Predicted label')
    plt.show()
```

We use the `imshow` function to plot the confusion matrix. Everything else in the function is straightforward! We just set the title, color bar, ticks, and the labels using the relevant functions. The `tick_marks` argument range from 0 to 3 because we have four distinct labels in our dataset. The `np.arange` function gives us this `numpy` array.

3. If you run the preceding code, you will see the following figure:

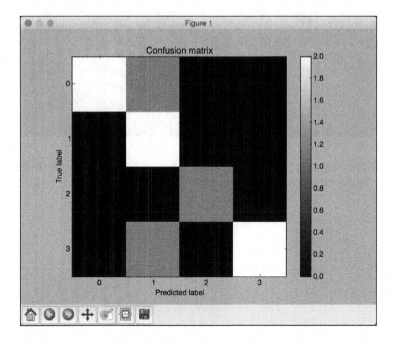

The diagonal colors are strong, and we want them to be strong. The black color indicates zero. There are a couple of gray colors in the nondiagonal spaces, which indicate misclassification. For example, when the real label is 0, the predicted label is 1, as we can see in the first row. In fact, all the misclassifications belong to **class-1** in the sense that the second column contains three rows that are non-zero. It's easy to see this from the figure.

Extracting the performance report

We also have a function in scikit-learn that can directly print the precision, recall, and F1 scores for us. Let's see how to do this.

How to do it...

1. Add the following lines to a new Python file:

```
from sklearn.metrics import classification_report
y_true = [1, 0, 0, 2, 1, 0, 3, 3, 3]
y_pred = [1, 1, 0, 2, 1, 0, 1, 3, 3]
target_names = ['Class-0', 'Class-1', 'Class-2', 'Class-3']
print(classification_report(y_true, y_pred, target_names=target_
names))
```

2. If you run this code, you will see the following on your Terminal:

	precision	recall	f1-score	support
Class-0	1.00	0.67	0.80	3
Class-1	0.50	1.00	0.67	2
Class-2	1.00	1.00	1.00	1
Class-3	1.00	0.67	0.80	3
avg / total	0.89	0.78	0.79	9

Instead of computing these metrics separately, you can directly use this function to extract those statistics from your model.

Evaluating cars based on their characteristics

Let's see how we can apply classification techniques to a real-world problem. We will use a dataset that contains some details about cars, such as number of doors, boot space, maintenance costs, and so on. Our goal is to determine the quality of the car. For the purposes of classification, the quality can take four values: unacceptable, acceptable, good, and very good.

Getting ready

You can download the dataset at `https://archive.ics.uci.edu/ml/datasets/Car+Evaluation`.

You need to treat each value in the dataset as a string. We consider six attributes in the dataset. Here are the attributes along with the possible values they can take:

- `buying`: These will be `vhigh`, `high`, `med`, and `low`
- `maint`: These will be `vhigh`, `high`, `med`, and `low`
- `doors`: These will be 2, 3, 4, 5, and more
- `persons`: These will be 2, 4, more
- `lug_boot`: These will be `small`, `med`, and `big`
- `safety`: These will be `low`, `med`, and `high`

Given that each line contains strings, we need to assume that all the features are strings and design a classifier. In the previous chapter, we used random forests to build a regressor. In this recipe, we will use random forests as a classifier.

How to do it...

1. We will use the `car.py` file that we already provided to you as reference. Let's go ahead and import a couple of packages:

   ```
   from sklearn import preprocessing
   from sklearn.ensemble import RandomForestClassifier
   ```

2. Let's load the dataset:

   ```
   input_file = 'path/to/dataset/car.data.txt'

   # Reading the data
   X = []
   count = 0
   ```

```
with open(input_file, 'r') as f:
    for line in f.readlines():
        data = line[:-1].split(',')
        X.append(data)

X = np.array(X)
```

Each line contains a comma-separated list of words. Therefore, we parse the input file, split each line, and then append the list to the main data. We ignore the last character on each line because it's a newline character. The Python packages only work with numerical data, so we need to transform these attributes into something that those packages will understand.

3. In the previous chapter, we discussed label encoding. That is what we will use here to convert strings to numbers:

```
# Convert string data to numerical data
label_encoder = []
X_encoded = np.empty(X.shape)
for i,item in enumerate(X[0]):
    label_encoder.append(preprocessing.LabelEncoder())
    X_encoded[:, i] = label_encoder[-1].fit_transform(X[:, i])

X = X_encoded[:, :-1].astype(int)
y = X_encoded[:, -1].astype(int)
```

As each attribute can take a limited number of values, we can use the label encoder to transform them into numbers. We need to use different label encoders for each attribute. For example, the `lug_boot` attribute can take three distinct values, and we need a label encoder that knows how to encode this attribute. The last value on each line is the class, so we assign it to the `y` variable.

4. Let's train the classifier:

```
# Build a Random Forest classifier
params = {'n_estimators': 200, 'max_depth': 8, 'random_state': 7}
classifier = RandomForestClassifier(**params)
classifier.fit(X, y)
```

You can play around with the `n_estimators` and `max_depth` parameters to see how they affect the classification accuracy. We will actually do this soon in a standardized way.

5. Let's perform cross-validation:

```
# Cross validation
from sklearn import cross_validation
```

```
accuracy = cross_validation.cross_val_score(classifier,
        X, y, scoring='accuracy', cv=3)
print "Accuracy of the classifier: " + str(round(100*accuracy.
mean(), 2)) + "%"
```

Once we train the classifier, we need to see how it performs. We use three-fold cross-validation to calculate the accuracy here.

6. One of the main goals of building a classifier is to use it on isolated and unknown data instances. Let's use a single datapoint and see how we can use this classifier to categorize it:

```
# Testing encoding on single data instance
input_data = ['vhigh', 'vhigh', '2', '2', 'small', 'low']
input_data_encoded = [-1] * len(input_data)
for i,item in enumerate(input_data):
    input_data_encoded[i] = int(label_encoder[i].transform(input_
data[i]))

input_data_encoded = np.array(input_data_encoded)
```

The first step was to convert that data into numerical data. We need to use the label encoders that we used during training because we want it to be consistent. If there are unknown values in the input datapoint, the label encoder will complain because it doesn't know how to handle that data. For example, if you change the first value in the list from vhigh to abcd, then the label encoder won't work because it doesn't know how to interpret this string. This acts like an error check to see if the input datapoint is valid.

7. We are now ready to predict the output class for this datapoint:

```
# Predict and print output for a particular datapoint
output_class = classifier.predict(input_data_encoded)
print "Output class:", label_encoder[-1].inverse_transform(output_
class)[0]
```

We use the predict method to estimate the output class. If we output the encoded output label, it wouldn't mean anything to us. Therefore, we use the inverse_transform method to convert this label back to its original form and print out the output class.

Extracting validation curves

We used random forests to build a classifier in the previous recipe, but we don't exactly know how to define the parameters. In our case, we dealt with two parameters: n_estimators and max_depth. They are called **hyperparameters**, and the performance of the classifier depends on them. It would be nice to see how the performance gets affected as we change the hyperparameters. This is where validation curves come into picture. These curves help us understand how each hyperparameter influences the training score. Basically, all other parameters are kept constant and we vary the hyperparameter of interest according to our range. We will then be able to visualize how this affects the score.

How to do it...

1. Add the following code to the same Python file, as in the previous recipe:

```
# Validation curves

from sklearn.learning_curve import validation_curve

classifier = RandomForestClassifier(max_depth=4, random_state=7)
parameter_grid = np.linspace(25, 200, 8).astype(int)
train_scores, validation_scores = validation_curve(classifier, X,
y,
        "n_estimators", parameter_grid, cv=5)
print "\n##### VALIDATION CURVES #####"
print "\nParam: n_estimators\nTraining scores:\n", train_scores
print "\nParam: n_estimators\nValidation scores:\n", validation_
scores
```

In this case, we defined the classifier by fixing the max_depth parameter. We want to estimate the optimal number of estimators to use, and so have defined our search space using parameter_grid. It is going to extract training and validation scores by iterating from 25 to 200 in eight steps.

2. If you run it, you will see the following on your Terminal:

```
##### VALIDATION CURVES #####

Param: n_estimators
Training scores:
[[ 0.80680174  0.80824891  0.80752533  0.80463097  0.81358382]
 [ 0.79522431  0.80535456  0.81041968  0.8089725   0.81069364]
 [ 0.80101302  0.80680174  0.81114327  0.81476122  0.8150289 ]
 [ 0.8024602   0.80535456  0.81186686  0.80752533  0.80346821]
 [ 0.80028944  0.80463097  0.81114327  0.80824891  0.81069364]
 [ 0.80390738  0.80535456  0.81041968  0.80969609  0.81647399]
 [ 0.80390738  0.80463097  0.81114327  0.81476122  0.81719653]
 [ 0.80390738  0.80607815  0.81114327  0.81403763  0.81647399]]

Param: n_estimators
Validation scores:
[[ 0.71098266  0.76589595  0.72543353  0.76300578  0.75290698]
 [ 0.71098266  0.75433526  0.71965318  0.75722543  0.74127907]
 [ 0.71098266  0.72254335  0.71965318  0.75722543  0.74418605]
 [ 0.71098266  0.71387283  0.71965318  0.75722543  0.72674419]
 [ 0.71098266  0.74277457  0.71965318  0.75722543  0.74127907]
 [ 0.71098266  0.74277457  0.71965318  0.75722543  0.74127907]
 [ 0.71098266  0.74566474  0.71965318  0.75722543  0.74418605]
 [ 0.71098266  0.75144509  0.71965318  0.75722543  0.74127907]]
```

3. Let's plot it:

```
# Plot the curve
plt.figure()
plt.plot(parameter_grid, 100*np.average(train_scores, axis=1),
color='black')
plt.title('Training curve')
plt.xlabel('Number of estimators')
plt.ylabel('Accuracy')
plt.show()
```

4. Here is the figure that you'll get:

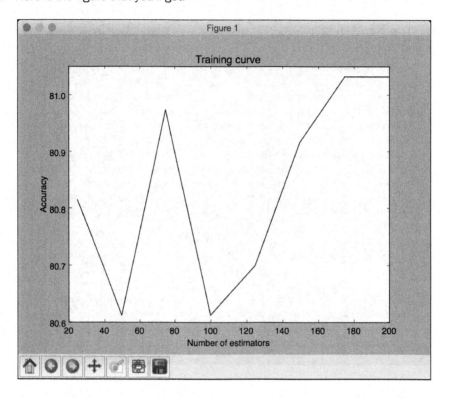

5. Let's do the same for the `max_depth` parameter:

```
classifier = RandomForestClassifier(n_estimators=20, random_
state=7)
parameter_grid = np.linspace(2, 10, 5).astype(int)
train_scores, valid_scores = validation_curve(classifier, X, y,
        "max_depth", parameter_grid, cv=5)
print "\nParam: max_depth\nTraining scores:\n", train_scores
print "\nParam: max_depth\nValidation scores:\n", validation_
scores
```

We fixed the `n_estimators` parameter at 20 to see how the performance varies with `max_depth`. Here is the output on the Terminal:

```
Param: max_depth
Training scores:
[[ 0.71852388  0.70043415  0.70043415  0.70043415  0.69942197]
 [ 0.80607815  0.80535456  0.80752533  0.79450072  0.81069364]
 [ 0.90665702  0.91027496  0.92836469  0.89797395  0.90679191]
 [ 0.97467438  0.96743849  0.97105644  0.97829233  0.96820809]
 [ 0.99421129  0.99782923  0.99782923  0.99855282  0.99421965]]

Param: max_depth
Validation scores:
[[ 0.71098266  0.76589595  0.72543353  0.76300578  0.75290698]
 [ 0.71098266  0.75433526  0.71965318  0.75722543  0.74127907]
 [ 0.71098266  0.72254335  0.71965318  0.75722543  0.74418605]
 [ 0.71098266  0.71387283  0.71965318  0.75722543  0.72674419]
 [ 0.71098266  0.74277457  0.71965318  0.75722543  0.74127907]
 [ 0.71098266  0.74277457  0.71965318  0.75722543  0.74127907]
 [ 0.71098266  0.74566474  0.71965318  0.75722543  0.74418605]
 [ 0.71098266  0.75144509  0.71965318  0.75722543  0.74127907]]
```

6. Let's plot it:

```
# Plot the curve
plt.figure()
plt.plot(parameter_grid, 100*np.average(train_scores, axis=1),
color='black')
plt.title('Validation curve')
plt.xlabel('Maximum depth of the tree')
plt.ylabel('Accuracy')
plt.show()
```

7. If you run this code, you will get the following figure:

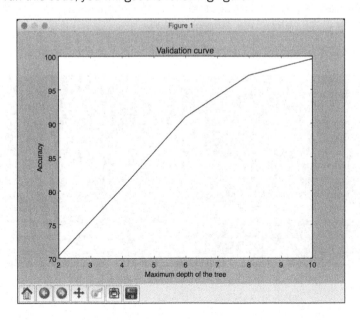

Extracting learning curves

Learning curves help us understand how the size of our training dataset influences the machine learning model. This is very useful when you have to deal with computational constraints. Let's go ahead and plot the learning curves by varying the size of our training dataset.

How to do it...

1. Add the following code to the same Python file, as in the previous recipe:

```
# Learning curves

from sklearn.learning_curve import learning_curve

classifier = RandomForestClassifier(random_state=7)

parameter_grid = np.array([200, 500, 800, 1100])
train_sizes, train_scores, validation_scores = learning_
curve(classifier,
        X, y, train_sizes=parameter_grid, cv=5)
print "\n##### LEARNING CURVES #####"
print "\nTraining scores:\n", train_scores
print "\nValidation scores:\n", validation_scores
```

We want to evaluate the performance metrics using training datasets of size 200, 500, 800, and 1100. We use five-fold cross-validation, as specified by the `cv` parameter in the `learning_curve` method.

2. If you run this code, you will get the following output on the Terminal:

```
##### LEARNING CURVES #####

Training scores:
[[ 1.         1.         1.         1.         1.        ]
 [ 1.         1.         0.998     0.998     0.998     ]
 [ 0.99875   0.99875   0.99875   0.99875   0.99875   ]
 [ 0.99909091 0.99545455 0.99909091 0.99818182 0.99818182]]

Validation scores:
[[ 0.69942197 0.69942197 0.69942197 0.69942197 0.70348837]
 [ 0.75433526 0.65028902 0.76878613 0.76589595 0.70348837]
 [ 0.70520231 0.78612717 0.52312139 0.76878613 0.77034884]
 [ 0.6416185  0.75722543 0.64450867 0.75433526 0.76744186]]
```

3. Let's plot it:

```
# Plot the curve
plt.figure()
plt.plot(parameter_grid, 100*np.average(train_scores, axis=1),
color='black')
plt.title('Learning curve')
plt.xlabel('Number of training samples')
plt.ylabel('Accuracy')
plt.show()
```

4. Here is the output figure:

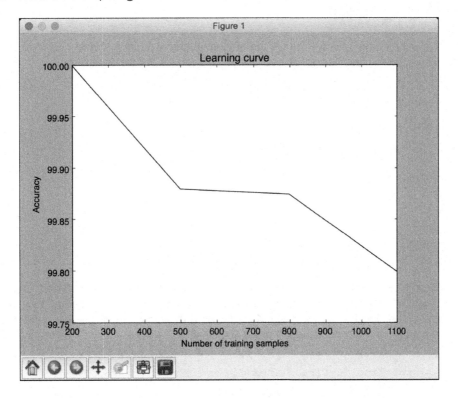

Although smaller training sets seem to give better accuracy, they are prone to overfitting. If we choose a bigger training dataset, it consumes more resources. Therefore, we need to make a trade-off here to pick the right size of the training dataset.

Estimating the income bracket

We will build a classifier to estimate the income bracket of a person based on 14 attributes. The possible output classes are *higher than 50K* or *lower than or equal to 50K*. There is a slight twist in this dataset in the sense that each datapoint is a mixture of numbers and strings. Numerical data is valuable, and we cannot use a label encoder in these situations. We need to design a system that can deal with numerical and non-numerical data at the same time. We will use the census income dataset available at `https://archive.ics.uci.edu/ml/datasets/Census+Income`.

How to do it...

1. We will use the `income.py` file already provided to you as a reference. We will use a Naive Bayes classifier to achieve this. Let's import a couple of packages:

```
from sklearn import preprocessing
from sklearn.naive_bayes import GaussianNB
```

2. Let's load the dataset:

```
input_file = 'path/to/adult.data.txt'

# Reading the data
X = []
y = []
count_lessthan50k = 0
count_morethan50k = 0
num_images_threshold = 10000
```

3. We will use 20,000 datapoints from the datasets—10,000 for each class to avoid class imbalance. During training, if you use many datapoints that belong to a single class, the classifier tends to get biased toward this class. Therefore, it's better to use the same number of datapoints for each class:

```
with open(input_file, 'r') as f:
    for line in f.readlines():
        if '?' in line:
            continue

        data = line[:-1].split(', ')

        if data[-1] == '<=50K' and count_lessthan50k < num_images_
threshold:
            X.append(data)
            count_lessthan50k = count_lessthan50k + 1
```

```
      elif data[-1] == '>50K' and count_morethan50k < num_
images_threshold:
            X.append(data)
            count_morethan50k = count_morethan50k + 1

      if count_lessthan50k >= num_images_threshold and count_
morethan50k >= num_images_threshold:
            break

X = np.array(X)
```

It's a comma-separated file again. We just loaded the data in the X variable just like before.

4. We need to convert string attributes to numerical data while leaving out the original numerical data:

```
# Convert string data to numerical data
label_encoder = []
X_encoded = np.empty(X.shape)
for i,item in enumerate(X[0]):
    if item.isdigit():
        X_encoded[:, i] = X[:, i]
    else:
        label_encoder.append(preprocessing.LabelEncoder())
        X_encoded[:, i] = label_encoder[-1].fit_transform(X[:, i])

X = X_encoded[:, :-1].astype(int)
y = X_encoded[:, -1].astype(int)
```

The isdigit() function helps us in identifying numerical data. We converted string data to numerical data and stored all the label encoders in a list so that we can use it when we want to classify unknown data.

5. Let's train the classifier:

```
# Build a classifier
classifier_gaussiannb = GaussianNB()
classifier_gaussiannb.fit(X, y)
```

6. Let's split the data into training and testing to extract performance metrics:

```
# Cross validation
from sklearn import cross_validation

X_train, X_test, y_train, y_test = cross_validation.train_test_
split(X, y, test_size=0.25, random_state=5)
classifier_gaussiannb = GaussianNB()
```

```
classifier_gaussiannb.fit(X_train, y_train)
y_test_pred = classifier_gaussiannb.predict(X_test)
```

7. Let's extract performance metrics:

```
# compute F1 score of the classifier
f1 = cross_validation.cross_val_score(classifier_gaussiannb,
        X, y, scoring='f1_weighted', cv=5)
print "F1 score: " + str(round(100*f1.mean(), 2)) + "%"
```

8. Let's see how to classify a single datapoint. We need to convert the datapoint into something that our classifier can understand:

```
# Testing encoding on single data instance
input_data = ['39', 'State-gov', '77516', 'Bachelors', '13',
'Never-married', 'Adm-clerical', 'Not-in-family', 'White', 'Male',
'2174', '0', '40', 'United-States']
count = 0
input_data_encoded = [-1] * len(input_data)
for i,item in enumerate(input_data):
    if item.isdigit():
        input_data_encoded[i] = int(input_data[i])
    else:
        input_data_encoded[i] = int(label_encoder[count].
transform(input_data[i]))
        count = count + 1


input_data_encoded = np.array(input_data_encoded)
```

9. We are now ready to classify it:

```
# Predict and print output for a particular datapoint
output_class = classifier_gaussiannb.predict(input_data_encoded)
print label_encoder[-1].inverse_transform(output_class)[0]
```

Just like before, we use the `predict` method to get the output class and the `inverse_transform` method to convert this label back to its original form to print it out on the Terminal.

3
Predictive Modeling

In this chapter, we will cover the following recipes:

- ▸ Building a linear classifier using Support Vector Machines (SVMs)
- ▸ Building a nonlinear classifier using SVMs
- ▸ Tackling class imbalance
- ▸ Extracting confidence measurements
- ▸ Finding optimal hyperparameters
- ▸ Building an event predictor
- ▸ Estimating traffic

Introduction

Predictive modeling is probably one of the most exciting fields in data analytics. It has gained a lot of attention in recent years due to massive amounts of data being available in many different verticals. It is very commonly used in areas concerning data mining to forecast future trends.

Predictive modeling is an analysis technique that is used to predict the future behavior of a system. It is a collection of algorithms that can identify the relationship between independent input variables and the target responses. We create a mathematical model, based on observations, and then use this model to estimate what's going to happen in the future.

In predictive modeling, we need to collect data with known responses to train our model. Once we create this model, we validate it using some metrics, and then use it to predict future values. We can use many different types of algorithms to create a predictive model. In this chapter, we will use Support Vector Machines to build linear and nonlinear models.

A predictive model is built using a number of features that are likely to influence the behavior of the system. For example, to estimate the weather conditions, we may use various types of data, such as temperature, barometric pressure, precipitation, and other atmospheric processes. Similarly, when we deal with other types of systems, we need to decide what factors are likely to influence its behavior and include them as part of the feature vector before training our model.

Building a linear classifier using Support Vector Machine (SVMs)

SVMs are supervised learning models that are used to build classifiers and regressors. An SVM finds the best separating boundary between the two sets of points by solving a system of mathematical equations. If you are not familiar with SVMs, here are a couple of good tutorials to get started:

▶ http://web.mit.edu/zoya/www/SVM.pdf

▶ http://www.support-vector.net/icml-tutorial.pdf

▶ http://www.svms.org/tutorials/Berwick2003.pdf

Let's see how to build a linear classifier using an SVM.

Getting ready

Let's visualize our data to understand the problem at hand. We will use `svm.py` that's already provided to you as a reference. Before we build the SVM, let's understand our data. We will use the `data_multivar.txt` file that's already provided to you. Let's see how to to visualize the data. Create a new Python file and add the following lines to it:

```
import numpy as np
import matplotlib.pyplot as plt

import utilities

# Load input data
input_file = 'data_multivar.txt'
X, y = utilities.load_data(input_file)
```

We just imported a couple of packages and named the input file. Let's look at the `load_data()` method:

```
# Load multivar data in the input file
def load_data(input_file):
    X = []
    y = []
    with open(input_file, 'r') as f:
        for line in f.readlines():
            data = [float(x) for x in line.split(',')]
            X.append(data[:-1])
            y.append(data[-1])

    X = np.array(X)
    y = np.array(y)

    return X, y
```

We need to separate the data into classes, as follows:

```
class_0 = np.array([X[i] for i in range(len(X)) if y[i]==0])
class_1 = np.array([X[i] for i in range(len(X)) if y[i]==1])
```

Now that we have separated the data, let's plot it:

```
plt.figure()
plt.scatter(class_0[:,0], class_0[:,1], facecolors='black',
edgecolors='black', marker='s')
plt.scatter(class_1[:,0], class_1[:,1], facecolors='None',
edgecolors='black', marker='s')
plt.title('Input data')
plt.show()
```

If you run this code, you will see the following figure:

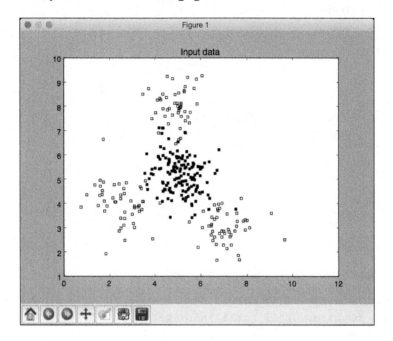

The preceding figure consists of two types of points – **solid squares** and **empty squares**. In machine learning lingo, we say that our data consists of two classes. Our goal is to build a model that can separate the solid squares from the empty squares.

How to do it...

1. We need to split our dataset into training and testing datasets. Add the following lines to the same Python file:

    ```
    # Train test split and SVM training
    from sklearn import cross_validation
    from sklearn.svm import SVC

    X_train, X_test, y_train, y_test = cross_validation.train_test_
    split(X, y, test_size=0.25, random_state=5)
    ```

2. Let's initialize the SVM object using a linear kernel. If you don't know what kernels are, you can check out http://www.eric-kim.net/eric-kim-net/posts/1/kernel_trick.html. Add the following lines to the file:

    ```
    params = {'kernel': 'linear'}
    classifier = SVC(**params)
    ```

3. We are now ready to train the linear SVM classifier:

```
classifier.fit(X_train, y_train)
```

4. We can now see how the classifier performs:

```
utilities.plot_classifier(classifier, X_train, y_train, 'Training
dataset')
plt.show()
```

5. If you run this code, you will get the following figure:

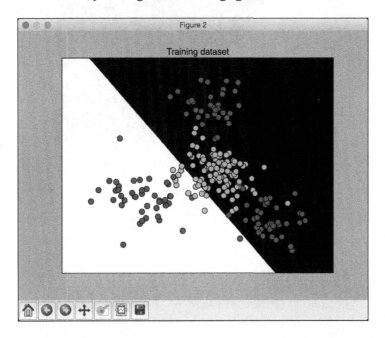

The `plot_classifier` function is the same that we discussed in the previous chapter. It has a couple of minor additions. You can check out the `utilities.py` file already provided to you for more details.

6. Let's see how this performs on the test dataset. Add the following lines to the same file:

```
y_test_pred = classifier.predict(X_test)
utilities.plot_classifier(classifier, X_test, y_test, 'Test
dataset')
plt.show()
```

7. If you run this code, you will see the following figure:

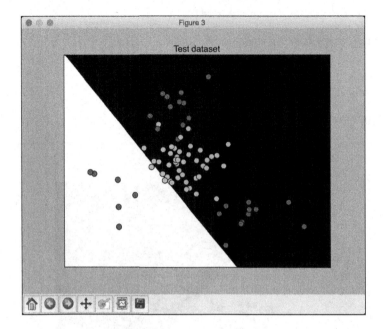

8. Let's compute the accuracy for the training set. Add the following lines to the same file:

```
from sklearn.metrics import classification_report

target_names = ['Class-' + str(int(i)) for i in set(y)]
print "\n" + "#"*30
print "\nClassifier performance on training dataset\n"
print classification_report(y_train, classifier.predict(X_train),
target_names=target_names)
print "#"*30 + "\n"
```

9. If you run this code, you will see the following on your Terminal:

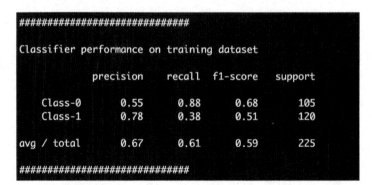

10. Finally, let's see the classification report for the testing dataset:

```
print "#"*30
print "\nClassification report on test dataset\n"
print classification_report(y_test, y_test_pred, target_
names=target_names)
print "#"*30 + "\n"
```

11. If you run this code, you will see the following on the Terminal:

```
##############################

Classification report on test dataset

                precision     recall   f1-score    support

    Class-0         0.64       0.96       0.77        45
    Class-1         0.75       0.20       0.32        30

avg / total         0.69       0.65       0.59        75

##############################
```

From the figure where we visualized the data, we can see that the solid squares are completely surrounded by empty squares. This means that the data is not linearly separable. We cannot draw a nice straight line to separate the two sets of points! Hence, we need a nonlinear classifier to separate these datapoints.

Building a nonlinear classifier using SVMs

An SVM provides a variety of options to build a nonlinear classifier. We need to build a nonlinear classifier using various kernels. For the sake of simplicity, let's consider two cases here. When we want to represent a curvy boundary between two sets of points, we can either do this using a polynomial function or a radial basis function.

How to do it...

1. For the first case, let's use a polynomial kernel to build a nonlinear classifier. In the same Python file, search for the following line:

```
params = {'kernel': 'linear'}
```

Replace this line with the following:

```
params = {'kernel': 'poly', 'degree': 3}
```

This means that we use a polynomial function with degree 3. If you increase the degree, this means we allow the polynomial to be curvier. However, curviness comes at a cost in the sense that it will take more time to train because it's more computationally expensive.

2. If you run this code now, you will get the following figure:

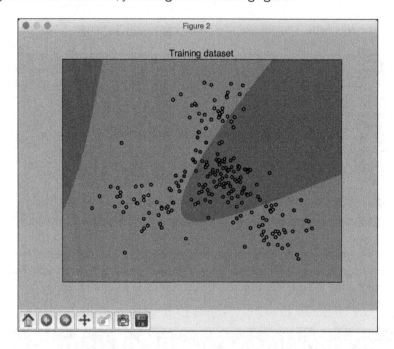

3. You will also see the following classification report printed on your Terminal:

```
###############################
Classifier performance on training dataset

             precision   recall  f1-score   support

    Class-0       0.92     0.84      0.88       105
    Class-1       0.87     0.93      0.90       120

avg / total       0.89     0.89      0.89       225

###############################
```

4. We can also use a radial basis function kernel to build a nonlinear classifier. In the same Python file, search for the following line:

```
params = {'kernel': 'poly', 'degree': 3}
```

Replace this line with the following one:

```
params = {'kernel': 'rbf'}
```

5. If you run this code now, you will get the following figure:

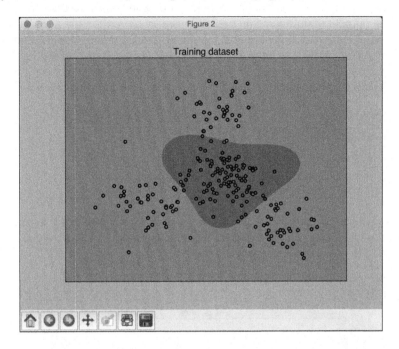

6. You will also see the following classification report printed on your Terminal:

```
#############################

Classifier performance on training dataset

                precision    recall  f1-score   support

      Class-0        0.95      0.98      0.97       105
      Class-1        0.98      0.96      0.97       120

  avg / total        0.97      0.97      0.97       225

#############################
```

Tackling class imbalance

Until now, we dealt with problems where we had a similar number of datapoints in all our classes. In the real world, we might not be able to get data in such an orderly fashion. Sometimes, the number of datapoints in one class is a lot more than the number of datapoints in other classes. If this happens, then the classifier tends to get biased. The boundary won't reflect of the true nature of your data just because there is a big difference in the number of datapoints between the two classes. Therefore, it becomes important to account for this discrepancy and neutralize it so that our classifier remains impartial.

How to do it...

1. Let's load the data:

```
input_file = 'data_multivar_imbalance.txt'
X, y = utilities.load_data(input_file)
```

2. Let's visualize the data. The code for visualization is exactly the same as it was in the previous recipe. You can also find it in the file named `svm_imbalance.py` already provided to you. If you run it, you will see the following figure:

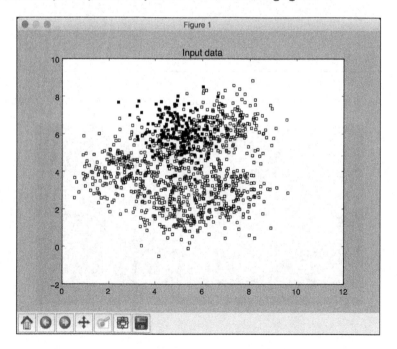

3. Let's build an SVM with a linear kernel. The code is the same as it was in the previous recipe. If you run it, you will see the following figure:

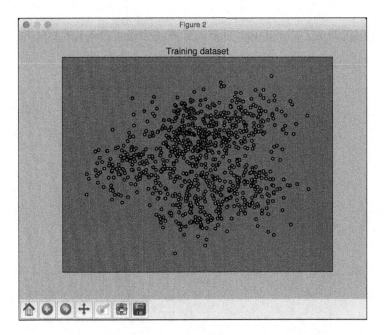

4. You might wonder why there's no boundary here! Well, this is because the classifier is unable to separate the two classes at all, resulting in 0% accuracy for Class-0. You will also see a classification report printed on your Terminal, as shown in the following screenshot:

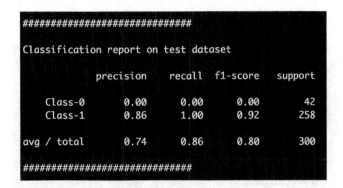

As we expected, Class-0 has 0% precision.

5. Let's go ahead and fix this! In the Python file, search for the following line:

```
params = {'kernel': 'linear'}
```

Replace the preceding line with the following:

```
params = {'kernel': 'linear', 'class_weight': 'auto'}
```

The `class_weight` parameter will count the number of datapoints in each class to adjust the weights so that the imbalance doesn't adversely affect the performance.

6. You will get the following figure once you run this code:

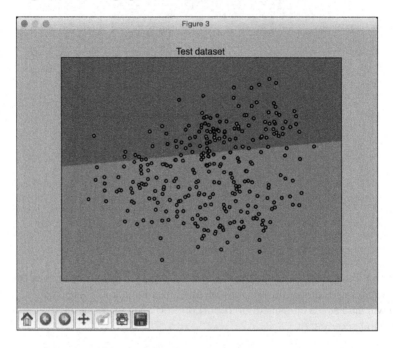

7. Let's look at the classification report, as follows:

```
##############################

Classification report on test dataset

                precision    recall   f1-score    support

    Class-0        0.29        0.76       0.42         42
    Class-1        0.95        0.70       0.80        258

avg / total        0.86        0.71       0.75        300

##############################
```

As we can see, `Class-0` is now detected with nonzero percentage accuracy.

Extracting confidence measurements

It would be nice to know the confidence with which we classify unknown data. When a new datapoint is classified into a known category, we can train the SVM to compute the confidence level of this output as well.

How to do it...

1. The full code is given in the `svm_confidence.py` file already provided to you. We will only discuss the core of the recipe here. Let's define some input data:

```
# Measure distance from the boundary
input_datapoints = np.array([[2, 1.5], [8, 9], [4.8, 5.2], [4, 4],
[2.5, 7], [7.6, 2], [5.4, 5.9]])
```

2. Let's measure the distance from the boundary:

```
print "\nDistance from the boundary:"
for i in input_datapoints:
    print i, '-->', classifier.decision_function(i)[0]
```

3. You will see the following printed on your Terminal:

```
Distance from the boundary:
[ 2.    1.5] --> 0.92489688282
[ 8.    9.] --> 0.642239002462
[ 4.8  5.2] --> -2.03541766793
[ 4.    4.] --> -0.07623172175
[ 2.5  7. ] --> 0.734559329252
[ 7.6  2. ] --> 1.09824378145
[ 5.4  5.9] --> -1.21145495531
```

4. Distance from the boundary gives us some information about the datapoint, but it doesn't exactly tell us how confident the classifier is about the output tag. To do this, we need **Platt scaling**. This is a method that converts the distance measure into probability measure between classes. You can check out the following tutorial to learn more about Platt scaling: `http://fastml.com/classifier-calibration-with-platts-scaling-and-isotonic-regression`. Let's go ahead and train an SVM using Platt scaling:

```
# Confidence measure
params = {'kernel': 'rbf', 'probability': True}
classifier = SVC(**params)
```

The `probability` parameter tells the SVM that it should train to compute the probabilities as well.

5. Let's train the classifier:

```
classifier.fit(X_train, y_train)
```

6. Let's compute the confidence measurements for these input datapoints:

```
print "\nConfidence measure:"
for i in input_datapoints:
    print i, '-->', classifier.predict_proba(i)[0]
```

The `predict_proba` function measures the confidence value.

7. You will see the following on your Terminal:

```
Confidence measure:
[ 2.    1.5] --> [ 0.05126939  0.94873061]
[ 8.    9.] --> [ 0.11146888  0.88853112]
[ 4.8  5.2] --> [ 0.99728099  0.00271901]
[ 4.    4.] --> [ 0.51684952  0.48315048]
[ 2.5  7. ] --> [ 0.08697132  0.91302868]
[ 7.6  2. ] --> [ 0.03124531  0.96875469]
[ 5.4  5.9] --> [ 0.96844526  0.03155474]
```

8. Let's see where the points are with respect to the boundary:

```
utilities.plot_classifier(classifier, input_datapoints,
[0]*len(input_datapoints), 'Input datapoints', 'True')
```

9. If you run this, you will get the following figure:

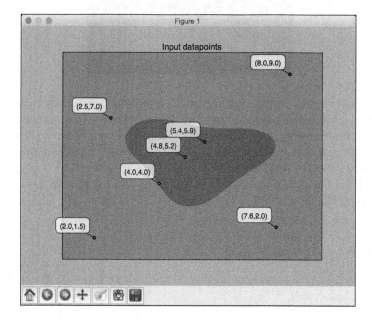

Finding optimal hyperparameters

As discussed in the previous chapter, hyperparameters are important in determining the performance of a classifier. Let's see how to extract optimal hyperparameters for SVMs.

How to do it...

1. The full code is given in the `perform_grid_search.py` file that's already provided to you. We will only discuss the core parts of the recipe here. We will use cross-validation here, which we covered in the previous recipes. Once you load the data and split it into training and testing datasets, add the following to the file:

```
# Set the parameters by cross-validation
parameter_grid = [  {'kernel': ['linear'], 'C': [1, 10, 50, 600]},
                    {'kernel': ['poly'], 'degree': [2, 3]},
                    {'kernel': ['rbf'], 'gamma': [0.01, 0.001],
'C': [1, 10, 50, 600]},
                  ]
```

2. Let's define the metrics that we want to use:

```
metrics = ['precision', 'recall_weighted']
```

3. Let's start the search for optimal hyperparameters for each of the metrics:

```
for metric in metrics:
    print "\n#### Searching optimal hyperparameters for", metric

    classifier = grid_search.GridSearchCV(svm.SVC(C=1),
            parameter_grid, cv=5, scoring=metric)
    classifier.fit(X_train, y_train)
```

4. Let's look at the scores:

```
    print "\nScores across the parameter grid:"
    for params, avg_score, _ in classifier.grid_scores_:
        print params, '-->', round(avg_score, 3)
```

5. Let's print the best parameter set:

```
    print "\nHighest scoring parameter set:", classifier.best_
params_
```

6. If you run this code, you will see the following on your Terminal:

```
#### Searching optimal hyperparameters for precision

Scores across the parameter grid:
{'kernel': 'linear', 'C': 1} --> 0.676
{'kernel': 'linear', 'C': 10} --> 0.676
{'kernel': 'linear', 'C': 50} --> 0.676
{'kernel': 'linear', 'C': 600} --> 0.676
{'kernel': 'poly', 'degree': 2} --> 0.872
{'kernel': 'poly', 'degree': 3} --> 0.872
{'kernel': 'rbf', 'C': 1, 'gamma': 0.01} --> 0.98
{'kernel': 'rbf', 'C': 1, 'gamma': 0.001} --> 0.533
{'kernel': 'rbf', 'C': 10, 'gamma': 0.01} --> 0.983
{'kernel': 'rbf', 'C': 10, 'gamma': 0.001} --> 0.543
{'kernel': 'rbf', 'C': 50, 'gamma': 0.01} --> 0.959
{'kernel': 'rbf', 'C': 50, 'gamma': 0.001} --> 0.806
{'kernel': 'rbf', 'C': 600, 'gamma': 0.01} --> 0.967
{'kernel': 'rbf', 'C': 600, 'gamma': 0.001} --> 0.983

Highest scoring parameter set: {'kernel': 'rbf', 'C': 10, 'gamma': 0.01}
```

7. As we can see in the preceding figure, it searches for all the optimal hyperparameters. In this case, the hyperparameters are the type of kernel, the C value, and gamma. It will try out various combinations of these parameters to find the best parameters. Let's test it out on the testing dataset:

```
y_true, y_pred = y_test, classifier.predict(X_test)
print "\nFull performance report:\n"
print classification_report(y_true, y_pred)
```

8. If you run this code, you will see the following on your Terminal:

```
Full performance report:

             precision    recall  f1-score   support

        0.0       0.92      0.98      0.95        45
        1.0       0.96      0.87      0.91        30

avg / total       0.94      0.93      0.93        75
```

Building an event predictor

Let's apply all of this knowledge to a real-world problem. We will build an SVM to predict the number of people going in and out of a building. The dataset is available at `https://archive.ics.uci.edu/ml/datasets/CalIt2+Building+People+Counts`. We will use a slightly modified version of this dataset so that it's easier to analyze. The modified data is available in the `building_event_binary.txt` and `building_event_multiclass.txt` files that are already provided to you.

Getting ready

Let's understand the data format before we start building the model. Each line in `building_event_binary.txt` consists of six comma-separated strings. The ordering of these six strings is as follows:

- ▸ Day
- ▸ Date
- ▸ Time
- ▸ The number of people going out of the building
- ▸ The number of people coming into the building
- ▸ The output indicating whether or not it's an event

The first five strings form the input data, and our task is to predict whether or not an event is going on in the building.

Each line in `building_event_multiclass.txt` consists of six comma-separated strings. This is more granular than the previous file in the sense that the output is the exact type of event going on in the building. The ordering of these six strings is as follows:

- ▸ Day
- ▸ Date
- ▸ Time
- ▸ The number of people going out of the building
- ▸ The number of people coming into the building
- ▸ The output indicating the type of event

The first five strings form the input data and our task is to predict what type of event is going on in the building.

How to do it...

1. We will use `event.py` that's already provided to you for reference. Create a new Python file, and add the following lines:

```python
import numpy as np
from sklearn import preprocessing
from sklearn.svm import SVC

input_file = 'building_event_binary.txt'

# Reading the data
X = []
count = 0
with open(input_file, 'r') as f:
    for line in f.readlines():
        data = line[:-1].split(',')
        X.append([data[0]] + data[2:])

X = np.array(X)
```

We just loaded all the data into X.

2. Let's convert the data into numerical form:

```python
# Convert string data to numerical data
label_encoder = []
X_encoded = np.empty(X.shape)
for i,item in enumerate(X[0]):
    if item.isdigit():
        X_encoded[:, i] = X[:, i]
    else:
        label_encoder.append(preprocessing.LabelEncoder())
        X_encoded[:, i] = label_encoder[-1].fit_transform(X[:, i])

X = X_encoded[:, :-1].astype(int)
y = X_encoded[:, -1].astype(int)
```

3. Let's train the SVM using the radial basis function, Platt scaling, and class balancing:

```python
# Build SVM
params = {'kernel': 'rbf', 'probability': True, 'class_weight':
'auto'}
classifier = SVC(**params)
classifier.fit(X, y)
```

4. We are now ready to perform cross-validation:

```
# Cross validation
from sklearn import cross_validation

accuracy = cross_validation.cross_val_score(classifier,
        X, y, scoring='accuracy', cv=3)
print "Accuracy of the classifier: " + str(round(100*accuracy.
mean(), 2)) + "%"
```

5. Let's test our SVM on a new datapoint:

```
# Testing on single data instance
input_data = ['Tuesday', '12:30:00','21','23']
input_data_encoded = [-1] * len(input_data)
count = 0
for i,item in enumerate(input_data):
    if item.isdigit():
        input_data_encoded[i] = int(input_data[i])
    else:
        input_data_encoded[i] = int(label_encoder[count].
transform(input_data[i]))
        count = count + 1

input_data_encoded = np.array(input_data_encoded)

# Predict and print output for a particular datapoint
output_class = classifier.predict(input_data_encoded)
print "Output class:", label_encoder[-1].inverse_transform(output_
class)[0]
```

6. If you run this code, you will see the following output on your Terminal:

   Accuracy of the classifier: 89.88%

   Output class: event

7. If you use the `building_event_multiclass.txt` file as the input data file instead of `building_event_binary.txt`, you will see the following output on your Terminal:

   Accuracy of the classifier: 65.9%

   Output class: eventA

Estimating traffic

An interesting application of SVMs is to predict the traffic, based on related data. In the previous recipe, we used an SVM as a classifier. In this recipe, we will use it as a regressor to estimate the traffic.

Getting ready

We will use the dataset available at `https://archive.ics.uci.edu/ml/datasets/Dodgers+Loop+Sensor`. This is a dataset that counts the number of cars passing by during baseball games at Los Angeles Dodgers home stadium. We will use a slightly modified form of that dataset so that it's easier to analyze. You can use the `traffic_data.txt` file already provided to you. Each line in this file contains comma-separated strings formatted in the following manner:

  ▶ Day
  ▶ Time
  ▶ The opponent team
  ▶ Whether or not a baseball game is going on
  ▶ The number of cars passing by

How to do it...

1. Let's see how to build an SVM regressor. We will use `traffic.py` that's already provided to you as a reference. Create a new Python file, and add the following lines:

```
# SVM regressor to estimate traffic

import numpy as np
from sklearn import preprocessing
from sklearn.svm import SVR

input_file = 'traffic_data.txt'

# Reading the data
X = []
count = 0
with open(input_file, 'r') as f:
    for line in f.readlines():
        data = line[:-1].split(',')
        X.append(data)

X = np.array(X)
```

We loaded all the input data into X.

2. Let's encode this data:

```
# Convert string data to numerical data
label_encoder = []
X_encoded = np.empty(X.shape)
for i,item in enumerate(X[0]):
    if item.isdigit():
        X_encoded[:, i] = X[:, i]
    else:
        label_encoder.append(preprocessing.LabelEncoder())
        X_encoded[:, i] = label_encoder[-1].fit_transform(X[:, i])

X = X_encoded[:, :-1].astype(int)
y = X_encoded[:, -1].astype(int)
```

3. Let's build and train the SVM regressor using the radial basis function:

```
# Build SVR
params = {'kernel': 'rbf', 'C': 10.0, 'epsilon': 0.2}
regressor = SVR(**params)
regressor.fit(X, y)
```

In the preceding lines, the C parameter specifies the penalty for misclassification and epsilon specifies the limit within which no penalty is applied.

4. Let's perform cross-validation to check the performance of the regressor:

```
# Cross validation
import sklearn.metrics as sm

y_pred = regressor.predict(X)
print "Mean absolute error =", round(sm.mean_absolute_error(y, y_
pred), 2)
```

5. Let's test it on a datapoint:

```
# Testing encoding on single data instance
input_data = ['Tuesday', '13:35', 'San Francisco', 'yes']
input_data_encoded = [-1] * len(input_data)
count = 0
for i,item in enumerate(input_data):
    if item.isdigit():
        input_data_encoded[i] = int(input_data[i])
    else:
        input_data_encoded[i] = int(label_encoder[count].
transform(input_data[i]))
        count = count + 1
```

```
input_data_encoded = np.array(input_data_encoded)

# Predict and print output for a particular datapoint
print "Predicted traffic:", int(regressor.predict(input_data_
encoded)[0])
```

6. If you run this code, you will see the following printed on your Terminal:

Mean absolute error = 4.08

Predicted traffic: 29

4
Clustering with Unsupervised Learning

In this chapter, we will cover the following recipes:

- ▶ Clustering data using the k-means algorithm
- ▶ Compressing an image using vector quantization
- ▶ Building a Mean Shift clustering model
- ▶ Grouping data using agglomerative clustering
- ▶ Evaluating the performance of clustering algorithms
- ▶ Automatically estimating the number of clusters using DBSCAN algorithm
- ▶ Finding patterns in stock market data
- ▶ Building a customer segmentation model

Introduction

Unsupervised learning is a paradigm in machine learning where we build models without relying on labeled training data. Until this point, we dealt with data that was labeled in some way. This means that learning algorithms can look at this data and learn to categorize them based on labels. In the world of unsupervised learning, we don't have this luxury! These algorithms are used when we want to find subgroups within datasets using some similarity metric.

One of the most common methods is **clustering**. You must have heard this term being used quite frequently. We mainly use it for data analysis where we want to find clusters in our data. These clusters are usually found using certain kind of similarity measure such as Euclidean distance. Unsupervised learning is used extensively in many fields, such as data mining, medical imaging, stock market analysis, computer vision, market segmentation, and so on.

Clustering data using the k-means algorithm

The **k-means algorithm** is one of the most popular clustering algorithms. This algorithm is used to divide the input data into *k* subgroups using various attributes of the data. Grouping is achieved using an optimization technique where we try to minimize the sum of squares of distances between the datapoints and the corresponding centroid of the cluster. If you need a quick refresher, you can learn more about k-means at http://www.onmyphd.com/?p=k-means.clustering&ckattempt=1.

How to do it...

1. The full code for this recipe is given in the kmeans.py file already provided to you. Let's look at how it's built. Create a new Python file, and import the following packages:

```python
import numpy as np
import matplotlib.pyplot as plt
from sklearn import metrics
from sklearn.cluster import KMeans

import utilities
```

2. Let's load the input data and define the number of clusters. We will use the data_multivar.txt file that's already provided to you:

```python
data = utilities.load_data('data_multivar.txt')
num_clusters = 4
```

3. We need to see what the input data looks like. Let's go ahead and add the following lines of the code to the Python file:

```python
plt.figure()
plt.scatter(data[:,0], data[:,1], marker='o',
        facecolors='none', edgecolors='k', s=30)
x_min, x_max = min(data[:, 0]) - 1, max(data[:, 0]) + 1
y_min, y_max = min(data[:, 1]) - 1, max(data[:, 1]) + 1
plt.title('Input data')
plt.xlim(x_min, x_max)
plt.ylim(y_min, y_max)
plt.xticks(())
plt.yticks(())
```

If you run this code, you will get the following figure:

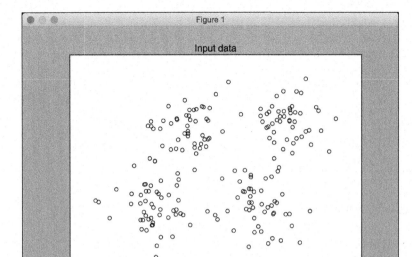

4. We are now ready to train the model. Let's initialize the k-means object and train it:

```
kmeans = KMeans(init='k-means++', n_clusters=num_clusters, n_
init=10)
kmeans.fit(data)
```

5. Now that the data is trained, we need to visualize the boundaries. Let's go ahead and add the following lines of code to the Python file:

```
# Step size of the mesh
step_size = 0.01

# Plot the boundaries
x_min, x_max = min(data[:, 0]) - 1, max(data[:, 0]) + 1
y_min, y_max = min(data[:, 1]) - 1, max(data[:, 1]) + 1
x_values, y_values = np.meshgrid(np.arange(x_min, x_max, step_
size), np.arange(y_min, y_max, step_size))

# Predict labels for all points in the mesh
predicted_labels = kmeans.predict(np.c_[x_values.ravel(), y_
values.ravel()])
```

6. We just evaluated the model across a grid of points. Let's plot these results to view the boundaries:

```
# Plot the results
predicted_labels = predicted_labels.reshape(x_values.shape)
plt.figure()
plt.clf()
plt.imshow(predicted_labels, interpolation='nearest',
        extent=(x_values.min(), x_values.max(), y_values.min(),
y_values.max()),
        cmap=plt.cm.Paired,
        aspect='auto', origin='lower')

plt.scatter(data[:,0], data[:,1], marker='o',
        facecolors='none', edgecolors='k', s=30)
```

7. Let's overlay the centroids on top of it:

```
centroids = kmeans.cluster_centers_
plt.scatter(centroids[:,0], centroids[:,1], marker='o', s=200,
linewidths=3,
        color='k', zorder=10, facecolors='black')
x_min, x_max = min(data[:, 0]) - 1, max(data[:, 0]) + 1
y_min, y_max = min(data[:, 1]) - 1, max(data[:, 1]) + 1
plt.title('Centoids and boundaries obtained using KMeans')
plt.xlim(x_min, x_max)
plt.ylim(y_min, y_max)
plt.xticks(())
plt.yticks(())
plt.show()
```

If you run this code, you should see the following figure:

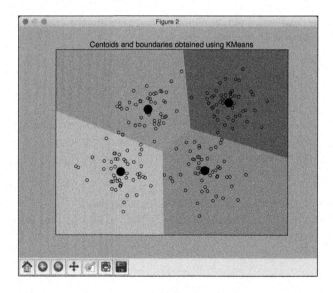

Compressing an image using vector quantization

One of the main applications of k-means clustering is **vector quantization**. Simply speaking, vector quantization is the *N*-dimensional version of "rounding off". When we deal with 1D data, such as numbers, we use the rounding-off technique to reduce the memory needed to store that value. For example, instead of storing 23.73473572, we just store 23.73 if we want to be accurate up to the second decimal place. Or, we can just store 24 if we don't care about decimal places. It depends on our needs and the trade-off that we are willing to make.

Similarly, when we extend this concept to *N*-dimensional data, it becomes vector quantization. Of course there are more nuances to it! You can learn more about it at http://www.data-compression.com/vq.shtml. Vector quantization is popularly used in image compression where we store each pixel using fewer bits than the original image to achieve compression.

How to do it...

1. The full code for this recipe is given in the vector_quantization.py file already provided to you. Let's look at how it's built. We'll start by importing the required packages. Create a new Python file, and add the following lines:

```
import argparse

import numpy as np
from scipy import misc
from sklearn import cluster
import matplotlib.pyplot as plt
```

2. Let's create a function to parse the input arguments. We will be able to pass the image and the number of bits per pixel as input arguments:

```
def build_arg_parser():
    parser = argparse.ArgumentParser(description='Compress the
input image \
            using clustering')
    parser.add_argument("--input-file", dest="input_file",
required=True,
            help="Input image")
    parser.add_argument("--num-bits", dest="num_bits",
required=False,
            type=int, help="Number of bits used to represent each
pixel")
    return parser
```

3. Let's create a function to compress the input image:

```
def compress_image(img, num_clusters):
    # Convert input image into (num_samples, num_features)
    # array to run kmeans clustering algorithm
    X = img.reshape((-1, 1))

    # Run kmeans on input data
    kmeans = cluster.KMeans(n_clusters=num_clusters, n_init=4,
random_state=5)
    kmeans.fit(X)
    centroids = kmeans.cluster_centers_.squeeze()
    labels = kmeans.labels_

    # Assign each value to the nearest centroid and
    # reshape it to the original image shape
    input_image_compressed = np.choose(labels, centroids).
reshape(img.shape)

    return input_image_compressed
```

4. Once we compress the image, we need to see how it affects the quality. Let's define a function to plot the output image:

```
def plot_image(img, title):
    vmin = img.min()
    vmax = img.max()
    plt.figure()
    plt.title(title)
    plt.imshow(img, cmap=plt.cm.gray, vmin=vmin, vmax=vmax)
```

5. We are now ready to use all these functions. Let's define the `main` function that takes the input arguments, processes them, and extracts the output image:

```
if __name__=='__main__':
    args = build_arg_parser().parse_args()
    input_file = args.input_file
    num_bits = args.num_bits

    if not 1 <= num_bits <= 8:
        raise TypeError('Number of bits should be between 1 and
8')

    num_clusters = np.power(2, num_bits)

    # Print compression rate
    compression_rate = round(100 * (8.0 - args.num_bits) / 8.0, 2)
```

```
        print "\nThe size of the image will be reduced by a factor
of", 8.0/args.num_bits
        print "\nCompression rate = " + str(compression_rate) + "%"
```

6. Let's load the input image:

```
# Load input image
input_image = misc.imread(input_file, True).astype(np.uint8)

# original image
plot_image(input_image, 'Original image')
```

7. Let's compress this image using the input argument:

```
# compressed image
input_image_compressed = compress_image(input_image, num_
clusters)
plot_image(input_image_compressed, 'Compressed image;
compression rate = '
            + str(compression_rate) + '%')

plt.show()
```

8. We are now ready to run the code. Run the following command on your Terminal:

```
$ python vector_quantization.py --input-file flower_image.jpg
--num-bits 4
```

The input image looks like the following:

You should get the following compressed image as the output:

9. Let's compress the image further by reducing the number of bits to 2. Run the following command on your Terminal:

```
$ python vector_quantization.py --input-file flower_image.jpg
--num-bits 2
```

You should get the following compressed image as the output:

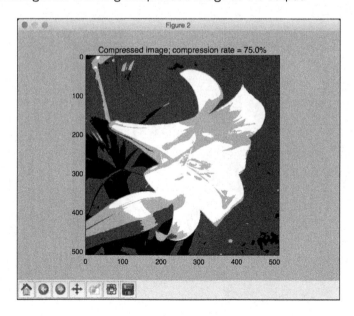

10. If you reduce the number of bits to 1, you can see that it will become a binary image with black and white as the only two colors. Run the following command:

```
$ python vector_quantization.py --input-file flower_image.jpg
--num-bits 1
```

You will get the following output:

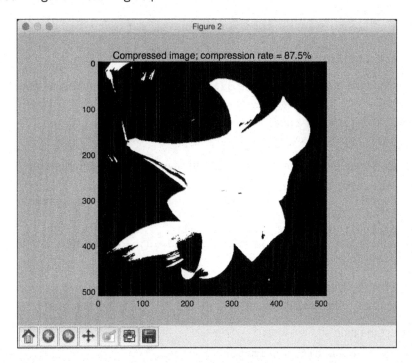

Building a Mean Shift clustering model

The **Mean Shift** is a powerful unsupervised learning algorithm that's used to cluster datapoints. It considers the distribution of datapoints as a probability-density function and tries to find the _modes_ in the feature space. These _modes_ are basically points corresponding to local maxima. The main advantage of Mean Shift algorithm is that we are not required to know the number of clusters beforehand.

Let's say that we have a set of input points, and we are trying to find clusters in them without knowing how many clusters we are looking for. Mean Shift algorithm considers these points to be sampled from a probability density function. If there are clusters in the datapoints, then they correspond to the peaks of that probability-density function. The algorithm starts from random points and iteratively converges toward these peaks. You can learn more about it at `http://homepages.inf.ed.ac.uk/rbf/CVonline/LOCAL_COPIES/TUZEL1/MeanShift.pdf`.

How to do it...

1. The full code for this recipe is given in the `mean_shift.py` file that's already provided to you. Let's look at how it's built. Create a new Python file, and import a couple of required packages:

    ```python
    import numpy as np
    from sklearn.cluster import MeanShift, estimate_bandwidth

    import utilities
    ```

2. Let's load the input data from the `data_multivar.txt` file that's already provided to you:

    ```python
    # Load data from input file
    X = utilities.load_data('data_multivar.txt')
    ```

3. Build a Mean Shift clustering model by specifying the input parameters:

    ```python
    # Estimating the bandwidth
    bandwidth = estimate_bandwidth(X, quantile=0.1, n_samples=len(X))

    # Compute clustering with MeanShift
    meanshift_estimator = MeanShift(bandwidth=bandwidth, bin_
    seeding=True)
    ```

4. Train the model:

    ```python
    meanshift_estimator.fit(X)
    ```

5. Extract the labels:

    ```python
    labels = meanshift_estimator.labels_
    ```

6. Extract the centroids of the clusters from the model and print out the number of clusters:

    ```python
    centroids = meanshift_estimator.cluster_centers_
    num_clusters = len(np.unique(labels))

    print "Number of clusters in input data =", num_clusters
    ```

7. Let's go ahead and visualize it:

    ```python
    # Plot the points and centroids
    import matplotlib.pyplot as plt
    from itertools import cycle

    plt.figure()

    # specify marker shapes for different clusters
    markers = '.*xv'
    ```

8. Iterate through the datapoints and plot them:

```
for i, marker in zip(range(num_clusters), markers):
    # plot the points belong to the current cluster
    plt.scatter(X[labels==i, 0], X[labels==i, 1], marker=marker,
color='k')

    # plot the centroid of the current cluster
    centroid = centroids[i]
    plt.plot(centroid[0], centroid[1], marker='o',
markerfacecolor='k',
            markeredgecolor='k', markersize=15)

plt.title('Clusters and their centroids')
plt.show()
```

9. If you run this code, you will get the following output:

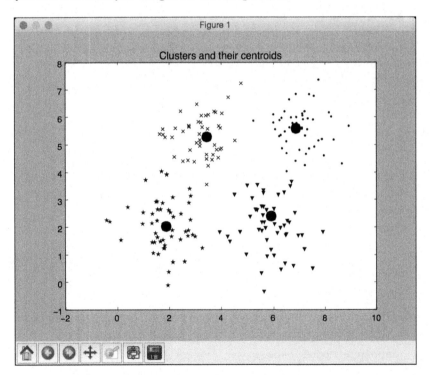

Grouping data using agglomerative clustering

Before we talk about agglomerative clustering, we need to understand hierarchical clustering. **Hierarchical clustering** refers to a set of clustering algorithms that build tree-like clusters by successively splitting or merging them. This hierarchical structure is represented using a tree.

Hierarchical clustering algorithms can be either bottom-up or top-down. Now what does this mean? In bottom-up algorithms, each datapoint is treated as a separate cluster with a single object. These clusters are then successively merged until all the clusters are merged into a single giant cluster. This is called **agglomerative clustering**. On the other hand, top-down algorithms start with a giant cluster and successively split these clusters until individual datapoints are reached. You can learn more about it at http://nlp.stanford.edu/IR-book/html/htmledition/hierarchical-agglomerative-clustering-1.html.

How to do it...

1. The full code for this recipe is given in the `agglomerative.py` file that's provided to you. Let's look at how it's built. Create a new Python file, and import the necessary packages:

```
import numpy as np
import matplotlib.pyplot as plt
from sklearn.cluster import AgglomerativeClustering
from sklearn.neighbors import kneighbors_graph
```

2. Let's define the function that we need to perform agglomerative clustering:

```
def perform_clustering(X, connectivity, title, num_clusters=3,
linkage='ward'):
    plt.figure()
    model = AgglomerativeClustering(linkage=linkage,
                    connectivity=connectivity, n_clusters=num_
clusters)
    model.fit(X)
```

3. Let's extract the labels and specify the shapes of the markers for the graph:

```
# extract labels
labels = model.labels_

# specify marker shapes for different clusters
markers = '.vx'
```

4. Iterate through the datapoints and plot them accordingly using different markers:

```
for i, marker in zip(range(num_clusters), markers):
    # plot the points belong to the current cluster
    plt.scatter(X[labels==i, 0], X[labels==i, 1], s=50,
                marker=marker, color='k', facecolors='none')

plt.title(title)
```

5. In order to demonstrate the advantage of agglomerative clustering, we need to run it on datapoints that are linked spatially but also located close to each other in space. We want the linked datapoints to belong to the same cluster as opposed to datapoints that are just spatially close to each other. Let's define a function to get a set of datapoints on a spiral:

```
def get_spiral(t, noise_amplitude=0.5):
    r = t
    x = r * np.cos(t)
    y = r * np.sin(t)

    return add_noise(x, y, noise_amplitude)
```

6. In the previous function, we added some noise the curve because it adds some uncertainty. Let's define this function:

```
def add_noise(x, y, amplitude):
    X = np.concatenate((x, y))
    X += amplitude * np.random.randn(2, X.shape[1])
    return X.T
```

7. Let's define another function to get datapoints located on a rose curve:

```
def get_rose(t, noise_amplitude=0.02):
    # Equation for "rose" (or rhodonea curve); if k is odd, then
    # the curve will have k petals, else it will have 2k petals
    k = 5
    r = np.cos(k*t) + 0.25
    x = r * np.cos(t)
    y = r * np.sin(t)

    return add_noise(x, y, noise_amplitude)
```

8. Just to add more variety, let's also define a **hypotrochoid**:

```
def get_hypotrochoid(t, noise_amplitude=0):
    a, b, h = 10.0, 2.0, 4.0
    x = (a - b) * np.cos(t) + h * np.cos((a - b) / b * t)
    y = (a - b) * np.sin(t) - h * np.sin((a - b) / b * t)

    return add_noise(x, y, 0)
```

9. We are now ready to define the `main` function:

```
if __name__=='__main__':
    # Generate sample data
    n_samples = 500
    np.random.seed(2)
    t = 2.5 * np.pi * (1 + 2 * np.random.rand(1, n_samples))
    X = get_spiral(t)

    # No connectivity
    connectivity = None
    perform_clustering(X, connectivity, 'No connectivity')

    # Create K-Neighbors graph
    connectivity = kneighbors_graph(X, 10, include_self=False)
    perform_clustering(X, connectivity, 'K-Neighbors
connectivity')

    plt.show()
```

10. If you run this code, you will get the following image if we don't use any connectivity:

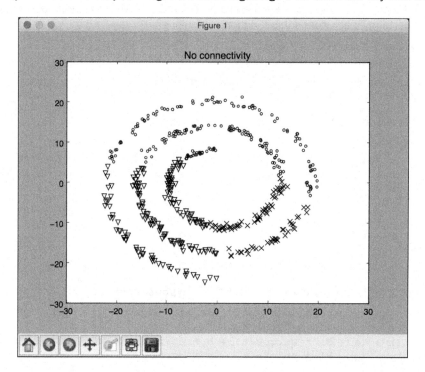

11. The second output image looks like the following:

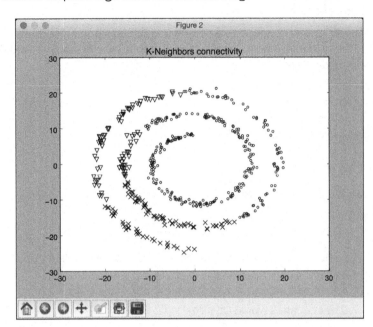

As we can see, using the connectivity feature enables us to the group datapoints that are linked to each other as opposed to clustering them, based on their spatial locations.

Evaluating the performance of clustering algorithms

So far, we built different clustering algorithms but didn't measure their performances. In supervised learning, we just compare the predicted values with the original labels to compute their accuracy. In unsupervised learning, we don't have any labels. Therefore, we need a way to measure the performance of our algorithms.

A good way to measure a clustering algorithm is by seeing how well the clusters are separated. Are the clusters well separated? Are the datapoints in a cluster tight enough? We need a metric that can quantify this behavior. We will use a metric, called **Silhouette Coefficient** score. This score is defined for each datapoint. This coefficient is defined as follows:

$score = (x - y) / max(x, y)$

Here, x is the average distance between the current datapoint and all the other datapoints in the same cluster; y is the average distance between the current datapoint and all the datapoints in the next nearest cluster.

How to do it...

1. The full code for this recipe is given in the `performance.py` file that's already provided to you. Let's look at how it's built. Create a new Python file, and import the following packages:

```python
import numpy as np
import matplotlib.pyplot as plt
from sklearn import metrics
from sklearn.cluster import KMeans

import utilities
```

2. Let's load the input data from the `data_perf.txt` file already provided to you:

```python
# Load data
data = utilities.load_data('data_perf.txt')
```

3. In order to determine the optimal number of clusters, let's iterate through a range of values and see where it peaks:

```python
scores = []
range_values = np.arange(2, 10)

for i in range_values:
    # Train the model
    kmeans = KMeans(init='k-means++', n_clusters=i, n_init=10)
    kmeans.fit(data)
    score = metrics.silhouette_score(data, kmeans.labels_,
                metric='euclidean', sample_size=len(data))

    print "\nNumber of clusters =", i
    print "Silhouette score =", score

    scores.append(score)
```

4. Let's plot the graph to see where it peaked:

```python
# Plot scores
plt.figure()
plt.bar(range_values, scores, width=0.6, color='k',
align='center')
plt.title('Silhouette score vs number of clusters')
```

```
# Plot data
plt.figure()
plt.scatter(data[:,0], data[:,1], color='k', s=30, marker='o',
facecolors='none')
x_min, x_max = min(data[:, 0]) - 1, max(data[:, 0]) + 1
y_min, y_max = min(data[:, 1]) - 1, max(data[:, 1]) + 1
plt.title('Input data')
plt.xlim(x_min, x_max)
plt.ylim(y_min, y_max)
plt.xticks(())
plt.yticks(())

plt.show()
```

5. If you run this code, you will get the following output on the Terminal:

```
Number of clusters = 2
Silhouette score = 0.529039717547

Number of clusters = 3
Silhouette score = 0.557246639118

Number of clusters = 4
Silhouette score = 0.583275751783

Number of clusters = 5
Silhouette score = 0.658279690976

Number of clusters = 6
Silhouette score = 0.582358411948

Number of clusters = 7
Silhouette score = 0.528610740989

Number of clusters = 8
Silhouette score = 0.459759448983

Number of clusters = 9
Silhouette score = 0.415953573837
```

6. The bar graph looks like the following:

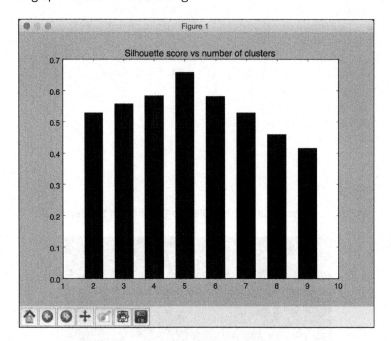

7. As per these scores, the best configuration is five clusters. Let's see what the data actually looks like:

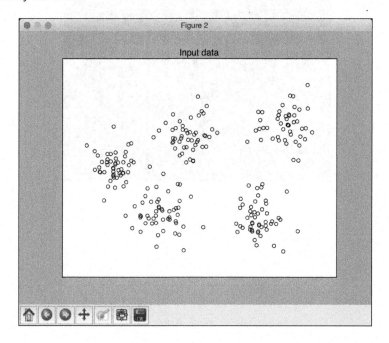

We can visually confirm that the data in fact has five clusters. We just took the example of a small dataset that contains five distinct clusters. This method becomes very useful when you are dealing with a huge dataset that contains high-dimensional data that cannot be visualized easily.

Automatically estimating the number of clusters using DBSCAN algorithm

When we discussed the k-means algorithm, we saw that we had to give the number of clusters as one of the input parameters. In the real world, we wouldn't have this information available. We can definitely sweep the parameter space to find out the optimal number of clusters using the silhouette coefficient score, but this would be an expensive process! Wouldn't it be nice if there were a method that can just tell us the number of clusters in our data? This is where **Density-Based Spatial Clustering of Applications with Noise** (**DBSCAN**) comes into the picture.

This works by treating datapoints as groups of dense clusters. If a point belongs to a cluster, then there should be a lot of others points that belong to the same cluster. One of the parameters that we can control is the maximum distance of this point from other points. This is called **epsilon**. No two points in a given cluster should be further away than epsilon. You can learn more about it at `http://staffwww.itn.liu.se/~aidvi/courses/06/dm/ Seminars2011/DBSCAN(4).pdf`. One of the main advantages of this method is that it can deal with outliers. If there are some points located alone in a low-density area, DBSCAN will detect these points as outliers as opposed to forcing them into a cluster.

How to do it...

1. The full code for this recipe is given in the `estimate_clusters.py` file that's already provided to you. Let's look at how it's built. Create a new Python file, and import the necessary packages:

```
from itertools import cycle

import numpy as np
from sklearn.cluster import DBSCAN
from sklearn import metrics
import matplotlib.pyplot as plt

from utilities import load_data
```

2. Load the input data from the `data_perf.txt` file. This is the same file that we used in the previous recipe, which will help us compare the methods on the same dataset:

```
# Load input data
input_file = 'data_perf.txt'
X = load_data(input_file)
```

3. We need to find the best parameter. Let's initialize a few variables:

```
# Find the best epsilon
eps_grid = np.linspace(0.3, 1.2, num=10)
silhouette_scores = []
eps_best = eps_grid[0]
silhouette_score_max = -1
model_best = None
labels_best = None
```

4. Let's sweep the parameter space:

```
for eps in eps_grid:
    # Train DBSCAN clustering model
    model = DBSCAN(eps=eps, min_samples=5).fit(X)

    # Extract labels
    labels = model.labels_
```

5. For each iteration, we need to extract the performance metric:

```
    # Extract performance metric
    silhouette_score = round(metrics.silhouette_score(X, labels),
4)
    silhouette_scores.append(silhouette_score)

    print "Epsilon:", eps, " --> silhouette score:", silhouette_
score
```

6. We need to store the best score and its associated epsilon value:

```
    if silhouette_score > silhouette_score_max:
        silhouette_score_max = silhouette_score
        eps_best = eps
        model_best = model
        labels_best = labels
```

7. Let's plot the bar graph:

```
# Plot silhouette scores vs epsilon
plt.figure()
plt.bar(eps_grid, silhouette_scores, width=0.05, color='k',
align='center')
plt.title('Silhouette score vs epsilon')

# Best params
print "\nBest epsilon =", eps_best
```

8. Let's store the best models and labels:

```
# Associated model and labels for best epsilon
model = model_best
labels = labels_best
```

9. Some datapoints may remain unassigned. We need to identify them, as follows:

```
# Check for unassigned datapoints in the labels
offset = 0
if -1 in labels:
    offset = 1
```

10. Extract the number of clusters:

```
# Number of clusters in the data
num_clusters = len(set(labels)) - offset

print "\nEstimated number of clusters =", num_clusters
```

11. We need to extract all core samples:

```
# Extracts the core samples from the trained model
mask_core = np.zeros(labels.shape, dtype=np.bool)
mask_core[model.core_sample_indices_] = True
```

12. Let's visualize the resultant clusters. We will start by extracting the set of unique labels and specifying different markers:

```
# Plot resultant clusters
plt.figure()
labels_uniq = set(labels)
markers = cycle('vo^s<>')
```

13. Let's iterate through the clusters and plot the datapoints using different markers:

```
for cur_label, marker in zip(labels_uniq, markers):
    # Use black dots for unassigned datapoints
    if cur_label == -1:
        marker = '.'

    # Create mask for the current label
    cur_mask = (labels == cur_label)

    cur_data = X[cur_mask & mask_core]
    plt.scatter(cur_data[:, 0], cur_data[:, 1], marker=marker,
            edgecolors='black', s=96, facecolors='none')

    cur_data = X[cur_mask & ~mask_core]
    plt.scatter(cur_data[:, 0], cur_data[:, 1], marker=marker,
```

```
                    edgecolors='black', s=32)

    plt.title('Data separated into clusters')
    plt.show()
```

14. If you run this code, you will get the following on your Terminal:

```
Epsilon: 0.3  --> silhouette score: 0.1287
Epsilon: 0.4  --> silhouette score: 0.3594
Epsilon: 0.5  --> silhouette score: 0.5134
Epsilon: 0.6  --> silhouette score: 0.6165
Epsilon: 0.7  --> silhouette score: 0.6322
Epsilon: 0.8  --> silhouette score: 0.6366
Epsilon: 0.9  --> silhouette score: 0.5142
Epsilon: 1.0  --> silhouette score: 0.5629
Epsilon: 1.1  --> silhouette score: 0.5629
Epsilon: 1.2  --> silhouette score: 0.5629

Best epsilon = 0.8

Estimated number of clusters = 5
```

15. You will get the following bar graph:

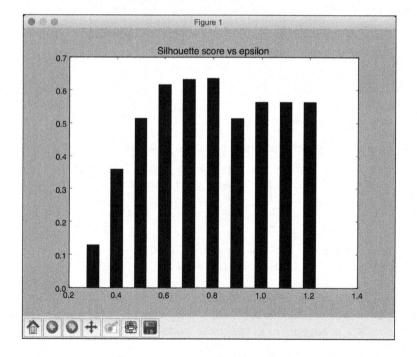

16. Let's look the labeled datapoints along with unassigned datapoints marked by solid points in the following figure:

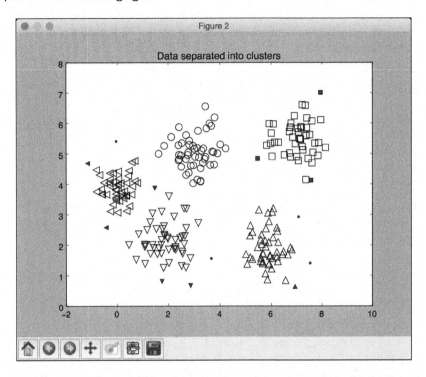

Finding patterns in stock market data

Let's see how we can use unsupervised learning for stock market analysis. We will operate with the assumption that we don't know how many clusters there are. As we don't know the number of clusters, we will use an algorithm called **Affinity Propagation** to cluster. It tries to find a representative datapoint for each cluster in our data. It tries to find measures of similarity between pairs of datapoints and considers all our datapoints as potential representatives, also called **exemplars**, of their respective clusters. You can learn more about it at http://www. cs.columbia.edu/~delbert/docs/DDueck-thesis_small.pdf

In this recipe, we will analyze the stock market variations of companies in a specified duration of time. Our goal is to then find out what companies behave similarly in terms of their quotes over time.

How to do it...

1. The full code for this recipe is given in the `stock_market.py` file that's already provided to you. Let's look at how it's built. Create a new Python file, and import the following packages:

```python
import json
import datetime

import numpy as np
import matplotlib.pyplot as plt
from sklearn import covariance, cluster
from matplotlib.finance import quotes_historical_yahoo_ochl as quotes_yahoo
```

2. We need a file that contains all the symbols and the associated names. This information is located in the `symbol_map.json` file provided to you. Let's load this, as follows:

```python
# Input symbol file
symbol_file = 'symbol_map.json'
```

3. Let's read the data from the symbol map file:

```python
# Load the symbol map
with open(symbol_file, 'r') as f:
    symbol_dict = json.loads(f.read())

symbols, names = np.array(list(symbol_dict.items())).T
```

4. Let's specify a time period for the purpose of this analysis. We will use these start and end dates to load the input data:

```python
# Choose a time period
start_date = datetime.datetime(2004, 4, 5)
end_date = datetime.datetime(2007, 6, 2)
```

5. Let's read the input data:

```python
quotes = [quotes_yahoo(symbol, start_date, end_date,
asobject=True)
                for symbol in symbols]
```

6. As we need some feature points for analysis, we will use the difference between the opening and closing quotes every day to analyze the data:

```python
# Extract opening and closing quotes
opening_quotes = np.array([quote.open for quote in quotes]).
astype(np.float)
```

```
closing_quotes = np.array([quote.close for quote in quotes]).
astype(np.float)

# The daily fluctuations of the quotes
delta_quotes = closing_quotes - opening_quotes
```

7. Let's build a graph model:

```
# Build a graph model from the correlations
edge_model = covariance.GraphLassoCV()
```

8. We need to standardize the data before we use it:

```
# Standardize the data
X = delta_quotes.copy().T
X /= X.std(axis=0)
```

9. Let's train the model using this data:

```
# Train the model
with np.errstate(invalid='ignore'):
    edge_model.fit(X)
```

10. We are now ready to build the clustering model:

```
# Build clustering model using affinity propagation
_, labels = cluster.affinity_propagation(edge_model.covariance_)
num_labels = labels.max()

# Print the results of clustering
for i in range(num_labels + 1):
    print "Cluster", i+1, "-->", ', '.join(names[labels == i])
```

11. If you run this code, you will get the following output on the Terminal:

```
Cluster 1 --> ConocoPhillips, Chevron, Total, Valero Energy, Exxon
Cluster 2 --> CVS, Walgreen
Cluster 3 --> IBM, Cisco, Microsoft, Texas instruments, Ford, HP, Dell
Cluster 4 --> Cablevision
Cluster 5 --> Pfizer, Apple, Caterpillar, Canon, Boeing, Toyota, SAP, Honda, Mitsubishi, Sony, Mc Donalds
, Unilever, Wal-Mart
Cluster 6 --> Kimberly-Clark, Colgate-Palmolive, Procter Gamble
Cluster 7 --> Yahoo, Amazon
Cluster 8 --> American express, Wells Fargo, Navistar, Bank of America, Time Warner, Ryder, Kellogg, Home
 Depot, AIG, Goldman Sachs, General Electrics, Marriott, Xerox, JPMorgan Chase, DuPont de Nemours, 3M, Co
mcast
Cluster 9 --> GlaxoSmithKline, Novartis, Sanofi-Aventis
Cluster 10 --> Pepsi, Coca Cola
Cluster 11 --> Raytheon, Lookheed Martin, General Dynamics, Northrop Grumman
Cluster 12 --> Kraft Foods
```

Building a customer segmentation model

One of the main applications of unsupervised learning is market segmentation. This is when we don't have labeled data available all the time, but it's important to segment the market so that people can target individual groups. This is very useful in advertising, inventory management, implementing strategies for distribution, mass media, and so on. Let's go ahead and apply unsupervised learning to one such case to see how it can be useful.

We will be dealing with a wholesale vendor and his customers. We will be using the data available at `https://archive.ics.uci.edu/ml/datasets/Wholesale+customers`. The spreadsheet contains data regarding the consumption of different types of items by their customers and our goal is to find clusters so that they can optimize their sales and distribution strategy.

How to do it...

1. The full code for this recipe is given in the `customer_segmentation.py` file that's already provided to you. Let's look at how it's built. Create a new Python file, and import the following packages:

    ```
    import csv

    import numpy as np
    from sklearn import cluster, covariance, manifold
    from sklearn.cluster import MeanShift, estimate_bandwidth
    import matplotlib.pyplot as plt
    ```

2. Let's load the input data from the `wholesale.csv` file that's already provided to you:

    ```
    # Load data from input file
    input_file = 'wholesale.csv'
    file_reader = csv.reader(open(input_file, 'rb'), delimiter=',')
    X = []
    for count, row in enumerate(file_reader):
        if not count:
            names = row[2:]
            continue

        X.append([float(x) for x in row[2:]])

    # Input data as numpy array
    X = np.array(X)
    ```

3. Let's build a Mean Shift model like we did in one of the earlier recipes:

```
# Estimating the bandwidth
bandwidth = estimate_bandwidth(X, quantile=0.8, n_samples=len(X))

# Compute clustering with MeanShift
meanshift_estimator = MeanShift(bandwidth=bandwidth, bin_
seeding=True)
meanshift_estimator.fit(X)
labels = meanshift_estimator.labels_
centroids = meanshift_estimator.cluster_centers_
num_clusters = len(np.unique(labels))

print "\nNumber of clusters in input data =", num_clusters
```

4. Let's print the centroids of clusters that we obtained, as follows:

```
print "\nCentroids of clusters:"
print '\t'.join([name[:3] for name in names])
for centroid in centroids:
    print '\t'.join([str(int(x)) for x in centroid])
```

5. Let's visualize a couple of features to get a sense of the output:

```
# Visualizing data

centroids_milk_groceries = centroids[:, 1:3]

# Plot the nodes using the coordinates of our centroids_milk_
groceries
plt.figure()
plt.scatter(centroids_milk_groceries[:,0], centroids_milk_
groceries[:,1],
        s=100, edgecolors='k', facecolors='none')

offset = 0.2
plt.xlim(centroids_milk_groceries[:,0].min() - offset * centroids_
milk_groceries[:,0].ptp(),
        centroids_milk_groceries[:,0].max() + offset * centroids_
milk_groceries[:,0].ptp(),)
plt.ylim(centroids_milk_groceries[:,1].min() - offset * centroids_
milk_groceries[:,1].ptp(),
        centroids_milk_groceries[:,1].max() + offset * centroids_
milk_groceries[:,1].ptp())

plt.title('Centroids of clusters for milk and groceries')
plt.show()
```

6. If you run this code, you will get the following output on the Terminal:

```
Number of clusters in input data = 8

Centroids of clusters:
Fre      Mil      Gro      Fro      Det      Del
9632     4671     6593     2570     2296     1248
40204    46314    57584    5518     25436    4241
8565     4980     67298    131      38102    1215
32717    16784    13626    60869    1272     5609
22925    73498    32114    987      20070    903
112151   29627    18148    16745    4948     8550
16117    46197    92780    1026     40827    2944
36847    43950    20170    36534    239      47943
```

7. You will get the following image that depicts the centroids for the features *milk* and *groceries*, where milk is on the X-axis and groceries is on the Y-axis:

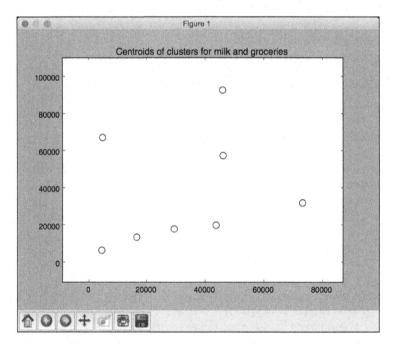

5
Building Recommendation Engines

In this chapter, we will cover the following recipes:

- ▶ Building function compositions for data processing
- ▶ Building machine learning pipelines
- ▶ Finding the nearest neighbors
- ▶ Constructing a k-nearest neighbors classifier
- ▶ Constructing a k-nearest neighbors regressor
- ▶ Computing the Euclidean distance score
- ▶ Computing the Pearson correlation score
- ▶ Finding similar users in the dataset
- ▶ Generating movie recommendations

Introduction

A recommendation engine is a model that can predict what a user may be interested in. When we apply this to the context of movies, this becomes a movie-recommendation engine. We filter items in our database by predicting how the current user might rate them. This helps us in connecting the users with the right content in our dataset. Why is this relevant? If you have a massive catalog, then the users may or may not find all the relevant content. By recommending the right content, you increase consumption. Companies such as Netflix heavily rely on recommendations to keep the user engaged.

Recommendation engines usually produce a set of recommendations using either collaborative filtering or content-based filtering. The difference between the two approaches is in the way the recommendations are mined. Collaborative filtering builds a model from the past behavior of the current user as well as ratings given by other users. We then use this model to predict what this user might be interested in. Content-based filtering, on the other hand, uses the characteristics of the item itself in order to recommend more items to the user. The similarity between items is the main driving force here. In this chapter, we will focus on collaborative filtering.

Building function compositions for data processing

One of the major parts of any machine learning system is the data processing pipeline. Before data is fed into the machine learning algorithm for training, we need to process it in different ways to make it suitable for that algorithm. Having a robust data processing pipeline goes a long way in building an accurate and scalable machine learning system. There are a lot of basic functionalities available, and data processing pipelines usually consist of a combination of these. Instead of calling these functions in a nested or loopy way, it's better to use the functional programming paradigm to build the combination. Let's take a look at how to combine these functions to form a reusable function composition. In this recipe, we will create three basic functions and look at how to compose a pipeline.

How to do it...

1. Create a new Python file, and add the following line:

```
import numpy as np
```

2. Let's define a function to add 3 to each element of the array:

```
def add3(input_array):
    return map(lambda x: x+3, input_array)
```

3. Let's define a second function to multiply 2 with each element of the array:

```
def mul2(input_array):
    return map(lambda x: x*2, input_array)
```

4. Let's define a third function to subtract 5 from each element of the array:

```
def sub5(input_array):
    return map(lambda x: x-5, input_array)
```

5. Let's define a function composer that takes functions as input arguments and returns a composed function. This composed function is basically a function that applies all the input functions in sequence:

```
def function_composer(*args):
    return reduce(lambda f, g: lambda x: f(g(x)), args)
```

We use the `reduce` function to combine all the input functions by successively applying the functions in sequence.

6. We are now ready to play with this function composer. Let's define some data and a sequence of operations:

```
if __name__=='__main__':
    arr = np.array([2,5,4,7])

    print "\nOperation: add3(mul2(sub5(arr)))"
```

7. If we were to use the regular method, we apply this successively, as follows:

```
    arr1 = add3(arr)
    arr2 = mul2(arr1)
    arr3 = sub5(arr2)
    print "Output using the lengthy way:", arr3
```

8. Let's use the function composer to achieve the same thing in a single line:

```
    func_composed = function_composer(sub5, mul2, add3)
    print "Output using function composition:", func_composed(arr)
```

9. We can do the same thing in a single line with the previous method as well, but the notation becomes really nested and unreadable. Also, this is not reusable! You have to write the whole thing again if you want to reuse this sequence of operations:

```
    print "\nOperation: sub5(add3(mul2(sub5(mul2(arr)))))\
nOutput:", \
            function_composer(mul2, sub5, mul2, add3, sub5)(arr)
```

10. If you run this code, you will get the following output on the Terminal:

```
Operation: add3(mul2(sub5(arr)))
Output using the lengthy way: [5, 11, 9, 15]
Output using function composition: [5, 11, 9, 15]

Operation: sub5(add3(mul2(sub5(mul2(arr)))))
Output: [-10, 2, -2, 10]
```

Building machine learning pipelines

The scikit-learn library has provisions to build machine learning pipelines. We just need to specify the functions, and it will build a composed object that makes the data go through the whole pipeline. This pipeline can include functions, such as preprocessing, feature selection, supervised learning, unsupervised learning, and so on. In this recipe, we will be building a pipeline to take the input feature vector, select the top *k* features, and then classify them using a random forest classifier.

How to do it...

1. Create a new Python file, and import the following packages:

```
from sklearn.datasets import samples_generator
from sklearn.ensemble import RandomForestClassifier
from sklearn.feature_selection import SelectKBest, f_regression
from sklearn.pipeline import Pipeline
```

2. Let's generate some sample data to play with:

```
# generate sample data
X, y = samples_generator.make_classification(
        n_informative=4, n_features=20, n_redundant=0, random_
state=5)
```

This line generated 20 dimensional feature vectors because this is the default value. You can change it using the n_features parameter in the previous line.

3. Our first step of the pipeline is to select the *k* best features and before the datapoint is used further. In this case, let's set k to 10:

```
# Feature selector
selector_k_best = SelectKBest(f_regression, k=10)
```

4. The next step is to use a random forest classifier to classify the data:

```
# Random forest classifier
classifier = RandomForestClassifier(n_estimators=50, max_depth=4)
```

5. We are now ready to build the pipeline. The pipeline method allows us to use predefined objects to build the pipeline:

```
# Build the machine learning pipeline
pipeline_classifier = Pipeline([('selector', selector_k_best),
('rf', classifier)])
```

We can also assign names to the blocks in our pipeline. In the preceding line, we assign the selector name to our feature selector and rf to our random forest classifier. You are free to use any other random names here!

6. We can also update these parameters as we go along. We can set the parameters using the names that we assigned in the previous step. For example, if we want to set k to 6 in the feature selector and set n_estimators to 25 in the random forest classifier, we can do it like in the following code. Note that these are the variable names given in the previous step:

```
pipeline_classifier.set_params(selector__k=6,
        rf__n_estimators=25)
```

7. Let's go ahead and train the classifier:

```
# Training the classifier
pipeline_classifier.fit(X, y)
```

8. Let's predict the outputs for the training data:

```
# Predict the output
prediction = pipeline_classifier.predict(X)
print "\nPredictions:\n", prediction
```

9. Let's estimate the performance of this classifier:

```
# Print score
print "\nScore:", pipeline_classifier.score(X, y)
```

10. We can also see which features get selected. Let's go ahead and print them:

```
# Print the selected features chosen by the selector
features_status = pipeline_classifier.named_steps['selector'].get_
support()
selected_features = []
for count, item in enumerate(features_status):
    if item:
```

```
        selected_features.append(count)
```

```
print "\nSelected features (0-indexed):", ', '.join([str(x) for x
in selected_features])
```

11. If you run this code, you will get the following output on your Terminal:

```
Predictions:
[0 0 0 1 1 0 1 1 0 1 0 0 0 0 1 0 1 1 1 0 0 1 0 1 1 1 0 0 1 0 1 0 1 0 0 0 0
 0 0 0 0 0 1 0 1 0 1 1 1 1 1 1 0 0 1 0 0 1 0 0 1 1 1 1 0 1 1 0 1 1 0 0 1
 0 0 1 1 1 1 0 0 0 1 1 1 1 0 1 0 0 0 0 1 0 0 1 1 0 1 0 1]

Score: 0.96

Selected features (0-indexed): 4, 8, 11, 15, 17, 19
```

How it works...

The advantage of selecting the *k* best features is that we will be able to work with low-dimensional data. This is helpful in reducing the computational complexity. The way in which we select the *k* best features is based on univariate feature selection. This performs univariate statistical tests and then extracts the top performing features from the feature vector. Univariate statistical tests refer to analysis techniques where a single variable is involved.

Once these tests are performed, each feature in the feature vector is assigned a score. Based on these scores, we select the top *k* features. We do this as a preprocessing step in our classifier pipeline. Once we extract the top *k* features, a *k*-dimensional feature vector is formed, and we use it as the input training data for the random forest classifier.

Finding the nearest neighbors

Nearest neighbors model refers to a general class of algorithms that aim to make a decision based on the number of nearest neighbors in the training dataset. Let's see how to find the nearest neighbors.

How to do it...

1. Create a new Python file, and import the following packages:

```
import numpy as np
import matplotlib.pyplot as plt
from sklearn.neighbors import NearestNeighbors
```

2. Let's create some sample two-dimensional data:

```
# Input data
X = np.array([[1, 1], [1, 3], [2, 2], [2.5, 5], [3, 1],
        [4, 2], [2, 3.5], [3, 3], [3.5, 4]])
```

3. Our goal is to find the three closest neighbors to any given point. Let's define this parameter:

```
# Number of neighbors we want to find
num_neighbors = 3
```

4. Let's define a random datapoint that's not present in the input data:

```
# Input point
input_point = [2.6, 1.7]
```

5. We need to see what this data looks like. Let's plot it, as follows:

```
# Plot datapoints
plt.figure()
plt.scatter(X[:,0], X[:,1], marker='o', s=25, color='k')
```

6. In order to find the nearest neighbors, we need to define the `NearestNeighbors` object with the right parameters and train it on the input data:

```
# Build nearest neighbors model
knn = NearestNeighbors(n_neighbors=num_neighbors, algorithm='ball_
tree').fit(X)
```

7. We can now find the distances of the input point to all the points in the input data:

```
distances, indices = knn.kneighbors(input_point)
```

8. We can print the k-nearest neighbors, as follows:

```
# Print the 'k' nearest neighbors
print "\nk nearest neighbors"
for rank, index in enumerate(indices[0][:num_neighbors]):
    print str(rank+1) + " -->", X[index]
```

The `indices` array is already sorted, so we just need to parse it and print the datapoints.

9. Let's plot the input datapoint and highlight the k-nearest neighbors:

```
# Plot the nearest neighbors
plt.figure()
plt.scatter(X[:,0], X[:,1], marker='o', s=25, color='k')
plt.scatter(X[indices][0][:][:,0], X[indices][0][:][:,1],
```

```
                marker='o', s=150, color='k', facecolors='none')
    plt.scatter(input_point[0], input_point[1],
                marker='x', s=150, color='k', facecolors='none')

    plt.show()
```

10. If you run this code, you will get the following output on your Terminal:

```
k nearest neighbors
1 --> [ 2.  2.]
2 --> [ 3.  1.]
3 --> [ 3.  3.]
```

11. Here is the plot of the input datapoints:

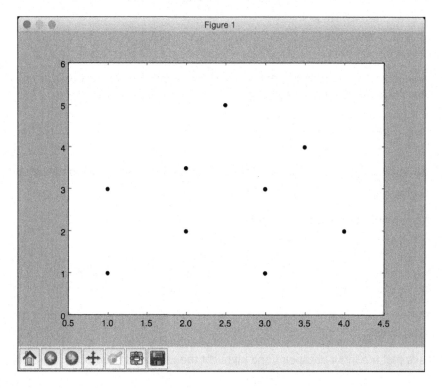

12. The second output figure depicts the location of the test datapoint and the three nearest neighbors, as shown in the following screenshot:

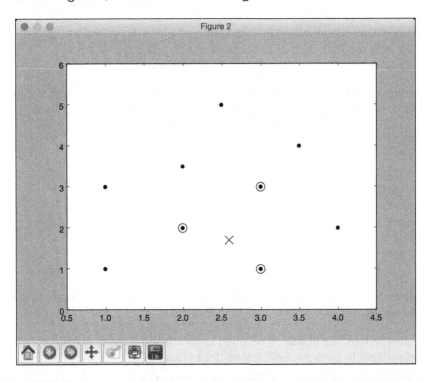

Constructing a k-nearest neighbors classifier

The **k-nearest neighbors** is an algorithm that uses *k*-nearest neighbors in the training dataset to find the category of an unknown object. When we want to find the class to which an unknown point belongs to, we find the k-nearest neighbors and take a majority vote. Let's take a look at how to construct this.

How to do it...

1. Create a new Python file, and import the following packages:

```
import numpy as np
import matplotlib.pyplot as plt
import matplotlib.cm as cm
from sklearn import neighbors, datasets

from utilities import load_data
```

2. We will use the `data_nn_classifier.txt` file for input data. Let's load this input data:

```
# Load input data
input_file = 'data_nn_classifier.txt'
data = load_data(input_file)
X, y = data[:,:-1], data[:,-1].astype(np.int)
```

The first two columns contain input data and the last column contains the labels. Hence, we separated them into X and y, as shown in the preceding code.

3. Let's visualize the input data:

```
# Plot input data
plt.figure()
plt.title('Input datapoints')
markers = '^sov<>hp'
mapper = np.array([markers[i] for i in y])
for i in range(X.shape[0]):
    plt.scatter(X[i, 0], X[i, 1], marker=mapper[i],
            s=50, edgecolors='black', facecolors='none')
```

We iterate through all the datapoints and use the appropriate markers to separate the classes.

4. In order to build the classifier, we need to specify the number of nearest neighbors that we want to consider. Let's define this parameter:

```
# Number of nearest neighbors to consider
num_neighbors = 10
```

5. In order to visualize the boundaries, we need to define a grid and evaluate the classifier on that grid. Let's define the step size:

```
# step size of the grid
h = 0.01
```

6. We are now ready to build the k-nearest neighbors classifier. Let's define this and train it:

```
# Create a K-Neighbours Classifier model and train it
classifier = neighbors.KNeighborsClassifier(num_neighbors,
weights='distance')
classifier.fit(X, y)
```

7. We need to create a mesh to plot the boundaries. Let's define this, as follows:

```
# Create the mesh to plot the boundaries
x_min, x_max = X[:, 0].min() - 1, X[:, 0].max() + 1
y_min, y_max = X[:, 1].min() - 1, X[:, 1].max() + 1
```

```
x_grid, y_grid = np.meshgrid(np.arange(x_min, x_max, h),
np.arange(y_min, y_max, h))
```

8. Let's evaluate the classifier output for all the points:

```
# Compute the outputs for all the points on the mesh
predicted_values = classifier.predict(np.c_[x_grid.ravel(), y_
grid.ravel()])
```

9. Let's plot it, as follows:

```
# Put the computed results on the map
predicted_values = predicted_values.reshape(x_grid.shape)
plt.figure()
plt.pcolormesh(x_grid, y_grid, predicted_values, cmap=cm.Pastel1)
```

10. Now that we plotted the color mesh, let's overlay the training datapoints to see where they lie in relation to the boundaries:

```
# Overlay the training points on the map
for i in range(X.shape[0]):
    plt.scatter(X[i, 0], X[i, 1], marker=mapper[i],
            s=50, edgecolors='black', facecolors='none')

plt.xlim(x_grid.min(), x_grid.max())
plt.ylim(y_grid.min(), y_grid.max())
plt.title('k nearest neighbors classifier boundaries')
```

11. Now, we can consider a test datapoint and see whether the classifier performs correctly. Let's define it and plot it:

```
# Test input datapoint
test_datapoint = [4.5, 3.6]
plt.figure()
plt.title('Test datapoint')
for i in range(X.shape[0]):
    plt.scatter(X[i, 0], X[i, 1], marker=mapper[i],
            s=50, edgecolors='black', facecolors='none')

plt.scatter(test_datapoint[0], test_datapoint[1], marker='x',
        linewidth=3, s=200, facecolors='black')
```

12. We need to extract the k-nearest neighbors using the following model:

```
# Extract k nearest neighbors
dist, indices = classifier.kneighbors(test_datapoint)
```

13. Let's plot the k-nearest neighbors and highlight them:

```
# Plot k nearest neighbors
plt.figure()
plt.title('k nearest neighbors')

for i in indices:
    plt.scatter(X[i, 0], X[i, 1], marker='o',
            linewidth=3, s=100, facecolors='black')

plt.scatter(test_datapoint[0], test_datapoint[1], marker='x',
        linewidth=3, s=200, facecolors='black')

for i in range(X.shape[0]):
    plt.scatter(X[i, 0], X[i, 1], marker=mapper[i],
            s=50, edgecolors='black', facecolors='none')

plt.show()
```

14. Let's print the classifier output on the Terminal:

```
print "Predicted output:", classifier.predict(test_datapoint)[0]
```

15. If you run this code, the first output figure depicts the distribution of the input datapoints:

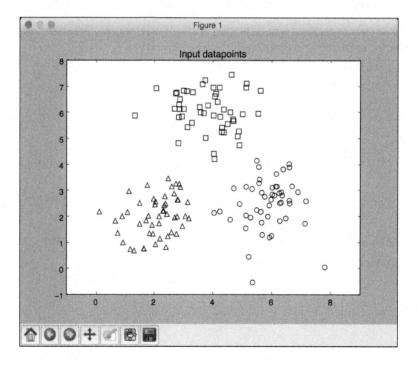

16. The second output figure depicts the boundaries obtained using the k-nearest neighbors classifier:

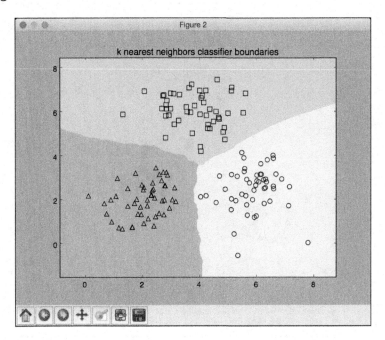

17. The third output figure depicts the location of the test datapoint:

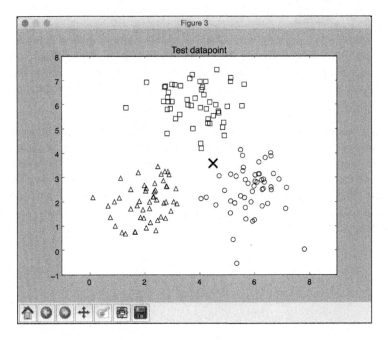

18. The fourth output figure depicts the location of the 10 nearest neighbors:

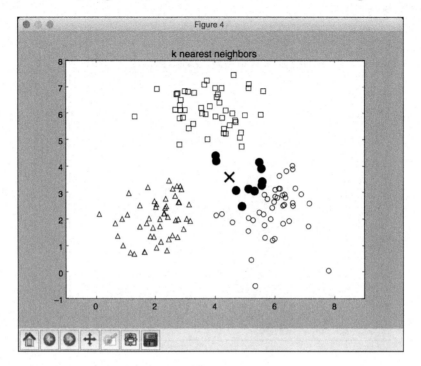

How it works...

The k-nearest neighbors classifier stores all the available datapoints and classifies new datapoints based on a similarity metric. This similarity metric usually appears in the form of a distance function. This algorithm is a nonparametric technique, which means it doesn't need to find out any underlying parameters before formulation. All we need to do is select a value of k that works for us.

Once we find out the k-nearest neighbors, we take a majority vote. A new datapoint is classified by this majority vote of the k-nearest neighbors. This datapoint is assigned to the class that is most common among its k-nearest neighbors. If we set the value of k to 1, then this simply becomes a case of a nearest neighbor classifier where we just assign the datapoint to the class of its nearest neighbor in the training dataset. You can learn more about it at http://www.fon.hum.uva.nl/praat/manual/kNN_classifiers_1__What_is_a_kNN_classifier_.html.

Constructing a k-nearest neighbors regressor

We learned how to use k-nearest neighbors algorithm to build a classifier. The good thing is that we can also use this algorithm as a regressor. Let's see how to use it as a regressor.

How to do it...

1. Create a new Python file, and import the following packages:

```
import numpy as np
import matplotlib.pyplot as plt
from sklearn import neighbors
```

2. Let's generate some sample Gaussian-distributed data:

```
# Generate sample data
amplitude = 10
num_points = 100
X = amplitude * np.random.rand(num_points, 1) - 0.5 * amplitude
```

3. We need to add some noise into the data to introduce some randomness into it. The goal of adding noise is to see whether our algorithm can get past it and still function in a robust way:

```
# Compute target and add noise
y = np.sinc(X).ravel()
y += 0.2 * (0.5 - np.random.rand(y.size))
```

4. Let's visualize it as follows:

```
# Plot input data
plt.figure()
plt.scatter(X, y, s=40, c='k', facecolors='none')
plt.title('Input data')
```

5. We just generated some data and evaluated a continuous-valued function on all these points. Let's define a denser grid of points:

```
# Create the 1D grid with 10 times the density of the input data
x_values = np.linspace(-0.5*amplitude, 0.5*amplitude, 10*num_points)[:, np.newaxis]
```

We defined this denser grid because we want to evaluate our regressor on all these points and look at how well it approximates our function.

6. Let's define the number of nearest neighbors that we want to consider:

```
# Number of neighbors to consider
n_neighbors = 8
```

7. Let's initialize and train the k-nearest neighbors regressor using the parameters that we defined earlier:

```
# Define and train the regressor
knn_regressor = neighbors.KNeighborsRegressor(n_neighbors,
weights='distance')
y_values = knn_regressor.fit(X, y).predict(x_values)
```

8. Let's see how the regressor performs by overlapping the input and output data on top of each other:

```
plt.figure()
plt.scatter(X, y, s=40, c='k', facecolors='none', label='input
data')
plt.plot(x_values, y_values, c='k', linestyle='--',
label='predicted values')
plt.xlim(X.min() - 1, X.max() + 1)
plt.ylim(y.min() - 0.2, y.max() + 0.2)
plt.axis('tight')
plt.legend()
plt.title('K Nearest Neighbors Regressor')

plt.show()
```

9. If you run this code, the first figure depicts the input datapoints:

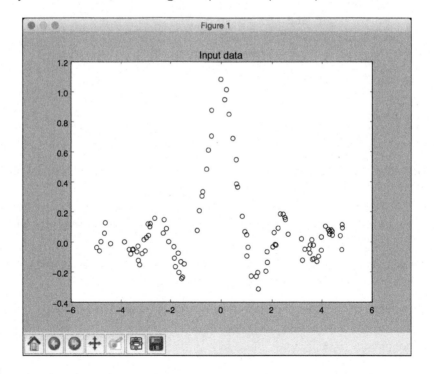

10. The second figure depicts the predicted values by the regressor:

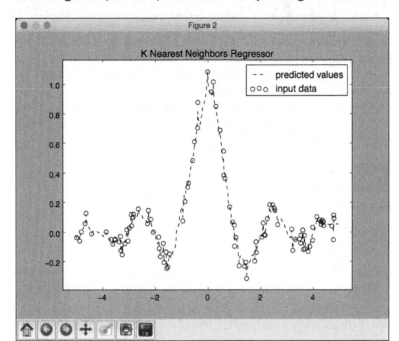

How it works...

The goal of a regressor is to predict continuous valued outputs. We don't have a fixed number of output categories in this case. We just have a set of real-valued output values, and we want our regressor to predict the output values for unknown datapoints. In this case, we used a sinc function to demonstrate the k-nearest neighbors regressor. This is also referred to as the **cardinal sine function**. A sinc function is defined by the following:

sinc(x) = sin(x)/x when x is not 0

> *= 1 when x is 0*

When x is 0, *sin(x)/x* takes the indeterminate form of *0/0*. Hence, we have to compute the limit of this function as x tends to 0. We used a set of values for training, and we defined a denser grid for testing. As we can see in the preceding figure, the output curve is close to the training outputs.

Computing the Euclidean distance score

Now that we have sufficient background in machine learning pipelines and nearest neighbors classifier, let's start the discussion on recommendation engines. In order to build a recommendation engine, we need to define a similarity metric so that we can find users in the database who are similar to a given user. Euclidean distance score is one such metric that we can use to compute the distance between datapoints. We will focus the discussion towards movie recommendation engines. Let's see how to compute the Euclidean score between two users.

How to do it...

1. Create a new Python file, and import the following packages:

    ```
    import json
    import numpy as np
    ```

2. We will now define a function to compute the Euclidean score between two users. The first step is to check whether the users are present in the database:

    ```
    # Returns the Euclidean distance score between user1 and user2
    def euclidean_score(dataset, user1, user2):
        if user1 not in dataset:
            raise TypeError('User ' + user1 + ' not present in the
    dataset')

        if user2 not in dataset:
            raise TypeError('User ' + user2 + ' not present in the
    dataset')
    ```

3. In order to compute the score, we need to extract the movies that both the users rated:

    ```
    # Movies rated by both user1 and user2
    rated_by_both = {}

    for item in dataset[user1]:
        if item in dataset[user2]:
            rated_by_both[item] = 1
    ```

4. If there are no common movies, then there is no similarity between the users (or at least we cannot compute it given the ratings in the database):

    ```
    # If there are no common movies, the score is 0
    if len(rated_by_both) == 0:
        return 0
    ```

5. For each of the common ratings, we just compute the square root of the sum of squared differences and normalize it so that the score is between 0 and 1:

```
squared_differences = []

for item in dataset[user1]:
    if item in dataset[user2]:
        squared_differences.append(np.square(dataset[user1]
[item] - dataset[user2][item]))

return 1 / (1 + np.sqrt(np.sum(squared_differences)))
```

If the ratings are similar, then the sum of squared differences will be very low. Hence, the score will become high, which is what we want from this metric.

6. We will use the `movie_ratings.json` file as our data file. Let's load it:

```
if __name__=='__main__':
    data_file = 'movie_ratings.json'

    with open(data_file, 'r') as f:
        data = json.loads(f.read())
```

7. Let's consider two random users and compute the Euclidean distance score:

```
user1 = 'John Carson'
user2 = 'Michelle Peterson'

print "\nEuclidean score:"
print euclidean_score(data, user1, user2)
```

8. When you run this code, you will see the Euclidean distance score printed on the Terminal.

Computing the Pearson correlation score

The Euclidean distance score is a good metric, but it has some shortcomings. Hence, Pearson correlation score is frequently used in recommendation engines. Let's see how to compute it.

How to do it...

1. Create a new Python file, and import the following packages:

```
import json
import numpy as np
```

2. We will define a function to compute the Pearson correlation score between two users in the database. Our first step is to confirm that these users exist in the database:

```
# Returns the Pearson correlation score between user1 and user2
def pearson_score(dataset, user1, user2):
    if user1 not in dataset:
        raise TypeError('User ' + user1 + ' not present in the
dataset')

    if user2 not in dataset:
        raise TypeError('User ' + user2 + ' not present in the
dataset')
```

3. The next step is to get the movies that both these users rated:

```
# Movies rated by both user1 and user2
rated_by_both = {}

for item in dataset[user1]:
    if item in dataset[user2]:
        rated_by_both[item] = 1

num_ratings = len(rated_by_both)
```

4. If there are no common movies, then there is no discernible similarity between these users; hence, we return 0:

```
# If there are no common movies, the score is 0
if num_ratings == 0:
    return 0
```

5. We need to compute the sum of squared values of common movie ratings:

```
# Compute the sum of ratings of all the common preferences
user1_sum = np.sum([dataset[user1][item] for item in rated_by_
both])
user2_sum = np.sum([dataset[user2][item] for item in rated_by_
both])
```

6. Let's compute the sum of squared ratings of all the common movie ratings:

```
# Compute the sum of squared ratings of all the common
preferences
user1_squared_sum = np.sum([np.square(dataset[user1][item])
for item in rated_by_both])
user2_squared_sum = np.sum([np.square(dataset[user2][item])
for item in rated_by_both])
```

7. Let's compute the sum of the products:

```
# Compute the sum of products of the common ratings
product_sum = np.sum([dataset[user1][item] * dataset[user2]
[item] for item in rated_by_both])
```

8. We are now ready to compute the various elements that we require to calculate the Pearson correlation score:

```
# Compute the Pearson correlation
Sxy = product_sum - (user1_sum * user2_sum / num_ratings)
Sxx = user1_squared_sum - np.square(user1_sum) / num_ratings
Syy = user2_squared_sum - np.square(user2_sum) / num_ratings
```

9. We need to take care of the case where the denominator becomes 0:

```
if Sxx * Syy == 0:
    return 0
```

10. If everything is good, we return the Pearson correlation score, as follows:

```
return Sxy / np.sqrt(Sxx * Syy)
```

11. Let's define the main function and compute the Pearson correlation score between two users:

```
if __name__=='__main__':
    data_file = 'movie_ratings.json'

    with open(data_file, 'r') as f:
        data = json.loads(f.read())

    user1 = 'John Carson'
    user2 = 'Michelle Peterson'

    print "\nPearson score:"
    print pearson_score(data, user1, user2)
```

12. If you run this code, you will see the Pearson correlation score printed on the Terminal.

Finding similar users in the dataset

One of the most important tasks in building a recommendation engine is finding users that are similar. This guides in creating the recommendations that will be provided to these users. Let's see how to build this.

How to do it...

1. Create a new Python file, and import the following packages:

```python
import json
import numpy as np

from pearson_score import pearson_score
```

2. Let's define a function to find similar users to the input user. It takes three input arguments: the database, input user, and the number of similar users that we are looking for. Our first step is to check whether the user is present in the database. If the user exists, we need to compute the Pearson correlation score between this user and all the other users in the database:

```python
# Finds a specified number of users who are similar to the input user
def find_similar_users(dataset, user, num_users):
    if user not in dataset:
        raise TypeError('User ' + user + ' not present in the dataset')

    # Compute Pearson scores for all the users
    scores = np.array([[x, pearson_score(dataset, user, x)] for x in dataset if user != x])
```

3. The next step is to sort these scores in descending order:

```python
    # Sort the scores based on second column
    scores_sorted = np.argsort(scores[:, 1])

    # Sort the scores in decreasing order (highest score first)
    scored_sorted_dec = scores_sorted[::-1]
```

4. Let's extract the *k* top scores and return them:

```python
    # Extract top 'k' indices
    top_k = scored_sorted_dec[0:num_users]

    return scores[top_k]
```

5. Let's define the `main` function and load the input database:

```python
if __name__=='__main__':
    data_file = 'movie_ratings.json'

    with open(data_file, 'r') as f:
        data = json.loads(f.read())
```

6. We want to find three similar users to, for example, `John Carson`. We do this using the following steps:

```
user = 'John Carson'
print "\nUsers similar to " + user + ":\n"
similar_users = find_similar_users(data, user, 3)
print "User\t\t\tSimilarity score\n"
for item in similar_users:
    print item[0], '\t\t', round(float(item[1]), 2)
```

7. If you run this code, you will see the following printed on your Terminal:

```
Users similar to John Carson:

User                    Similarity score

Michael Henry           0.99
Alex Roberts            0.75
Melissa Jones           0.59
```

Generating movie recommendations

Now that we built all of the different parts of a recommendation engine, we are ready to generate movie recommendations. We will use all the functionality that we built in the previous recipes to build a movie recommendation engine. Let's see how to build it.

How to do it...

1. Create a new Python file, and import the following packages:

```
import json
import numpy as np

from euclidean_score import euclidean_score
from pearson_score import pearson_score
from find_similar_users import find_similar_users
```

2. We will define a function to generate movie recommendations for a given user. The first step is to check whether the user exists in the dataset:

```
# Generate recommendations for a given user
def generate_recommendations(dataset, user):
    if user not in dataset:
        raise TypeError('User ' + user + ' not present in the
dataset')
```

3. Let's compute the Pearson score of this user with all the other users in the dataset:

```
total_scores = {}
similarity_sums = {}

for u in [x for x in dataset if x != user]:
    similarity_score = pearson_score(dataset, user, u)

    if similarity_score <= 0:
        continue
```

4. We need to find the movies that haven't been rated by this user:

```
for item in [x for x in dataset[u] if x not in
dataset[user] or dataset[user][x] == 0]:
        total_scores.update({item: dataset[u][item] *
similarity_score})
        similarity_sums.update({item: similarity_score})
```

5. If the user has watched every single movie in the database, then we cannot recommend anything to this user. Let's take care of this condition:

```
if len(total_scores) == 0:
    return ['No recommendations possible']
```

6. We now have a list of these scores. Let's create a normalized list of movie ranks:

```
# Create the normalized list
movie_ranks = np.array([[total/similarity_sums[item], item]
            for item, total in total_scores.items()])
```

7. We need to sort it in descending order based on the score:

```
# Sort in decreasing order based on the first column
movie_ranks = movie_ranks[np.argsort(movie_ranks[:, 0])[::-1]]
```

8. We are finally ready to extract the movie recommendations:

```
# Extract the recommended movies
recommendations = [movie for _, movie in movie_ranks]

return recommendations
```

9. Let's define the `main` function and load the dataset:

```
if __name__=='__main__':
    data_file = 'movie_ratings.json'

    with open(data_file, 'r') as f:
        data = json.loads(f.read())
```

10. Let's generate recommendations for `Michael Henry`:

```
user = 'Michael Henry'
print "\nRecommendations for " + user + ":"
movies = generate_recommendations(data, user)
for i, movie in enumerate(movies):
    print str(i+1) + '. ' + movie
```

11. The user `John Carson` has watched all the movies. Therefore, if we try to generate recommendations for him, it should display 0 recommendations. Let's see whether this happens:

```
user = 'John Carson'
print "\nRecommendations for " + user + ":"
movies = generate_recommendations(data, user)
for i, movie in enumerate(movies):
    print str(i+1) + '. ' + movie
```

12. If you run this code, you will see the following on your Terminal:

```
Recommendations for Michael Henry:
1. Jerry Maguire
2. Anger Management
3. Inception

Recommendations for John Carson:
1. No recommendations possible
```

6
Analyzing Text Data

In this chapter, we will cover the following recipes:

- ▶ Preprocessing data using tokenization
- ▶ Stemming text data
- ▶ Converting text to its base form using lemmatization
- ▶ Dividing text using chunking
- ▶ Building a bag-of-words model
- ▶ Building a text classifier
- ▶ Identifying the gender
- ▶ Analyzing the sentiment of a sentence
- ▶ Identifying patterns in text using topic modeling

Introduction

Text analysis and **natural language processing** (**NLP**) is an integral part of modern artificial intelligence systems. Computers are good at understanding rigidly-structured data with limited variety. However, when we deal with unstructured free-form text, things begin to get difficult. Developing NLP applications is challenging because computers have a hard time understanding underlying concepts. There are also many subtle variations to the way in which we communicate things. These can be in the form of dialects, context, slang, and so on.

In order to solve this problem, NLP applications are developed based on machine learning. These algorithms detect patterns in text data so that we can extract insights from it. Artificial intelligence companies make heavy use of NLP and text analysis to deliver relevant results. Some of the most common applications of NLP include search engines, sentiment analysis, topic modeling, part-of-speech tagging, entity recognition, and so on. The goal of NLP is to develop a set of algorithms so that we can interact with computers in plain English. If we can achieve this, then we wouldn't need programming languages to instruct computers about what they should do. In this chapter, we will look at a few recipes that focus on text analysis and how we can extract meaningful information from text data. We will use a Python package called **Natural Language Toolkit** (**NLTK**) heavily in this chapter. Make sure that you install this before you proceed. You can find the installation steps at http://www.nltk.org/install.html. You also need to install NLTK Data, which contains many corpora and trained models. This is an integral part of text analysis! You can find the installation steps at http://www.nltk.org/data.html.

Preprocessing data using tokenization

Tokenization is the process of dividing text into a set of meaningful pieces. These pieces are called **tokens**. For example, we can divide a chunk of text into words, or we can divide it into sentences. Depending on the task at hand, we can define our own conditions to divide the input text into meaningful tokens. Let's take a look at how to do this.

How to do it...

1. Create a new Python file and add the following lines. Let's define some sample text for analysis:

    ```
    text = "Are you curious about tokenization? Let's see how it
    works! We need to analyze a couple of sentences with punctuations
    to see it in action."
    ```

2. Let's start with sentence tokenization. NLTK provides a sentence tokenizer, so let's import this:

    ```
    # Sentence tokenization
    from nltk.tokenize import sent_tokenize
    ```

3. Run the sentence tokenizer on the input text and extract the tokens:

    ```
    sent_tokenize_list = sent_tokenize(text)
    ```

4. Print the list of sentences to see whether it works correctly:

    ```
    print "\nSentence tokenizer:"
    print sent_tokenize_list
    ```

5. Word tokenization is very commonly used in NLP. NLTK comes with a couple of different word tokenizers. Let's start with the basic word tokenizer:

```
# Create a new word tokenizer
from nltk.tokenize import word_tokenize

print "\nWord tokenizer:"
print word_tokenize(text)
```

6. There is another word tokenizer that is available called `PunktWord` Tokenizer. This splits the text on punctuation, but this keeps it within the words:

```
# Create a new punkt word tokenizer
from nltk.tokenize import PunktWordTokenizer

punkt_word_tokenizer = PunktWordTokenizer()
print "\nPunkt word tokenizer:"
print punkt_word_tokenizer.tokenize(text)
```

7. If you want to split these punctuations into separate tokens, then we need to use `WordPunct` Tokenizer:

```
# Create a new WordPunct tokenizer
from nltk.tokenize import WordPunctTokenizer

word_punct_tokenizer = WordPunctTokenizer()
print "\nWord punct tokenizer:"
print word_punct_tokenizer.tokenize(text)
```

8. The full code is in the `tokenizer.py` file. If you run this code, you will see the following output on your Terminal:

```
Sentence tokenizer:
['Are you curious about tokenization?', "Let's see how it works!", 'We need to analyze a couple of senten
ces with punctuations to see it in action.']

Word tokenizer:
['Are', 'you', 'curious', 'about', 'tokenization', '?', 'Let', "'s", 'see', 'how', 'it', 'works', '!', 'W
e', 'need', 'to', 'analyze', 'a', 'couple', 'of', 'sentences', 'with', 'punctuations', 'to', 'see', 'it',
'in', 'action', '.']

Punkt word tokenizer:
['Are', 'you', 'curious', 'about', 'tokenization', '?', 'Let', "'s", 'see', 'how', 'it', 'works', '!', 'W
e', 'need', 'to', 'analyze', 'a', 'couple', 'of', 'sentences', 'with', 'punctuations', 'to', 'see', 'it',
'in', 'action.']

Word punct tokenizer:
['Are', 'you', 'curious', 'about', 'tokenization', '?', 'Let', "'", 's', 'see', 'how', 'it', 'works', '!'
, 'We', 'need', 'to', 'analyze', 'a', 'couple', 'of', 'sentences', 'with', 'punctuations', 'to', 'see', '
it', 'in', 'action', '.']
```

Stemming text data

When we deal with a text document, we encounter different forms of a word. Consider the word "play". This word can appear in various forms, such as "play", "plays", "player", "playing", and so on. These are basically families of words with similar meanings. During text analysis, it's useful to extract the base form of these words. This will help us in extracting some statistics to analyze the overall text. The goal of stemming is to reduce these different forms into a common base form. This uses a heuristic process to cut off the ends of words to extract the base form. Let's see how to do this in Python.

How to do it...

1. Create a new Python file, and import the following packages:

    ```
    from nltk.stem.porter import PorterStemmer
    from nltk.stem.lancaster import LancasterStemmer
    from nltk.stem.snowball import SnowballStemmer
    ```

2. Let's define a few words to play with, as follows:

    ```
    words = ['table', 'probably', 'wolves', 'playing', 'is',

            'dog', 'the', 'beaches', 'grounded', 'dreamt', 'envision']
    ```

3. We'll define a list of stemmers that we want to use:

    ```
    # Compare different stemmers
    stemmers = ['PORTER', 'LANCASTER', 'SNOWBALL']
    ```

4. Initialize the required objects for all three stemmers:

    ```
    stemmer_porter = PorterStemmer()
    stemmer_lancaster = LancasterStemmer()
    stemmer_snowball = SnowballStemmer('english')
    ```

5. In order to print the output data in a neat tabular form, we need to format it in the right way:

    ```
    formatted_row = '{:>16}' * (len(stemmers) + 1)
    print '\n', formatted_row.format('WORD', *stemmers), '\n'
    ```

6. Let's iterate through the list of words and stem them using the three stemmers:

    ```
    for word in words:
        stemmed_words = [stemmer_porter.stem(word),
                stemmer_lancaster.stem(word),
                stemmer_snowball.stem(word)]
        print formatted_row.format(word, *stemmed_words)
    ```

7. The full code is in the `stemmer.py` file. If you run this code, you will see the following output on your Terminal. Observe how the Lancaster stemmer behaves differently for a couple of words:

WORD	PORTER	LANCASTER	SNOWBALL
table	tabl	tabl	tabl
probably	probabl	prob	probabl
wolves	wolv	wolv	wolv
playing	play	play	play
is	is	is	is
dog	dog	dog	dog
the	the	the	the
beaches	beach	beach	beach
grounded	ground	ground	ground
dreamt	dreamt	dreamt	dreamt
envision	envis	envid	envis

How it works...

All three stemming algorithms basically aim to achieve the same thing. The difference between the three stemming algorithms is basically the level of strictness with which they operate. If you observe the outputs, you will see that the Lancaster stemmer is stricter than the other two stemmers. The Porter stemmer is the least in terms of strictness and Lancaster is the strictest. The stemmed words that we get from Lancaster stemmer tend to get confusing and obfuscated. The algorithm is really fast but it will reduce the words a lot. So, a good rule of thumb is to use the Snowball stemmer.

Converting text to its base form using lemmatization

The goal of lemmatization is also to reduce words to their base forms, but this is a more structured approach. In the previous recipe, we saw that the base words that we obtained using stemmers don't really make sense. For example, the word "wolves" was reduced to "wolv", which is not a real word. Lemmatization solves this problem by doing things using a vocabulary and morphological analysis of words. It removes inflectional word endings, such as "ing" or "ed", and returns the base form of a word. This base form is known as the lemma. If you lemmatize the word "wolves", you will get "wolf" as the output. The output depends on whether the token is a verb or a noun. Let's take a look at how to do this in this recipe.

How to do it...

1. Create a new Python file, and import the following package:

```
from nltk.stem import WordNetLemmatizer
```

2. Let's define the same set of words that we used during stemming:

```
words = ['table', 'probably', 'wolves', 'playing', 'is',
        'dog', 'the', 'beaches', 'grounded', 'dreamt', 'envision']
```

3. We will compare two lemmatizers, the NOUN and VERB lemmatizers. Let's list them as follows:

```
# Compare different lemmatizers
lemmatizers = ['NOUN LEMMATIZER', 'VERB LEMMATIZER']
```

4. Create the object based on WordNet lemmatizer:

```
lemmatizer_wordnet = WordNetLemmatizer()
```

5. In order to print the output in a tabular form, we need to format it in the right way:

```
formatted_row = '{:>24}' * (len(lemmatizers) + 1)
print '\n', formatted_row.format('WORD', *lemmatizers), '\n'
```

6. Iterate through the words and lemmatize them:

```
for word in words:
    lemmatized_words = [lemmatizer_wordnet.lemmatize(word,
pos='n'),
            lemmatizer_wordnet.lemmatize(word, pos='v')]
    print formatted_row.format(word, *lemmatized_words)
```

7. The full code is in the lemmatizer.py file. If you run this code, you will see the following output. Observe how NOUN and VERB lemmatizers differ when they lemmatize the word "is" in the following image:

WORD	NOUN LEMMATIZER	VERB LEMMATIZER
table	table	table
probably	probably	probably
wolves	wolf	wolves
playing	playing	play
is	is	be
dog	dog	dog
the	the	the
beaches	beach	beach
grounded	grounded	ground
dreamt	dreamt	dream
envision	envision	envision

Dividing text using chunking

Chunking refers to dividing the input text into pieces, which are based on any random condition. This is different from tokenization in the sense that there are no constraints and the chunks do not need to be meaningful at all. This is used very frequently during text analysis. When you deal with really large text documents, you need to divide it into chunks for further analysis. In this recipe, we will divide the input text into a number of pieces, where each piece has a fixed number of words.

How to do it...

1. Create a new Python file, and import the following packages:

```
import numpy as np
from nltk.corpus import brown
```

2. Let's define a function to split text into chunks. The first step is to divide the text based on spaces:

```
# Split a text into chunks
def splitter(data, num_words):
    words = data.split(' ')
    output = []
```

3. Initialize a couple of required variables:

```
cur_count = 0
cur_words = []
```

4. Let's iterate through the words:

```
for word in words:
    cur_words.append(word)
    cur_count += 1
```

5. Once you hit the required number of words, reset the variables:

```
if cur_count == num_words:
    output.append(' '.join(cur_words))
    cur_words = []
    cur_count = 0
```

6. Append the chunks to the output variable, and return it:

```
output.append(' '.join(cur_words) )

return output
```

7. We can now define the `main` function. Load the data from Brown corpus. We will use the first 10,000 words:

```
if __name__=='__main__':
    # Read the data from the Brown corpus
    data = ' '.join(brown.words()[:10000])
```

8. Define the number of words in each chunk:

```
    # Number of words in each chunk
    num_words = 1700
```

9. Initialize a couple of relevant variables:

```
    chunks = []
    counter = 0
```

10. Call the `splitter` function on this text data and print the output:

```
    text_chunks = splitter(data, num_words)

    print "Number of text chunks =", len(text_chunks)
```

11. The full code is in the `chunking.py` file. If you run this code, you will see the number of chunks generated printed on the Terminal. It should be 6!

Building a bag-of-words model

When we deal with text documents that contain millions of words, we need to convert them into some kind of numeric representation. The reason for this is to make them usable for machine learning algorithms. These algorithms need numerical data so that they can analyze them and output meaningful information. This is where the **bag-of-words** approach comes into picture. This is basically a model that learns a vocabulary from all the words in all the documents. After this, it models each document by building a histogram of all the words in the document.

How to do it...

1. Create a new Python file, and import the following packages:

```
import numpy as np
from nltk.corpus import brown
from chunking import splitter
```

2. Let's define the `main` function. Load the input data from the Brown corpus:

```
if __name__=='__main__':
    # Read the data from the Brown corpus
    data = ' '.join(brown.words()[:10000])
```

3. Divide the text data into five chunks:

```
# Number of words in each chunk
num_words = 2000

chunks = []
counter = 0

text_chunks = splitter(data, num_words)
```

4. Create a dictionary that is based on these text chunks:

```
for text in text_chunks:
    chunk = {'index': counter, 'text': text}
    chunks.append(chunk)
    counter += 1
```

5. The next step is to extract a document term matrix. This is basically a matrix that counts the number of occurrences of each word in the document. We will use scikit-learn to do this because it has better provisions as compared to NLTK for this particular task. Import the following package:

```
# Extract document term matrix
from sklearn.feature_extraction.text import CountVectorizer
```

6. Define the object, and extract the document term matrix:

```
vectorizer = CountVectorizer(min_df=5, max_df=.95)
doc_term_matrix = vectorizer.fit_transform([chunk['text'] for
chunk in chunks])
```

7. Extract the vocabulary from the `vectorizer` object and print it:

```
vocab = np.array(vectorizer.get_feature_names())
print "\nVocabulary:"
print vocab
```

8. Print the document term matrix:

```
print "\nDocument term matrix:"
chunk_names = ['Chunk-0', 'Chunk-1', 'Chunk-2', 'Chunk-3',
'Chunk-4']
```

9. To print in tabular form, we need to format this, as follows:

```
formatted_row = '{:>12}' * (len(chunk_names) + 1)
print '\n', formatted_row.format('Word', *chunk_names), '\n'
```

10. Iterate through the words, and print the number of times each word has occurred in different chunks:

```
for word, item in zip(vocab, doc_term_matrix.T):
    # 'item' is a 'csr_matrix' data structure
    output = [str(x) for x in item.data]
    print formatted_row.format(word, *output)
```

11. The full code is in the `bag_of_words.py` file. If you run this code, you will see two main things printed on the Terminal. The first output is the vocabulary as shown in the following image:

```
Vocabulary:
[u'about' u'after' u'against' u'aid' u'all' u'also' u'an' u'and' u'are'
 u'as' u'at' u'be' u'been' u'before' u'but' u'by' u'committee' u'congress'
 u'did' u'each' u'education' u'first' u'for' u'from' u'general' u'had'
 u'has' u'have' u'he' u'health' u'his' u'house' u'in' u'increase' u'is'
 u'it' u'last' u'made' u'make' u'may' u'more' u'no' u'not' u'of' u'on'
 u'one' u'only' u'or' u'other' u'out' u'over' u'pay' u'program' u'proposed'
 u'said' u'similar' u'state' u'such' u'take' u'than' u'that' u'the' u'them'
 u'there' u'they' u'this' u'time' u'to' u'two' u'under' u'up' u'was'
 u'were' u'what' u'which' u'who' u'will' u'with' u'would' u'year' u'years']
```

12. The second thing is the document term matrix, which is a pretty long. The first few lines will look like the following:

```
Document term matrix:
```

Word	Chunk-0	Chunk-1	Chunk-2	Chunk-3	Chunk-4
about	1	1	1	1	3
after	2	3	2	1	3
against	1	2	2	1	1
aid	1	1	1	3	5
all	2	2	5	2	1
also	3	3	3	4	3
an	5	7	5	7	10
and	34	27	36	36	41
are	5	3	6	3	2
as	13	4	14	18	4
at	5	7	9	3	6
be	20	14	7	10	18
been	7	1	6	15	5
before	2	2	1	1	2
but	3	3	2	9	5
by	8	22	15	14	12
committee	2	10	3	1	7

How it works...

Consider the following sentences:

- ▶ **Sentence 1**: The brown dog is running.
- ▶ **Sentence 2**: The black dog is in the black room.
- ▶ **Sentence 3**: Running in the room is forbidden.

If you consider all the three sentences, we have the following nine unique words:

- ▶ the
- ▶ brown
- ▶ dog
- ▶ is
- ▶ running
- ▶ black
- ▶ in
- ▶ room
- ▶ forbidden

Now, let's convert each sentence into a histogram using the count of words in each sentence. Each feature vector will be 9-dimensional because we have nine unique words:

- ▶ **Sentence 1**: [1, 1, 1, 1, 1, 0, 0, 0, 0]
- ▶ **Sentence 2**: [2, 0, 1, 1, 0, 2, 1, 1, 0]
- ▶ **Sentence 3**: [0, 0, 0, 1, 1, 0, 1, 1, 1]

Once we extract these feature vectors, we can use machine learning algorithms to analyze them.

Building a text classifier

The goal of text classification is to categorize text documents into different classes. This is an extremely important analysis technique in NLP. We will use a technique, which is based on a statistic called **tf-idf**, which stands for **term frequency—inverse document frequency**. This is an analysis tool that helps us understand how important a word is to a document in a set of documents. This serves as a feature vector that's used to categorize documents. You can learn more about it at http://www.tfidf.com.

How to do it...

1. Create a new Python file, and import the following package:

```
from sklearn.datasets import fetch_20newsgroups
```

2. Let's select a list of categories and name them using a dictionary mapping. These categories are available as part of the news groups dataset that we just imported:

```
category_map = {'misc.forsale': 'Sales', 'rec.motorcycles':
'Motorcycles',
        'rec.sport.baseball': 'Baseball', 'sci.crypt':
'Cryptography',
        'sci.space': 'Space'}
```

3. Load the training data based on the categories that we just defined:

```
training_data = fetch_20newsgroups(subset='train',
        categories=category_map.keys(), shuffle=True, random_
state=7)
```

4. Import the feature extractor:

```
# Feature extraction
from sklearn.feature_extraction.text import CountVectorizer
```

5. Extract the features using the training data:

```
vectorizer = CountVectorizer()
X_train_termcounts = vectorizer.fit_transform(training_data.data)
print "\nDimensions of training data:", X_train_termcounts.shape
```

6. We are now ready to train the classifier. We will use the Multinomial Naive Bayes classifier:

```
# Training a classifier
from sklearn.naive_bayes import MultinomialNB
from sklearn.feature_extraction.text import TfidfTransformer
```

7. Define a couple of random input sentences:

```
input_data = [
    "The curveballs of right handed pitchers tend to curve to the
left",
    "Caesar cipher is an ancient form of encryption",
    "This two-wheeler is really good on slippery roads"
]
```

8. Define the tf-idf transformer object and train it:

```
# tf-idf transformer
tfidf_transformer = TfidfTransformer()
X_train_tfidf = tfidf_transformer.fit_transform(X_train_
termcounts)
```

9. Once we have the feature vectors, train the Multinomial Naive Bayes classifier using this data:

```
# Multinomial Naive Bayes classifier
classifier = MultinomialNB().fit(X_train_tfidf, training_data.
target)
```

10. Transform the input data using the word counts:

```
X_input_termcounts = vectorizer.transform(input_data)
```

11. Transform the input data using the tf-idf transformer:

```
X_input_tfidf = tfidf_transformer.transform(X_input_termcounts)
```

12. Predict the output categories of these input sentences using the trained classifier:

```
# Predict the output categories
predicted_categories = classifier.predict(X_input_tfidf)
```

13. Print the outputs, as follows:

```
# Print the outputs
for sentence, category in zip(input_data, predicted_categories):
    print '\nInput:', sentence, '\nPredicted category:', \
            category_map[training_data.target_names[category]]
```

14. The full code is in the `tfidf.py` file. If you run this code, you will see the following output printed on your Terminal:

```
Dimensions of training data: (2968, 40605)

Input: The curveballs of right handed pitchers tend to curve to the left
Predicted category: Baseball

Input: Caesar cipher is an ancient form of encryption
Predicted category: Cryptography

Input: This two-wheeler is really good on slippery roads
Predicted category: Motorcycles
```

How it works...

The tf-idf technique is used frequently in information retrieval. The goal is to understand the importance of each word within a document. We want to identify words that are occur many times in a document. At the same time, common words like "is" and "be" don't really reflect the nature of the content. So we need to extract the words that are true indicators. The importance of each word increases as the count increases. At the same time, as it appears a lot, the frequency of this word increases too. These two things tend to balance each other out. We extract the term counts from each sentence. Once we convert this to a feature vector, we train the classifier to categorize these sentences.

The **term frequency** (**TF**) measures how frequently a word occurs in a given document. As multiple documents differ in length, the numbers in the histogram tend to vary a lot. So, we need to normalize this so that it becomes a level playing field. To achieve normalization, we divide term-frequency by the total number of words in a given document. The **inverse document frequency** (**IDF**) measures the importance of a given word. When we compute TF, all words are considered to be equally important. To counter-balance the frequencies of commonly-occurring words, we need to weigh them down and scale up the rare ones. We need to calculate the ratio of the number of documents with the given word and divide it by the total number of documents. IDF is calculated by taking the negative algorithm of this ratio.

For example, simple words, such as "is" or "the" tend to appear a lot in various documents. However, this doesn't mean that we can characterize the document based on these words. At the same time, if a word appears a single time, this is not useful either. So, we look for words that appear a number of times, but not so much that they become noisy. This is formulated in the tf-idf technique and used to classify documents. Search engines frequently use this tool to order the search results by relevance.

Identifying the gender

Identifying the gender of a name is an interesting task in NLP. We will use the heuristic that the last few characters in a name is its defining characteristic. For example, if the name ends with "la", it's most likely a female name, such as "Angela" or "Layla". On the other hand, if the name ends with "im", it's most likely a male name, such as "Tim" or "Jim". As we are sure of the exact number of characters to use, we will experiment with this. Let's see how to do it.

How to do it...

1. Create a new Python file, and import the following packages:

```
import random
from nltk.corpus import names
from nltk import NaiveBayesClassifier
from nltk.classify import accuracy as nltk_accuracy
```

2. We need to define a function to extract features from input words:

```
# Extract features from the input word
def gender_features(word, num_letters=2):
    return {'feature': word[-num_letters:].lower()}
```

3. Let's define the `main` function. We need some labeled training data:

```
if __name__=='__main__':
    # Extract labeled names
    labeled_names = ([(name, 'male') for name in names.
words('male.txt')] +
            [(name, 'female') for name in names.words('female.
txt')])
```

4. Seed the random number generator, and shuffle the training data:

```
    random.seed(7)
    random.shuffle(labeled_names)
```

5. Define some input names to play with:

```
    input_names = ['Leonardo', 'Amy', 'Sam']
```

6. As we don't know how many ending characters we need to consider, we will sweep the parameter space from 1 to 5. Each time, we will extract the features, as follows:

```
    # Sweeping the parameter space
    for i in range(1, 5):
        print '\nNumber of letters:', i
        featuresets = [(gender_features(n, i), gender) for (n,
gender) in labeled_names]
```

7. Divide this into train and test datasets:

```
        train_set, test_set = featuresets[500:], featuresets[:500]
```

8. We will use the Naive Bayes classifier to do this:

```
        classifier = NaiveBayesClassifier.train(train_set)
```

9. Evaluate the classifier for each value in the parameter space:

```
        # Print classifier accuracy
        print 'Accuracy ==>', str(100 * nltk_accuracy(classifier,
test_set)) + str('%')

        # Predict outputs for new inputs
        for name in input_names:
            print name, '==>', classifier.classify(gender_
features(name, i))
```

10. The full code is in the `gender_identification.py` file. If you run this code, you will see the following output printed on your Terminal:

```
Number of letters: 1
Accuracy ==> 76.6%
Leonardo ==> male
Amy ==> female
Sam ==> male

Number of letters: 2
Accuracy ==> 80.2%
Leonardo ==> male
Amy ==> female
Sam ==> male

Number of letters: 3
Accuracy ==> 78.4%
Leonardo ==> male
Amy ==> female
Sam ==> female

Number of letters: 4
Accuracy ==> 71.6%
Leonardo ==> male
Amy ==> female
Sam ==> female
```

Analyzing the sentiment of a sentence

Sentiment analysis is one of the most popular applications of NLP. Sentiment analysis refers to the process of determining whether a given piece of text is positive or negative. In some variations, we consider "neutral" as a third option. This technique is commonly used to discover how people feel about a particular topic. This is used to analyze sentiments of users in various forms, such as marketing campaigns, social media, e-commerce customers, and so on.

How to do it...

1. Create a new Python file, and import the following packages:

```
import nltk.classify.util
from nltk.classify import NaiveBayesClassifier
from nltk.corpus import movie_reviews
```

2. Define a function to extract features:

```
def extract_features(word_list):
    return dict([(word, True) for word in word_list])
```

3. We need training data for this, so we will use movie reviews in NLTK:

```
if __name__=='__main__':
    # Load positive and negative reviews
    positive_fileids = movie_reviews.fileids('pos')
    negative_fileids = movie_reviews.fileids('neg')
```

4. Let's separate these into positive and negative reviews:

```
features_positive = [(extract_features(movie_reviews.
words(fileids=[f])),
            'Positive') for f in positive_fileids]
features_negative = [(extract_features(movie_reviews.
words(fileids=[f])),
            'Negative') for f in negative_fileids]
```

5. Divide the data into training and testing datasets:

```
# Split the data into train and test (80/20)
threshold_factor = 0.8
threshold_positive = int(threshold_factor * len(features_
positive))
threshold_negative = int(threshold_factor * len(features_
negative))
```

6. Extract the features:

```
features_train = features_positive[:threshold_positive] +
features_negative[:threshold_negative]
features_test = features_positive[threshold_positive:] +
features_negative[threshold_negative:]
print "\nNumber of training datapoints:", len(features_train)
print "Number of test datapoints:", len(features_test)
```

7. We will use a Naive Bayes classifier. Define the object and train it:

```
# Train a Naive Bayes classifier
classifier = NaiveBayesClassifier.train(features_train)
print "\nAccuracy of the classifier:", nltk.classify.util.
accuracy(classifier, features_test)
```

8. The classifier object contains the most informative words that it obtained during analysis. These words basically have a strong say in what's classified as a positive or a negative review. Let's print them out:

```
print "\nTop 10 most informative words:"
for item in classifier.most_informative_features()[:10]:
    print item[0]
```

9. Create a couple of random input sentences:

```
# Sample input reviews
input_reviews = [
    "It is an amazing movie",
    "This is a dull movie. I would never recommend it to
anyone.",
    "The cinematography is pretty great in this movie",
    "The direction was terrible and the story was all over the
place"
    ]
```

10. Run the classifier on those input sentences and obtain the predictions:

```
print "\nPredictions:"
for review in input_reviews:
    print "\nReview:", review
    probdist = classifier.prob_classify(extract_
features(review.split()))
    pred_sentiment = probdist.max()
```

11. Print the output:

```
    print "Predicted sentiment:", pred_sentiment
    print "Probability:", round(probdist.prob(pred_sentiment),
2)
```

12. The full code is in the `sentiment_analysis.py` file. If you run this code, you will see three main things printed on the Terminal. The first is the accuracy, as shown in the following image:

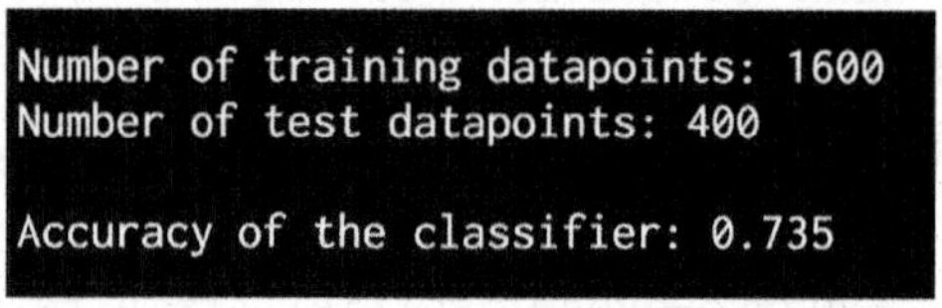

```
Number of training datapoints: 1600
Number of test datapoints: 400

Accuracy of the classifier: 0.735
```

13. The next is a list of most informative words:

```
Top 10 most informative words:
outstanding
insulting
vulnerable
ludicrous
uninvolving
astounding
avoids
fascination
animators
affecting
```

14. The last is the list of predictions, which are based on the input sentences:

```
Predictions:

Review: It is an amazing movie
Predicted sentiment: Positive
Probability: 0.61

Review: This is a dull movie. I would never recommend it to anyone.
Predicted sentiment: Negative
Probability: 0.77

Review: The cinematography is pretty great in this movie
Predicted sentiment: Positive
Probability: 0.67

Review: The direction was terrible and the story was all over the place
Predicted sentiment: Negative
Probability: 0.63
```

How it works...

We use NLTK's Naive Bayes classifier for our task here. In the feature extractor function, we basically extract all the unique words. However, the NLTK classifier needs the data to be arranged in the form of a dictionary. Hence, we arranged it in such a way that the NLTK classifier object can ingest it.

Once we divide the data into training and testing datasets, we train the classifier to categorize the sentences into positive and negative. If you look at the top informative words, you can see that we have words such as "outstanding" to indicate positive reviews and words such as "insulting" to indicate negative reviews. This is interesting information because it tells us what words are being used to indicate strong reactions.

Identifying patterns in text using topic modeling

The **topic modeling** refers to the process of identifying hidden patterns in text data. The goal is to uncover some hidden thematic structure in a collection of documents. This will help us in organizing our documents in a better way so that we can use them for analysis. This is an active area of research in NLP. You can learn more about it at `http://www.cs.columbia.edu/~blei/topicmodeling.html`. We will use a library called `gensim` during this recipe. Make sure that you install this before you proceed. The installation steps are given at `https://radimrehurek.com/gensim/install.html`.

How to do it...

1. Create a new Python file and import the following packages:

```
from nltk.tokenize import RegexpTokenizer
from nltk.stem.snowball import SnowballStemmer
from gensim import models, corpora
from nltk.corpus import stopwords
```

2. Define a function to load the input data. We will use the `data_topic_modeling.txt` text file that is already provided to you:

```
# Load input data
def load_data(input_file):
    data = []
    with open(input_file, 'r') as f:
        for line in f.readlines():
            data.append(line[:-1])

    return data
```

3. Let's define a class to preprocess text. This preprocessor takes care of creating the required objects and extracting the relevant features from input text:

```
# Class to preprocess text
class Preprocessor(object):
    # Initialize various operators
    def __init__(self):
        # Create a regular expression tokenizer
        self.tokenizer = RegexpTokenizer(r'\w+')
```

4. We need a list of stop words so that we can exclude them from analysis. These are common words, such as "in", "the", "is", and so on:

```
# get the list of stop words
self.stop_words_english = stopwords.words('english')
```

5. Define a snowball stemmer:

```
# Create a Snowball stemmer
self.stemmer = SnowballStemmer('english')
```

6. Define a processor function that takes care of tokenization, stop word removal, and stemming:

```
# Tokenizing, stop word removal, and stemming
def process(self, input_text):
    # Tokenize the string
    tokens = self.tokenizer.tokenize(input_text.lower())
```

7. Remove the stop words from the text:

```
# Remove the stop words
tokens_stopwords = [x for x in tokens if not x in self.
stop_words_english]
```

8. Perform stemming on tokens:

```
# Perform stemming on the tokens
tokens_stemmed = [self.stemmer.stem(x) for x in tokens_
stopwords]
```

9. Return the processed tokens:

```
return tokens_stemmed
```

10. We are now ready to define the `main` function. Load the input data from the text file:

```
if __name__=='__main__':
    # File containing linewise input data
    input_file = 'data_topic_modeling.txt'

    # Load data
    data = load_data(input_file)
```

11. Define an object that is based on the class that we defined:

```
# Create a preprocessor object
preprocessor = Preprocessor()
```

12. We need to process the text in the file, and extract the processed tokens:

```
# Create a list for processed documents
processed_tokens = [preprocessor.process(x) for x in data]
```

13. Create a dictionary, which is based on tokenized documents so that this can be used for topic modeling:

```
# Create a dictionary based on the tokenized documents
dict_tokens = corpora.Dictionary(processed_tokens)
```

14. We need to create a document-term matrix using the processed tokens, as follows:

```
# Create a document-term matrix
corpus = [dict_tokens.doc2bow(text) for text in processed_
tokens]
```

15. Let's say we know that the text can be divided into two topics. We will use a technique called **Latent Dirichlet Allocation** (**LDA**) for topic modeling. Define the required parameters and initialize the LDA model object:

```
# Generate the LDA model based on the corpus we just created
num_topics = 2
num_words = 4

ldamodel = models.ldamodel.LdaModel(corpus,
        num_topics=num_topics, id2word=dict_tokens, passes=25)
```

16. Once this identifies the two topics, we can see how it's separating these two topics by looking at the most-contributed words:

```
print "Most contributing words to the topics:"
for item in ldamodel.print_topics(num_topics=num_topics, num_
words=num_words):
    print "\nTopic", item[0], "==>", item[1]
```

17. The full code is in the `topic_modeling.py` file. If you run this code, you will see the following printed on your Terminal:

```
Most contributing words to the topics:

Topic 0 ==> 0.049*need + 0.030*younger + 0.030*talent + 0.030*train

Topic 1 ==> 0.064*need + 0.063*order + 0.038*encrypt + 0.038*understand
```

How it works...

Topic modeling works by identifying the important words of themes in a document. These words tend to determine what the topic is about. We use a regular expression tokenizer because we just want the words without any punctuation or other kinds of tokens. Hence, we use this to extract the tokens. Stop word removal is another important step because this helps us eliminate the noise caused due to words, such as "is" or "the". After this, we need to stem the words to get to their base forms. This entire thing is packaged as a preprocessing block in text analysis tools. This is what we are doing here as well!

We use a technique called Latent Dirichlet Allocation (LDA) to model the topics. LDA basically represents the documents as a mixture of different topics that tend to spit out words. These words are spat out with certain probabilities. The goal is to find these topics! This is a generative model that tries to find the set of topics that are responsible for the generation of the given set of documents. You can learn more about it at `http://blog.echen.me/2011/08/22/introduction-to-latent-dirichlet-allocation`.

As you can see from the output, we have words such as "talent" and "train" to characterize the sports topic, whereas we have "encrypt" to characterize the cryptography topic. We are working with a really small text file, which is the reason why some words might seem less relevant. Obviously, the accuracy will improve if you work with a larger dataset.

7

Speech Recognition

In this chapter, we will cover the following recipes:

- ▶ Reading and plotting audio data
- ▶ Transforming audio signals into the frequency domain
- ▶ Generating audio signals with custom parameters
- ▶ Synthesizing music
- ▶ Extracting frequency domain features
- ▶ Building Hidden Markov Models
- ▶ Building a speech recognizer

Introduction

Speech recognition refers to the process of recognizing and understanding spoken language. Input comes in the form of audio data, and the speech recognizers will process this data to extract meaningful information from it. This has a lot of practical uses, such as voice controlled devices, transcription of spoken language into words, security systems, and so on.

Speech signals are very versatile in nature. There are many variations of speech in the same language. There are different elements to speech, such as language, emotion, tone, noise, accent, and so on. It's difficult to rigidly define a set of rules that can constitute speech. Even with all these variations, humans are really good at understanding all of this with relative ease. Hence, we need machines to understand speech in the same way.

Over the last couple of decades, researchers have worked on various aspects of speech, such as identifying the speaker, understanding words, recognizing accents, translating speech, and so on. Among all these tasks, automatic speech recognition has been the focal point of attention for many researchers. In this chapter, we will learn how to build a **speech recognizer**.

Reading and plotting audio data

Let's take a look at how to read an audio file and visualize the signal. This will be a good starting point, and it will give us a good understanding about the basic structure of audio signals. Before we start, we need to understand that audio files are digitized versions of actual audio signals. Actual audio signals are complex continuous-valued waves. In order to save a digital version, we sample the signal and convert it into numbers. For example, speech is commonly sampled at 44100 Hz. This means that each second of the signal is broken down into 44100 parts, and the values at these timestamps are stored. In other words, you store a value every 1/44100 seconds. As the sampling rate is high, we feel that the signal is continuous when we listen to it on our media players.

How to do it...

1. Create a new Python file, and import the following packages:

   ```
   import numpy as np
   import matplotlib.pyplot as plt
   from scipy.io import wavfile
   ```

2. We will use the `wavfile` package to read the audio file from the `input_read.wav` input file that is already provided to you:

   ```
   # Read the input file
   sampling_freq, audio = wavfile.read('input_read.wav')
   ```

3. Let's print out the parameters of this signal:

   ```
   # Print the params
   print '\nShape:', audio.shape
   print 'Datatype:', audio.dtype
   print 'Duration:', round(audio.shape[0] / float(sampling_freq),
   3), 'seconds'
   ```

4. The audio signal is stored as 16-bit signed integer data. We need to normalize these values:

   ```
   # Normalize the values
   audio = audio / (2.**15)
   ```

5. Let's extract the first 30 values to plot, as follows:

   ```
   # Extract first 30 values for plotting
   audio = audio[:30]
   ```

6. The X-axis is the time axis. Let's build this axis, considering the fact that it should be scaled using the sampling frequency factor:

   ```
   # Build the time axis
   x_values = np.arange(0, len(audio), 1) / float(sampling_freq)
   ```

7. Convert the units to seconds:

```
# Convert to seconds
x_values *= 1000
```

8. Let's plot this as follows:

```
# Plotting the chopped audio signal
plt.plot(x_values, audio, color='black')
plt.xlabel('Time (ms)')
plt.ylabel('Amplitude')
plt.title('Audio signal')
plt.show()
```

9. The full code is in the `read_plot.py` file. If you run this code, you will see the following signal:

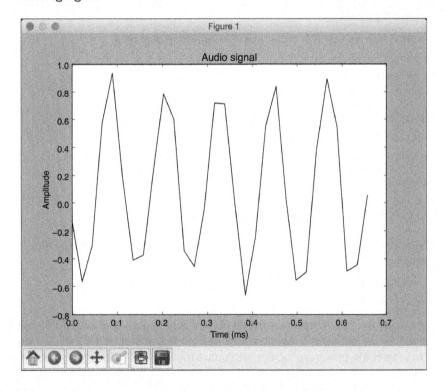

10. You will also see the following printed on your Terminal:

```
Shape: (132300,)
Datatype: int16
Duration: 3.0 seconds
```

Transforming audio signals into the frequency domain

Audio signals consist of a complex mixture of sine waves of different frequencies, amplitudes, and phases. Sine waves are also referred to as **sinusoids**. There is a lot of information that is hidden in the frequency content of an audio signal. In fact, an audio signal is heavily characterized by its frequency content. The whole world of speech and music is based on this fact. Before you proceed further, you will need some knowledge about **Fourier transforms**. A quick refresher can be found at http://www.thefouriertransform.com. Now, let's take a look at how to transform an audio signal into the frequency domain.

How to do it...

1. Create a new Python file, and import the following package:

```
import numpy as np
from scipy.io import wavfile
import matplotlib.pyplot as plt
```

2. Read the input_freq.wav file that is already provided to you:

```
# Read the input file
sampling_freq, audio = wavfile.read('input_freq.wav')
```

3. Normalize the signal, as follows:

```
# Normalize the values
audio = audio / (2.**15)
```

4. The audio signal is just a NumPy array. So, you can extract the length using the following code:

```
# Extract length
len_audio = len(audio)
```

5. Let's apply the Fourier transform. The Fourier transform signal is mirrored along the center, so we just need to take the first half of the transformed signal. Our end goal is to extract the power signal. So, we square the values in the signal in preparation for this:

```
# Apply Fourier transform
transformed_signal = np.fft.fft(audio)
half_length = np.ceil((len_audio + 1) / 2.0)
transformed_signal = abs(transformed_signal[0:half_length])
transformed_signal /= float(len_audio)
transformed_signal **= 2
```

6. Extract the length of the signal:

```
# Extract length of transformed signal
len_ts = len(transformed_signal)
```

7. We need to double the signal according to the length of the signal:

```
# Take care of even/odd cases
if len_audio % 2:
    transformed_signal[1:len_ts] *= 2
else:
    transformed_signal[1:len_ts-1] *= 2
```

8. The power signal is extracted using the following formula:

```
# Extract power in dB
power = 10 * np.log10(transformed_signal)
```

9. The X-axis is the time axis. We need to scale this according the sampling frequency and then convert this into seconds:

```
# Build the time axis
x_values = np.arange(0, half_length, 1) * (sampling_freq / len_
audio) / 1000.0
```

10. Plot the signal, as follows:

```
# Plot the figure
plt.figure()
plt.plot(x_values, power, color='black')
plt.xlabel('Freq (in kHz)')
plt.ylabel('Power (in dB)')
plt.show()
```

11. The full code is in the `freq_transform.py` file. If you run this code, you will see the following figure:

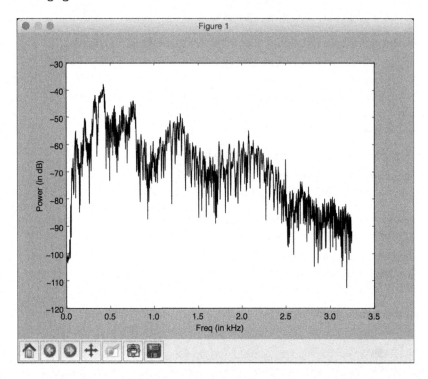

Generating audio signals with custom parameters

We can use NumPy to generate audio signals. As we discussed earlier, audio signals are complex mixtures of sinusoids. So, we will keep this in mind when we generate our own audio signal.

How to do it...

1. Create a new Python file, and import the following packages:

```
import numpy as np
import matplotlib.pyplot as plt
from scipy.io.wavfile import write
```

2. We need to define the output file where the generated audio will be stored:

```
# File where the output will be saved
output_file = 'output_generated.wav'
```

3. Let's specify the audio generation parameters. We want to generate a three-second long signal with a sampling frequency of `44100` and a tonal frequency of `587` Hz. The values on the time axis will go from *-2*pi* to *2*pi*:

```
# Specify audio parameters
duration = 3   # seconds
sampling_freq = 44100   # Hz
tone_freq = 587
min_val = -2 * np.pi
max_val = 2 * np.pi
```

4. Let's generate the time axis and the audio signal. The audio signal is a simple sinusoid with the previously mentioned parameters:

```
# Generate audio
t = np.linspace(min_val, max_val, duration * sampling_freq)
audio = np.sin(2 * np.pi * tone_freq * t)
```

5. Let's add some noise to the signal:

```
# Add some noise
noise = 0.4 * np.random.rand(duration * sampling_freq)
audio += noise
```

6. We need to scale the values to 16-bit integers before we store them:

```
# Scale it to 16-bit integer values
scaling_factor = pow(2,15) - 1
audio_normalized = audio / np.max(np.abs(audio))
audio_scaled = np.int16(audio_normalized * scaling_factor)
```

7. Write this signal to the output file:

```
# Write to output file
write(output_file, sampling_freq, audio_scaled)
```

8. Plot the signal using the first 100 values:

```
# Extract first 100 values for plotting
audio = audio[:100]
```

9. Generate the time axis:

```
# Build the time axis
x_values = np.arange(0, len(audio), 1) / float(sampling_freq)
```

10. Convert the time axis into seconds:

```
# Convert to seconds
x_values *= 1000
```

11. Plot the signal, as follows:

```
# Plotting the chopped audio signal
plt.plot(x_values, audio, color='black')
plt.xlabel('Time (ms)')
plt.ylabel('Amplitude')
plt.title('Audio signal')
plt.show()
```

12. The full code is in the `generate.py` file. If you run this code, you will get the following figure:

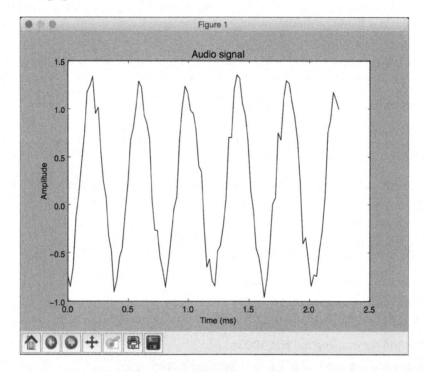

Synthesizing music

Now that we know how to generate audio, let's use this principle to synthesize some music. You can check out this link, `http://www.phy.mtu.edu/~suits/notefreqs.html`. This link lists various notes, such as *A*, *G*, *D*, and so on, along with their corresponding frequencies. We will use this to generate some simple music.

How to do it...

1. Create a new Python file, and import the following packages:

```
import json
import numpy as np
from scipy.io.wavfile import write
import matplotlib.pyplot as plt
```

2. Define a function to synthesize a tone, based on input parameters:

```
# Synthesize tone
def synthesizer(freq, duration, amp=1.0, sampling_freq=44100):
```

3. Build the time axis values:

```
        # Build the time axis
        t = np.linspace(0, duration, duration * sampling_freq)
```

4. Construct the audio sample using the input arguments, such as amplitude and frequency:

```
        # Construct the audio signal
        audio = amp * np.sin(2 * np.pi * freq * t)

        return audio.astype(np.int16)
```

5. Let's define the `main` function. You have been provided with a JSON file called `tone_freq_map.json`, which contains some notes along with their frequencies:

```
if __name__=='__main__':
    tone_map_file = 'tone_freq_map.json'
```

6. Load that file:

```
        # Read the frequency map
        with open(tone_map_file, 'r') as f:
            tone_freq_map = json.loads(f.read())
```

7. Let's assume that we want to generate a G note for a duration of 2 seconds:

```
        # Set input parameters to generate 'G' tone
        input_tone = 'G'
        duration = 2       # seconds
        amplitude = 10000
        sampling_freq = 44100       # Hz
```

8. Call the function with the following parameters:

```
        # Generate the tone
        synthesized_tone = synthesizer(tone_freq_map[input_tone],
    duration, amplitude, sampling_freq)
```

9. Write the generated signal into the output file:

```
# Write to the output file
write('output_tone.wav', sampling_freq, synthesized_tone)
```

10. Open this file in a media player and listen to it. That's the G note! Let's do something more interesting. Let's generate some notes in sequence to give it a musical feel. Define a note sequence along with their durations in seconds:

```
# Tone-duration sequence
tone_seq = [('D', 0.3), ('G', 0.6), ('C', 0.5), ('A', 0.3),
('Asharp', 0.7)]
```

11. Iterate through this list and call the synthesizer function for each of them:

```
# Construct the audio signal based on the chord sequence
output = np.array([])
for item in tone_seq:
    input_tone = item[0]
    duration = item[1]
    synthesized_tone = synthesizer(tone_freq_map[input_tone],
duration, amplitude, sampling_freq)
    output = np.append(output, synthesized_tone, axis=0)
```

12. Write the signal to the output file:

```
# Write to the output file
write('output_tone_seq.wav', sampling_freq, output)
```

13. The full code is in the `synthesize_music.py` file. You can open the `output_tone_seq.wav` file in your media player and listen to it. You can feel the music!

Extracting frequency domain features

We discussed earlier how to convert a signal into the frequency domain. In most modern speech recognition systems, people use frequency-domain features. After you convert a signal into the frequency domain, you need to convert it into a usable form. **Mel Frequency Cepstral Coefficients (MFCC)** is a good way to do this. MFCC takes the power spectrum of a signal and then uses a combination of filter banks and discrete cosine transform to extract features. If you need a quick refresher, you can check out `http://practicalcryptography. com/miscellaneous/machine-learning/guide-mel-frequency-cepstral-coefficients-mfccs`. Make sure that the `python_speech_features` package is installed before you start. You can find the installation instructions at `http://python-speech-features.readthedocs.org/en/latest`. Let's take a look at how to extract MFCC features.

How to do it...

1. Create a new Python file, and import the following packages:

```
import numpy as np
import matplotlib.pyplot as plt
from scipy.io import wavfile
from features import mfcc, logfbank
```

2. Read the `input_freq.wav` input file that is already provided to you:

```
# Read input sound file
sampling_freq, audio = wavfile.read("input_freq.wav")
```

3. Extract the MFCC and filter bank features:

```
# Extract MFCC and Filter bank features
mfcc_features = mfcc(audio, sampling_freq)
filterbank_features = logfbank(audio, sampling_freq)
```

4. Print the parameters to see how many windows were generated:

```
# Print parameters
print '\nMFCC:\nNumber of windows =', mfcc_features.shape[0]
print 'Length of each feature =', mfcc_features.shape[1]
print '\nFilter bank:\nNumber of windows =', filterbank_features.shape[0]
print 'Length of each feature =', filterbank_features.shape[1]
```

5. Let's visualize the MFCC features. We need to transform the matrix so that the time domain is horizontal:

```
# Plot the features
mfcc_features = mfcc_features.T
plt.matshow(mfcc_features)
plt.title('MFCC')
```

6. Let's visualize the filter bank features. Again, we need to transform the matrix so that the time domain is horizontal:

```
filterbank_features = filterbank_features.T
plt.matshow(filterbank_features)
plt.title('Filter bank')

plt.show()
```

7. The full code is in the `extract_freq_features.py` file. If you run this code, you will get the following figure for MFCC features:

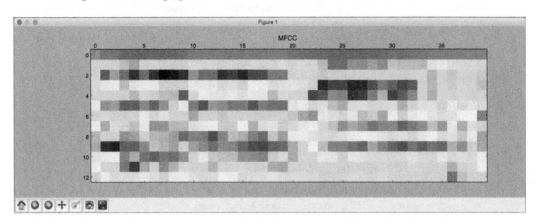

8. The filter bank features will look like the following:

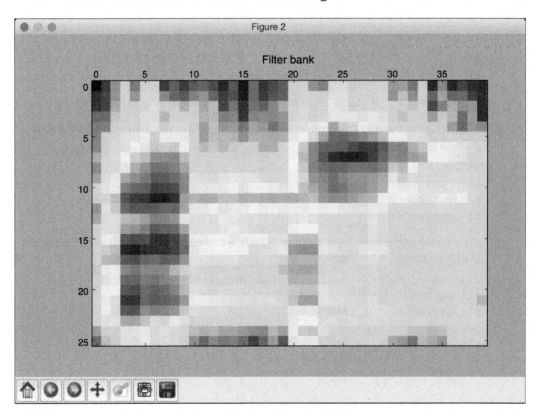

9. You will get the following output on your Terminal:

```
MFCC:
Number of windows = 40
Length of each feature = 13

Filter bank:
Number of windows = 40
Length of each feature = 26
```

Building Hidden Markov Models

We are now ready to discuss speech recognition. We will use **Hidden Markov Models** (**HMMs**) to perform speech recognition. HMMs are great at modeling time series data. As an audio signal is a time series signal, HMMs perfectly suit our needs. An HMM is a model that represents probability distributions over sequences of observations. We assume that the outputs are generated by hidden states. So, our goal is to find these hidden states so that we can model the signal. You can learn more about it at https://www.robots.ox.ac.uk/~vgg/rg/slides/hmm.pdf. Before you proceed, you need to install the hmmlearn package. You can find the installation instructions at http://hmmlearn.readthedocs.org/en/latest. Let's take a look at how to build HMMs.

How to do it...

1. Create a new Python file. Let's define a class to model HMMs:

```
# Class to handle all HMM related processing
class HMMTrainer(object):
```

2. Let's initialize the class. We will use Gaussian HMMs to model our data. The n_components parameter defines the number of hidden states. The cov_type defines the type of covariance in our transition matrix, and n_iter indicates the number of iterations it will go through before it stops training:

```
    def __init__(self, model_name='GaussianHMM', n_components=4,
cov_type='diag', n_iter=1000):
```

The choice of the preceding parameters depends on the problem at hand. You need to have an understanding of your data in order to select these parameters in a smart way.

3. Initialize the variables:

```
self.model_name = model_name
self.n_components = n_components
self.cov_type = cov_type
self.n_iter = n_iter
self.models = []
```

4. Define the model with the following parameters:

```
if self.model_name == 'GaussianHMM':
    self.model = hmm.GaussianHMM(n_components=self.n_
components,
            covariance_type=self.cov_type, n_iter=self.n_
iter)
    else:
        raise TypeError('Invalid model type')
```

5. The input data is a NumPy array, where each element is a feature vector consisting of *k*-dimensions:

```
# X is a 2D numpy array where each row is 13D
def train(self, X):
    np.seterr(all='ignore')
    self.models.append(self.model.fit(X))
```

6. Define a method to extract the score, based on the model:

```
# Run the model on input data
def get_score(self, input_data):
    return self.model.score(input_data)
```

7. We built a class to handle HMM training and prediction, but we need some data to see it in action. We will use it in the next recipe to build a speech recognizer. The full code is in the `speech_recognizer.py` file.

Building a speech recognizer

We need a database of speech files to build our speech recognizer. We will use the database available at `https://code.google.com/archive/p/hmm-speech-recognition/downloads`. This contains seven different words, where each word has 15 audio files associated with it. This is a small dataset, but this is sufficient to understand how to build a speech recognizer that can recognize seven different words. We need to build an HMM model for each class. When we want to identify the word in a new input file, we need to run all the models on this file and pick the one with the best score. We will use the HMM class that we built in the previous recipe.

How to do it...

1. Create a new Python file, and import the following packages:

```python
import os
import argparse

import numpy as np
from scipy.io import wavfile
from hmmlearn import hmm
from features import mfcc
```

2. Define a function to parse the input arguments in the command line:

```python
# Function to parse input arguments
def build_arg_parser():
    parser = argparse.ArgumentParser(description='Trains the HMM classifier')
    parser.add_argument("--input-folder", dest="input_folder", required=True,
            help="Input folder containing the audio files in subfolders")
    return parser
```

3. Define the `main` function, and parse the input arguments:

```python
if __name__=='__main__':
    args = build_arg_parser().parse_args()
    input_folder = args.input_folder
```

4. Initiate the variable that will hold all the HMM models:

```python
    hmm_models = []
```

5. Parse the input directory that contains all the database's audio files:

```python
    # Parse the input directory
    for dirname in os.listdir(input_folder):
```

6. Extract the name of the subfolder:

```python
        # Get the name of the subfolder
        subfolder = os.path.join(input_folder, dirname)

        if not os.path.isdir(subfolder):
            continue
```

7. The name of the subfolder is the label of this class. Extract it using the following:

```
# Extract the label
label = subfolder[subfolder.rfind('/') + 1:]
```

8. Initialize the variables for training:

```
# Initialize variables
X = np.array([])
y_words = []
```

9. Iterate through the list of audio files in each subfolder:

```
# Iterate through the audio files (leaving 1 file for
testing in each class)
for filename in [x for x in os.listdir(subfolder) if
x.endswith('.wav')][:-1]:
```

10. Read each audio file, as follows:

```
# Read the input file
filepath = os.path.join(subfolder, filename)
sampling_freq, audio = wavfile.read(filepath)
```

11. Extract the MFCC features:

```
# Extract MFCC features
mfcc_features = mfcc(audio, sampling_freq)
```

12. Keep appending this to the X variable:

```
# Append to the variable X
if len(X) == 0:
    X = mfcc_features
else:
    X = np.append(X, mfcc_features, axis=0)
```

13. Append the corresponding label too:

```
# Append the label
y_words.append(label)
```

14. Once you have extracted features from all the files in the current class, train and save the HMM model. As HMM is a generative model for unsupervised learning, we don't need labels to build HMM models for each class. We explicitly assume that separate HMM models will be built for each class:

```
# Train and save HMM model
hmm_trainer = HMMTrainer()
hmm_trainer.train(X)
hmm_models.append((hmm_trainer, label))
hmm_trainer = None
```

15. Get a list of test files that were not used for training:

```
# Test files
input_files = [
        'data/pineapple/pineapple15.wav',
        'data/orange/orange15.wav',
        'data/apple/apple15.wav',
        'data/kiwi/kiwi15.wav'
        ]
```

16. Parse the input files, as follows:

```
# Classify input data
for input_file in input_files:
```

17. Read in each audio file:

```
# Read input file
sampling_freq, audio = wavfile.read(input_file)
```

18. Extract the MFCC features:

```
# Extract MFCC features
mfcc_features = mfcc(audio, sampling_freq)
```

19. Define variables to store the maximum score and the output label:

```
# Define variables
max_score = None
output_label = None
```

20. Iterate through all the models and run the input file through each of them:

```
# Iterate through all HMM models and pick
# the one with the highest score
for item in hmm_models:
    hmm_model, label = item
```

21. Extract the score and store the maximum score:

```
score = hmm_model.get_score(mfcc_features)
if score > max_score:
    max_score = score
    output_label = label
```

22. Print the true and predicted labels:

```
# Print the output
print "\nTrue:", input_file[input_file.find('/')+1:input_file.rfind('/')]
print "Predicted:", output_label
```

23. The full code is in the `speech_recognizer.py` file. If you run this code, you will see the following on your Terminal:

```
True: pineapple
Predicted: pineapple

True: orange
Predicted: orange

True: apple
Predicted: apple

True: kiwi
Predicted: kiwi
```

8
Dissecting Time Series and Sequential Data

In this chapter, we will cover the following recipes:

- ▶ Transforming data into the time series format
- ▶ Slicing time series data
- ▶ Operating on time series data
- ▶ Extracting statistics from time series data
- ▶ Building Hidden Markov Models for sequential data
- ▶ Building Conditional Random Fields for sequential text data
- ▶ Analyzing stock market data using Hidden Markov Models

Introduction

Time series data is basically a sequence of measurements that are collected over time. These measurements are taken with respect to a predetermined variable and at regular time intervals. One of the main characteristics of time series data is that the ordering matters!

The list of observations that we collect is ordered on a timeline, and the order in which they appear says a lot about underlying patterns. If you change the order, this would totally change the meaning of the data. Sequential data is a generalized notion that encompasses any data that comes in a sequential form, including time series data.

Our objective here is to build a model that describes the pattern of the time series or any sequence in general. Such models are used to describe important features of the time series pattern. We can use these models to explain how the past might affect the future. We can also use them to see how two datasets can be correlated, to forecast future values, or to control a given variable that is based on some metric.

In order to visualize time series data, we tend to plot it using line charts or bar graphs. Time series data analysis is frequently used in finance, signal processing, weather prediction, trajectory forecasting, predicting earthquakes, or any field where we have to deal with temporal data. The models that we build in time series and sequential data analysis should take into account the ordering of data and extract the relationships between neighbors. Let's go ahead and check out a few recipes to analyze time series and sequential data in Python.

Transforming data into the time series format

We will start by understanding how to convert a sequence of observations into time series data and visualize it. We will use a library called **pandas** to analyze time series data. Make sure that you install pandas before you proceed further. You can find the installation instructions at `http://pandas.pydata.org/pandas-docs/stable/install.html`.

How to do it...

1. Create a new Python file, and import the following packages:

```
import numpy as np
import pandas as pd
import matplotlib.pyplot as plt
```

2. Let's define a function to read an input file that converts sequential observations into time-indexed data:

```
def convert_data_to_timeseries(input_file, column, verbose=False):
```

3. We will use a text file consisting of four columns. The first column denotes the year, the second column denotes the month, and the third and fourth columns denote data. Let's load this into a NumPy array:

```
# Load the input file
data = np.loadtxt(input_file, delimiter=',')
```

4. As this is arranged chronologically, the first row contains the start date and the last row contains the end date. Let's extract the starting and ending dates of this dataset:

```
# Extract the start and end dates
start_date = str(int(data[0,0])) + '-' + str(int(data[0,1]))
end_date = str(int(data[-1,0] + 1)) + '-' + str(int(data[-1,1]
% 12 + 1))
```

5. There is also a verbose mode for this function. So if this is set to true, it will print a few things. Let's print out the start and end dates:

```
if verbose:
    print "\nStart date =", start_date
    print "End date =", end_date
```

6. Let's create a pandas variable, which contains the date sequence with monthly intervals:

```
# Create a date sequence with monthly intervals
dates = pd.date_range(start_date, end_date, freq='M')
```

7. Our next step is to convert the given column into time series data. You can access this data using the month and year (as opposed to index):

```
# Convert the data into time series data
data_timeseries = pd.Series(data[:,column], index=dates)
```

8. Use the verbose mode to print out the first ten elements:

```
if verbose:
    print "\nTime series data:\n", data_timeseries[:10]
```

9. Return the time-indexed variable, as follows:

```
return data_timeseries
```

10. Define the `main` function, as follows:

```
if __name__=='__main__':
```

11. We will use the `data_timeseries.txt` file that is already provided to you:

```
# Input file containing data
input_file = 'data_timeseries.txt'
```

12. Load the third column from this text file and convert it to time series data:

```
# Load input data
column_num = 2
data_timeseries = convert_data_to_timeseries(input_file,
column_num)
```

13. The pandas library provides a nice plotting function that you can run directly on the variable:

```
# Plot the time series data
data_timeseries.plot()
plt.title('Input data')

plt.show()
```

14. The full code is given in the `convert_to_timeseries.py` file that is provided to you. If you run the code, you will see the following image:

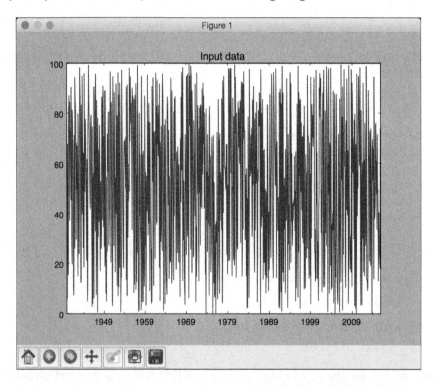

Slicing time series data

In this recipe, we will learn how to slice time series data using pandas. This will help you extract information from various intervals in the time series data. We will learn how to use dates to handle subsets of our data.

How to do it...

1. Create a new Python file, and import the following packages:

```
import numpy as np
import pandas as pd
import matplotlib.pyplot as plt

from convert_to_timeseries import convert_data_to_timeseries
```

2. We will use the same text file that we used in the previous recipe to slice and dice the data:

```
# Input file containing data
input_file = 'data_timeseries.txt'
```

3. We will use the third column again:

```
# Load data
column_num = 2
data_timeseries = convert_data_to_timeseries(input_file, column_
num)
```

4. Let's assume that we want to extract the data between given start and end years. Let's define these, as follows:

```
# Plot within a certain year range
start = '2008'
end = '2015'
```

5. Plot the data between the given year range:

```
plt.figure()
data_timeseries[start:end].plot()
plt.title('Data from ' + start + ' to ' + end)
```

6. We can also slice the data based on a certain range of months:

```
# Plot within a certain range of dates
start = '2007-2'
end = '2007-11'
```

7. Plot the data, as follows:

```
plt.figure()
data_timeseries[start:end].plot()
plt.title('Data from ' + start + ' to ' + end)

plt.show()
```

8. The full code is given in the `slicing_data.py` file that is provided to you. If you run the code, you will see the following image:

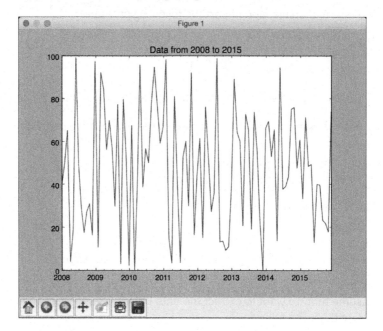

9. The next figure will display a smaller time frame; hence, it looks like we have zoomed into it:

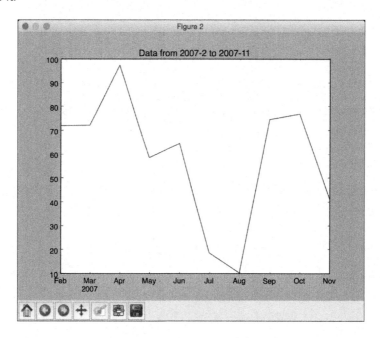

Operating on time series data

Now that we know how to slice data and extract various subsets, let's discuss how to operate on time series data. You can filter the data in many different ways. The pandas library allows you to operate on time series data in any way that you want.

How to do it...

1. Create a new Python file, and import the following packages:

```
import numpy as np
import pandas as pd
import matplotlib.pyplot as plt

from convert_to_timeseries import convert_data_to_timeseries
```

2. We will use the same text file that we used in the previous recipe:

```
# Input file containing data
input_file = 'data_timeseries.txt'
```

3. We will use both the third and fourth columns in this text file:

```
# Load data
data1 = convert_data_to_timeseries(input_file, 2)
data2 = convert_data_to_timeseries(input_file, 3)
```

4. Convert the data into a pandas data frame:

```
dataframe = pd.DataFrame({'first': data1, 'second': data2})
```

5. Plot the data in the given year range:

```
# Plot data
dataframe['1952':'1955'].plot()
plt.title('Data overlapped on top of each other')
```

6. Let's assume that we want to plot the difference between the two columns that we just loaded in the given year range. We can do this using the following lines:

```
# Plot the difference
plt.figure()
difference = dataframe['1952':'1955']['first'] -
dataframe['1952':'1955']['second']
difference.plot()
plt.title('Difference (first - second)')
```

7. If we want to filter the data based on different conditions for the first and second column, we can just specify these conditions and plot this:

```
# When 'first' is greater than a certain threshold
# and 'second' is smaller than a certain threshold
dataframe[(dataframe['first'] > 60) & (dataframe['second'] < 20)].
plot()
plt.title('first > 60 and second < 20')

plt.show()
```

8. The full code is in the `operating_on_data.py` file that is already provided to you. If you run the code, the first figure will look like the following:

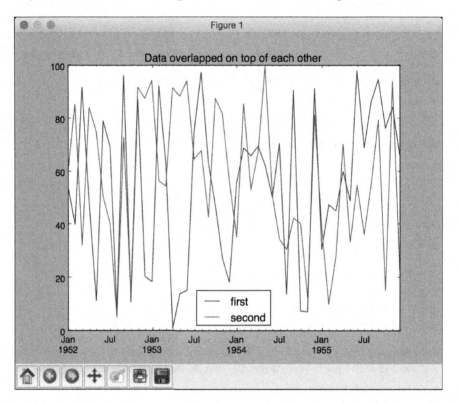

9. The second output figure denotes the difference, as follows:

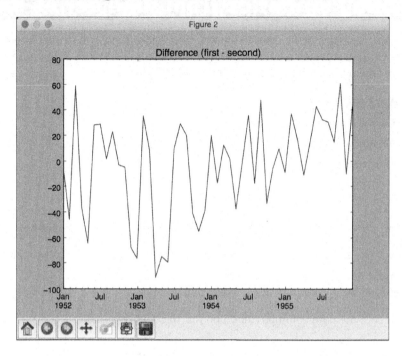

10. The third output figure denotes the filtered data, as follows:

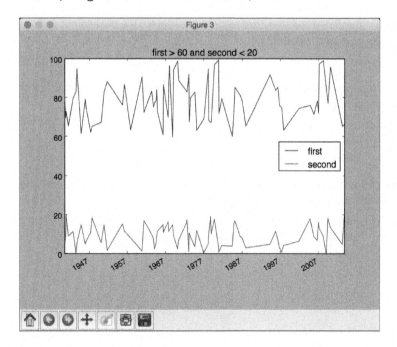

Extracting statistics from time series data

One of the main reasons that we want to analyze time series data is to extract interesting statistics from it. This provides a lot of information regarding the nature of the data. In this recipe, we will take a look at how to extract these stats.

How to do it...

1. Create a new Python file, and import the following packages:

```
import numpy as np
import pandas as pd
import matplotlib.pyplot as plt

from convert_to_timeseries import convert_data_to_timeseries
```

2. We will use the same text file that we used in the previous recipes for analysis:

```
# Input file containing data
input_file = 'data_timeseries.txt'
```

3. Load both the data columns (third and fourth columns):

```
# Load data
data1 = convert_data_to_timeseries(input_file, 2)
data2 = convert_data_to_timeseries(input_file, 3)
```

4. Create a pandas data structure to hold this data. This dataframe is like a dictionary that has keys and values:

```
dataframe = pd.DataFrame({'first': data1, 'second': data2})
```

5. Let's start extracting some stats now. To extract the maximum and minimum values, use the following code:

```
# Print max and min
print '\nMaximum:\n', dataframe.max()
print '\nMinimum:\n', dataframe.min()
```

6. To print the mean values of your data or just the row-wise mean, use the following code:

```
# Print mean
print '\nMean:\n', dataframe.mean()
print '\nMean row-wise:\n', dataframe.mean(1)[:10]
```

7. The rolling mean is an important statistic that's used a lot in time series processing. One of the most famous applications is smoothing a signal to remove noise. Rolling mean refers to computing the mean of a signal in a window that keeps sliding on the time scale. Let's consider a window size of 24 and plot this, as follows:

```
# Plot rolling mean
pd.rolling_mean(dataframe, window=24).plot()
```

8. Correlation coefficients are useful in understanding the nature of the data, as follows:

```
# Print correlation coefficients
print '\nCorrelation coefficients:\n', dataframe.corr()
```

9. Let's plot this using a window size of 60:

```
# Plot rolling correlation
plt.figure()
pd.rolling_corr(dataframe['first'], dataframe['second'],
window=60).plot()

plt.show()
```

10. The full code is given in the `extract_stats.py` file that is already provided to you. If you run the code, the rolling mean will look like the following:

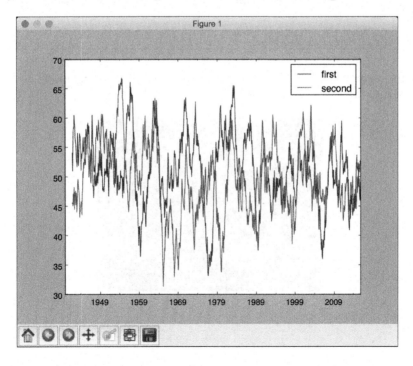

11. The second output figure indicates the rolling correlation:

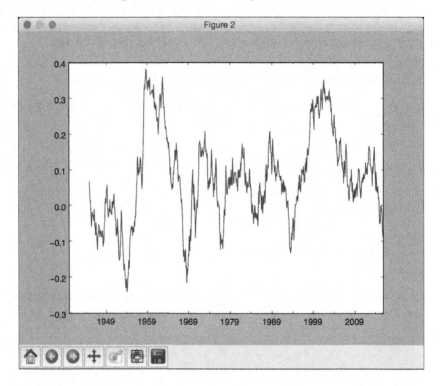

12. In the upper half of the Terminal, you will see max, min, and mean values printed, as shown in the following image:

```
Maximum:
first     99.82
second    99.97
dtype: float64

Minimum:
first     0.07
second    0.00
dtype: float64

Mean:
first     51.264529
second    49.695417
dtype: float64
```

13. In the lower half of the Terminal, you will see the row-wise mean stats and correlation coefficients printed, as seen in the following image:

```
Mean row-wise:
1940-01-31    81.885
1940-02-29    41.135
1940-03-31    10.305
1940-04-30    83.545
1940-05-31    18.395
1940-06-30    16.695
1940-07-31    86.875
1940-08-31    42.255
1940-09-30    55.880
1940-10-31    34.720
Freq: M, dtype: float64

Correlation coefficients:
            first     second
first    1.000000   0.077607
second   0.077607   1.000000
```

Building Hidden Markov Models for sequential data

The **Hidden Markov Models (HMMs)** are really powerful when it comes to sequential data analysis. They are used extensively in finance, speech analysis, weather forecasting, sequencing of words, and so on. We are often interested in uncovering hidden patterns that appear over time.

Any source of data that produces a sequence of outputs could produce patterns. Note that HMMs are generative models, which means that they can generate the data once they learn the underlying structure. HMMs cannot discriminate between classes in their base forms. This is in contrast to discriminative models that can learn to discriminate between classes but cannot generate data.

Getting ready

For example, let's say that we want to predict whether the weather will be sunny, chilly, or rainy tomorrow. To do this, we look at all the parameters, such as temperature, pressure, and so on, whereas the underlying state is hidden. Here, the underlying state refers to the three available options: sunny, chilly, or rainy. If you wish to learn more about HMMs, check out this tutorial at https://www.robots.ox.ac.uk/~vgg/rg/slides/hmm.pdf.

We will use hmmlearn to build and train HMMs. Make sure that you install this before you proceed. You can find the installation instructions at http://hmmlearn.readthedocs.org/en/latest.

How to do it...

1. Create a new Python file, and import the following packages:

    ```
    import datetime

    import numpy as np
    import matplotlib.pyplot as plt
    from hmmlearn.hmm import GaussianHMM

    from convert_to_timeseries import convert_data_to_timeseries
    ```

2. We will use the data from a file named `data_hmm.txt` that is already provided to you. This file contains comma-separated lines. Each line contains three values: a year, a month, and a floating point data. Let's load this into a NumPy array:

    ```
    # Load data from input file
    input_file = 'data_hmm.txt'
    data = np.loadtxt(input_file, delimiter=',')
    ```

3. Let's stack the data column-wise for analysis. We don't need to technically column-stack this because it's only one column. However, if you had more than one column to analyze, you can use this structure:

    ```
    # Arrange data for training
    X = np.column_stack([data[:,2]])
    ```

4. Create and train the HMM using four components. The number of components is a hyperparameter that we have to choose. Here, by selecting four, we say that the data is being generated using four underlying states. We will see how the performance varies with this parameter soon:

    ```
    # Create and train Gaussian HMM
    print "\nTraining HMM...."
    num_components = 4
    model = GaussianHMM(n_components=num_components, covariance_type="diag", n_iter=1000)
    model.fit(X)
    ```

5. Run the predictor to get the hidden states:

    ```
    # Predict the hidden states of HMM
    hidden_states = model.predict(X)
    ```

6. Compute the mean and variance of the hidden states:

```
print "\nMeans and variances of hidden states:"
for i in range(model.n_components):
    print "\nHidden state", i+1
    print "Mean =", round(model.means_[i][0], 3)
    print "Variance =", round(np.diag(model.covars_[i])[0], 3)
```

7. As we discussed earlier, HMMs are generative models. So, let's generate, for example, 1000 samples and plot this:

```
# Generate data using model
num_samples = 1000
samples, _ = model.sample(num_samples)
plt.plot(np.arange(num_samples), samples[:,0], c='black')
plt.title('Number of components = ' + str(num_components))

plt.show()
```

8. The full code is given in the hmm.py file that is already provided to you. If you run the code, you will see the following figure:

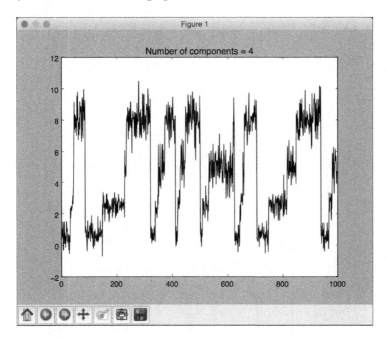

9. You can experiment with the `n_components` parameter to see how the curve gets nicer as you increase it. You can basically give it more freedom to train and customize by allowing a larger number of hidden states. If you increase it to `8`, you will see the following figure:

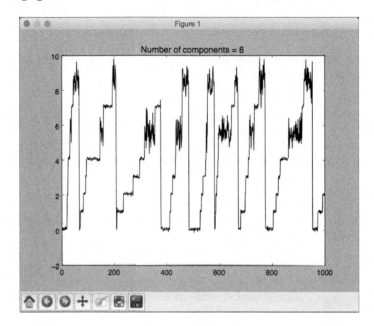

10. If you increase this to `12`, it will get even smoother:

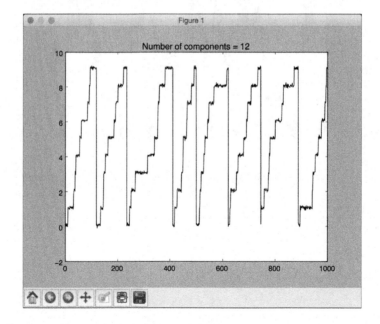

11. In the Terminal, you will get the following output:

```
Training HMM....

Means and variances of hidden states:

Hidden state 1
Mean = 5.092
Variance = 0.677

Hidden state 2
Mean = 0.6
Variance = 0.254

Hidden state 3
Mean = 8.099
Variance = 0.678

Hidden state 4
Mean = 2.601
Variance = 0.257
```

Building Conditional Random Fields for sequential text data

The **Conditional Random Fields (CRFs)** are probabilistic models used to analyze structured data. They are frequently used to label and segment sequential data. CRFs are discriminative models as opposed to HMMs, which are generative models. CRFs are used extensively to analyze sequences, stocks, speech, words, and so on. In these models, given a particular labeled observation sequence, we define a conditional probability distribution over this sequence. This is in contrast with HMMs where we define a joint distribution over the label and the observed sequence.

Getting ready

HMMs assume that the current output is statistically independent of the previous outputs. This is needed by HMMs to ensure that the inference works in a robust way. However, this assumption need not always be true! The current output in a time series setup, more often than not, depends on previous outputs. One of the main advantages of CRFs over HMMs is that they are conditional by nature, which means that we are not assuming any independence between output observations. There are a few other advantages of using CRFs over HMMs. CRFs tend to outperform HMMs in a number of applications, such as linguistics, bioinformatics, speech analysis, and so on. In this recipe, we will learn how to use CRFs to analyze sequences of letters.

We will use a library called pystruct to build and train CRFs. Make sure that you install this before you proceed. You can find the installation instructions at https://pystruct.github.io/installation.html.

How to do it...

1. Create a new Python file, and import the following packages:

```
import os
import argparse
import cPickle as pickle

import numpy as np
import matplotlib.pyplot as plt
from pystruct.datasets import load_letters
from pystruct.models import ChainCRF
from pystruct.learners import FrankWolfeSSVM
```

2. Define an argument parser to take the C value as an input argument. C is a hyperparameter that controls how specific you want your model to be without losing the power to generalize:

```
def build_arg_parser():
    parser = argparse.ArgumentParser(description='Trains the CRF classifier')
    parser.add_argument("--c-value", dest="c_value",
required=False, type=float,
            default=1.0, help="The C value that will be used for training")
    return parser
```

3. Define a class to handle all CRF-related processing:

```
class CRFTrainer(object):
```

4. Define an init function to initialize the values:

```
    def __init__(self, c_value, classifier_name='ChainCRF'):
        self.c_value = c_value
        self.classifier_name = classifier_name
```

5. We will use chain CRF to analyze the data. We need to add an error check for this, as follows:

```
        if self.classifier_name == 'ChainCRF':
            model = ChainCRF()
```

6. Define the classifier that we will use with our CRF model. We will use a type of **Support Vector Machine** to achieve this:

```
            self.clf = FrankWolfeSSVM(model=model, C=self.c_value,
max_iter=50)
        else:
            raise TypeError('Invalid classifier type')
```

7. Load the letters dataset. This dataset consists of segmented letters and their associated feature vectors. We will not analyze the images because we already have the feature vectors. The first letter from each word has been removed, so all we have are lowercase letters:

```
def load_data(self):
    letters = load_letters()
```

8. Load the data and labels into their respective variables:

```
    X, y, folds = letters['data'], letters['labels'],
letters['folds']
    X, y = np.array(X), np.array(y)
    return X, y, folds
```

9. Define a training method, as follows:

```
# X is a numpy array of samples where each sample
# has the shape (n_letters, n_features)
def train(self, X_train, y_train):
    self.clf.fit(X_train, y_train)
```

10. Define a method to evaluate the performance of the model:

```
def evaluate(self, X_test, y_test):
    return self.clf.score(X_test, y_test)
```

11. Define a method to classify new data:

```
# Run the classifier on input data
def classify(self, input_data):
    return self.clf.predict(input_data)[0]
```

12. The letters are indexed in a numbered array. In order to check the output and make it readable, we need to transform these numbers into alphabets. Define a function to do this:

```
def decoder(arr):

    alphabets = 'abcdefghijklmnopqrstuvwxyz'
    output = ''
    for i in arr:
        output += alphabets[i]

    return output
```

13. Define the `main` function and parse the input arguments:

```
if __name__=='__main__':
    args = build_arg_parser().parse_args()
    c_value = args.c_value
```

14. Initialize the variable with the class and the C value:

```
crf = CRFTrainer(c_value)
```

15. Load the letters data:

```
X, y, folds = crf.load_data()
```

16. Separate the data into training and testing datasets:

```
X_train, X_test = X[folds == 1], X[folds != 1]
y_train, y_test = y[folds == 1], y[folds != 1]
```

17. Train the CRF model, as follows:

```
print "\nTraining the CRF model..."
crf.train(X_train, y_train)
```

18. Evaluate the performance of the CRF model:

```
score = crf.evaluate(X_test, y_test)
print "\nAccuracy score =", str(round(score*100, 2)) + '%'
```

19. Let's take a random test vector and predict the output using the model:

```
print "\nTrue label =", decoder(y_test[0])
predicted_output = crf.classify([X_test[0]])
print "Predicted output =", decoder(predicted_output)
```

20. The full code is given in the `crf.py` file that is already provided to you. If you run this code, you will get the following output on your Terminal. As we can see, the word is supposed to be "commanding". The CRF does a pretty good job of predicting all the letters:

```
Training the CRF model...

Accuracy score = 78.05%

True label = ommanding
Predicted output = ommanging
```

Analyzing stock market data using Hidden Markov Models

Let's analyze stock market data using Hidden Markov Models. Stock market data is a good example of time series data where the data is organized in the form of dates. In the dataset that we will use, we can see how the stock values of various companies fluctuate over time. Hidden Markov Models are generative models that are used to analyze such time series data. In this recipe, we will use these models to analyze stock values.

How to do it...

1. Create a new Python file, and import the following packages:

```
import datetime

import numpy as np
import matplotlib.pyplot as plt
from matplotlib.finance import quotes_historical_yahoo_ochl
from hmmlearn.hmm import GaussianHMM
```

2. Get the stock quotes from Yahoo finance. There is a method available in `matplotlib` to load this directly:

```
# Get quotes from Yahoo finance
quotes = quotes_historical_yahoo_ochl("INTC",
        datetime.date(1994, 4, 5), datetime.date(2015, 7, 3))
```

3. There are six values in each quote. Let's extract the relevant data such as the closing value of the stock and the volume of stock that is traded along with their corresponding dates:

```
# Extract the required values
dates = np.array([quote[0] for quote in quotes], dtype=np.int)
closing_values = np.array([quote[2] for quote in quotes])
volume_of_shares = np.array([quote[5] for quote in quotes])[1:]
```

4. Let's compute the percentage change in the closing value of each type of data. We will use this as one of the features:

```
# Take diff of closing values and computing rate of change
diff_percentage = 100.0 * np.diff(closing_values) / closing_
values[:-1]

dates = dates[1:]
```

5. Stack the two arrays column-wise for training:

```
# Stack the percentage diff and volume values column-wise for
training
X = np.column_stack([diff_percentage, volume_of_shares])
```

6. Train the HMM using five components:

```
# Create and train Gaussian HMM
print "\nTraining HMM...."
model = GaussianHMM(n_components=5, covariance_type="diag", n_
iter=1000)

model.fit(X)
```

7. Generate 500 samples using the trained HMM and plot this, as follows:

```
# Generate data using model
num_samples = 500
samples, _ = model.sample(num_samples)
plt.plot(np.arange(num_samples), samples[:,0], c='black')

plt.show()
```

8. The full code is given in `hmm_stock.py` that is already provided to you. If you run this code, you will see the following figure:

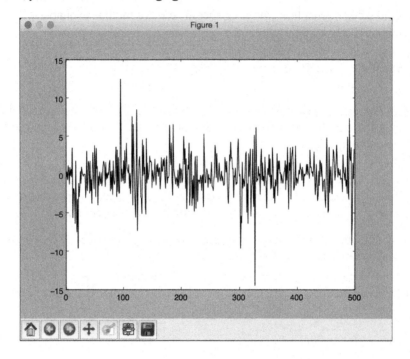

9
Image Content Analysis

In this chapter, we will cover the following recipes:

- ▸ Operating on images using OpenCV-Python
- ▸ Detecting edges
- ▸ Histogram equalization
- ▸ Detecting corners
- ▸ Detecting SIFT feature points
- ▸ Building Star feature detector
- ▸ Creating features using visual codebook and vector quantization
- ▸ Training an image classifier using Extremely Random Forests
- ▸ Building an object recognizer

Introduction

Computer Vision is a field that studies how to process, analyze, and understand the contents of visual data. In image content analysis, we use a lot of Computer Vision algorithms to build our understanding of the objects in the image. Computer Vision covers various aspects of image analysis, such as object recognition, shape analysis, pose estimation, 3D modeling, visual search, and so on. Humans are really good at identifying and recognizing things around them! The ultimate goal of Computer Vision is to accurately model the human vision system using computers.

Computer Vision consists of various levels of analysis. In low-level vision, we deal with pixel processing tasks, such as edge detection, morphological processing, and optical flow. In middle-level and high-level vision, we deal with things, such as object recognition, 3D modeling, motion analysis, and various other aspects of visual data. As we go higher, we tend to delve deeper into the conceptual aspects of our visual system and try to extract a description of visual data, based on activities and intentions. One thing to note is that higher levels tend to rely on the outputs of the lower levels for analysis.

One of the most common questions here is, "How is Computer Vision different from Image Processing?" Image Processing studies image transformations at the pixel level. Both the input and output of an Image Processing system are images. Some common examples are edge detection, histogram equalization, or image compression. Computer Vision algorithms heavily rely on Image Processing algorithms to perform their duties. In Computer Vision, we deal with more complex things that include understanding the visual data at a conceptual level. The reason for this is because we want to construct meaningful descriptions of the objects in the images. The output of a Computer Vision system is an interpretation of the 3D scene in the given image. This interpretation can come in various forms, depending on the task at hand.

In this chapter, we will use a library, called **OpenCV**, to analyze images. OpenCV is the world's most popular library for Computer Vision. As it has been highly optimized for many different platforms, it has become the de facto standard in the industry. Before you proceed, make sure that you install the library with Python support. You can download and install OpenCV at http://opencv.org. For detailed installation instructions on various operating systems, you can refer to the documentation section on the website.

Operating on images using OpenCV-Python

Let's take a look at how to operate on images using OpenCV-Python. In this recipe, we will see how to load and display an image. We will also look at how to crop, resize, and save an image to an output file.

How to do it...

1. Create a new Python file, and import the following packages:

```
import sys

import cv2
import numpy as np
```

2. Specify the input image as the first argument to the file, and read it using the image read function. We will use `forest.jpg`, as follows:

```
# Load and display an image -- 'forest.jpg'
input_file = sys.argv[1]
img = cv2.imread(input_file)
```

3. Display the input image, as follows:

```
cv2.imshow('Original', img)
```

4. We will now crop this image. Extract the height and width of the input image, and then specify the boundaries:

```
# Cropping an image
h, w = img.shape[:2]
start_row, end_row = int(0.21*h), int(0.73*h)
start_col, end_col= int(0.37*w), int(0.92*w)
```

5. Crop the image using NumPy style slicing and display it:

```
img_cropped = img[start_row:end_row, start_col:end_col]
cv2.imshow('Cropped', img_cropped)
```

6. Resize the image to `1.3` times its original size and display it:

```
# Resizing an image
scaling_factor = 1.3
img_scaled = cv2.resize(img, None, fx=scaling_factor, fy=scaling_
factor,
interpolation=cv2.INTER_LINEAR)
cv2.imshow('Uniform resizing', img_scaled)
```

7. The previous method will uniformly scale the image on both dimensions. Let's assume that we want to skew the image based on specific output dimensions. We use the following code:

```
img_scaled = cv2.resize(img, (250, 400), interpolation=cv2.INTER_
AREA)
cv2.imshow('Skewed resizing', img_scaled)
```

8. Save the image to an output file:

```
# Save an image
output_file = input_file[:-4] + '_cropped.jpg'
cv2.imwrite(output_file, img_cropped)

cv2.waitKey()
```

9. The `waitKey()` function displays the images until you hit a key on the keyboard.

10. The full code is given in the `operating_on_images.py` file that is already provided to you. If you run the code, you will see the following input image:

11. The second output is the cropped image:

12. The third output is the uniformly resized image:

13. The fourth output is the skewed image:

Detecting edges

Edge detection is one of the most popular techniques in Computer Vision. It is used as a preprocessing step in many applications. Let's look at how to use different edge detectors to detect edges in the input image.

How to do it...

1. Create a new Python file, and import the following packages:

   ```
   import sys

   import cv2
   import numpy as np
   ```

2. Load the input image. We will use `chair.jpg`:

   ```
   # Load the input image -- 'chair.jpg'
   # Convert it to grayscale
   input_file = sys.argv[1]
   img = cv2.imread(input_file, cv2.IMREAD_GRAYSCALE)
   ```

3. Extract the height and width of the image:

   ```
   h, w = img.shape
   ```

4. **Sobel filter** is a type of edge detector that uses a 3x3 kernel to detect horizontal and vertical edges separately. You can learn more about it at `http://www.tutorialspoint.com/dip/sobel_operator.htm`. Let's start with the horizontal detector:

   ```
   sobel_horizontal = cv2.Sobel(img, cv2.CV_64F, 1, 0, ksize=5)
   ```

5. Run the vertical Sobel detector:

   ```
   sobel_vertical = cv2.Sobel(img, cv2.CV_64F, 0, 1, ksize=5)
   ```

6. **Laplacian edge detector** detects edges in both the directions. You can learn more about it at `http://homepages.inf.ed.ac.uk/rbf/HIPR2/log.htm`. We use it as follows:

   ```
   laplacian = cv2.Laplacian(img, cv2.CV_64F)
   ```

7. Even though Laplacian addresses the shortcomings of Sobel, the output is still very noisy. **Canny edge detector** outperforms all of them because of the way it treats the problem. It is a multistage process, and it uses hysteresis to come up with clean edges. You can learn more about it at http://homepages.inf.ed.ac.uk/rbf/HIPR2/canny.htm:

```
canny = cv2.Canny(img, 50, 240)
```

8. Display all the output images:

```
cv2.imshow('Original', img)
cv2.imshow('Sobel horizontal', sobel_horizontal)
cv2.imshow('Sobel vertical', sobel_vertical)
cv2.imshow('Laplacian', laplacian)
cv2.imshow('Canny', canny)

cv2.waitKey()
```

9. The full code is given in the edge_detector.py file that is already provided to you. The original input image looks like the following:

10. Here is the horizontal Sobel edge detector output. Note how the detected lines tend to be vertical. This is due the fact that it's a horizontal edge detector, and it tends to detect changes in this direction:

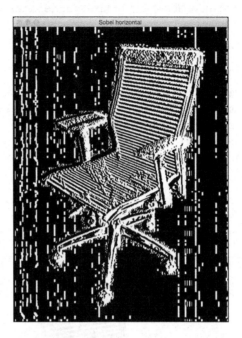

11. The vertical Sobel edge detector output looks like the following image:

12. Here is the Laplacian edge detector output:

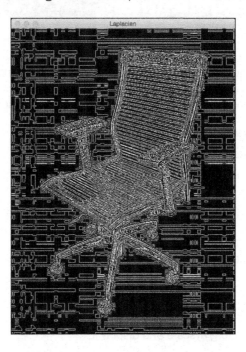

13. Canny edge detector detects all the edges nicely, as shown in the following image:

Histogram equalization

Histogram equalization is the process of modifying the intensities of the image pixels to enhance the contrast. The human eye likes contrast! This is the reason that almost all camera systems use histogram equalization to make images look nice. The interesting thing is that the histogram equalization process is different for grayscale and color images. There's a catch when dealing with color images, and we'll see it in this recipe. Let's see how to do it.

How to do it...

1. Create a new Python file, and import the following packages:

```
import sys

import cv2
import numpy as np
```

2. Load the input image. We will use the image, `sunrise.jpg`:

```
# Load input image -- 'sunrise.jpg'
input_file = sys.argv[1]
img = cv2.imread(input_file)
```

3. Convert the image to grayscale and display it:

```
# Convert it to grayscale
img_gray = cv2.cvtColor(img, cv2.COLOR_BGR2GRAY)
cv2.imshow('Input grayscale image', img_gray)
```

4. Equalize the histogram of the grayscale image and display it:

```
# Equalize the histogram
img_gray_histeq = cv2.equalizeHist(img_gray)
cv2.imshow('Histogram equalized - grayscale', img_gray_histeq)
```

5. In order to equalize the histogram of the color images, we need to follow a different procedure. Histogram equalization only applies to the intensity channel. An RGB image consists of three color channels, and we cannot apply the histogram equalization process on these channels separately. We need to separate the intensity information from the color information before we do anything. So, we convert it to YUV colorspace first, equalize the Y channel, and then convert it back to RGB to get the output. You can learn more about YUV colorspace at `http://softpixel.com/~cwright/programming/colorspace/yuv`. OpenCV loads images in the BGR format by default, so let's convert it from BGR to YUV first:

```
# Histogram equalization of color images
img_yuv = cv2.cvtColor(img, cv2.COLOR_BGR2YUV)
```

6. Equalize the Y channel, as follows:

```
img_yuv[:,:,0] = cv2.equalizeHist(img_yuv[:,:,0])
```

7. Convert it back to BGR:

```
img_histeq = cv2.cvtColor(img_yuv, cv2.COLOR_YUV2BGR)
```

8. Display the input and output images:

```
cv2.imshow('Input color image', img)
cv2.imshow('Histogram equalized - color', img_histeq)

cv2.waitKey()
```

9. The full code is given in the `histogram_equalizer.py` file that is already provided to you. The input image is shown, as follows:

10. The histogram equalized image looks like the following:

Detecting corners

Corner detection is an important process in Computer Vision. It helps us identify the salient points in the image. This was one of the earliest feature extraction techniques that was used to develop image analysis systems.

How to do it...

1. Create a new Python file, and import the following packages:

```
import sys

import cv2
import numpy as np
```

2. Load the input image. We will use box.png:

```
# Load input image -- 'box.png'
input_file = sys.argv[1]
img = cv2.imread(input_file)
cv2.imshow('Input image', img)
```

3. Convert the image to grayscale and cast it to floating point values. We need the floating point values for the corner detector to work:

```
img_gray = cv2.cvtColor(img, cv2.COLOR_BGR2GRAY)
img_gray = np.float32(img_gray)
```

4. Run the **Harris corner detector** function on the grayscale image. You can learn more about Harris corner detector at http://docs.opencv.org/3.0-beta/doc/py_tutorials/py_feature2d/py_features_harris/py_features_harris.html:

```
# Harris corner detector
img_harris = cv2.cornerHarris(img_gray, 7, 5, 0.04)
```

5. In order to mark the corners, we need to dilate the image, as follows:

```
# Resultant image is dilated to mark the corners
img_harris = cv2.dilate(img_harris, None)
```

6. Let's threshold the image to display the important points:

```
# Threshold the image
img[img_harris > 0.01 * img_harris.max()] = [0, 0, 0]
```

7. Display the output image:

```
cv2.imshow('Harris Corners', img)
cv2.waitKey()
```

8. The full code is given in the `corner_detector.py` file that is already provided to you. The input image is displayed, as follows:

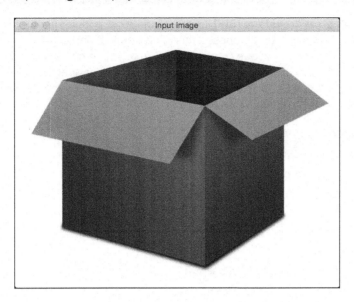

9. The output image after detecting corners is as follows:

Detecting SIFT feature points

Scale Invariant Feature Transform (**SIFT**) is one of the most popular features in the field of Computer Vision. David Lowe first proposed this in his seminal paper, which is available at `https://www.cs.ubc.ca/~lowe/papers/ijcv04.pdf`. It has since become one of the most effective features to use for image recognition and content analysis. It is robust against scale, orientation, intensity, and so on. This forms the basis of our object recognition system. Let's take a look at how to detect these feature points.

How to do it...

1. Create a new Python file, and import the following packages:

    ```
    import sys

    import cv2
    import numpy as np
    ```

2. Load the input image. We will use `table.jpg`:

    ```
    # Load input image -- 'table.jpg'
    input_file = sys.argv[1]
    img = cv2.imread(input_file)
    ```

3. Convert this image to grayscale:

    ```
    img_gray = cv2.cvtColor(img, cv2.COLOR_BGR2GRAY)
    ```

4. Initialize the SIFT detector object and extract the keypoints:

    ```
    sift = cv2.xfeatures2d.SIFT_create()
    keypoints = sift.detect(img_gray, None)
    ```

5. The keypoints are the salient points, but they are not the features. This basically gives us the location of the salient points. SIFT also functions as a very effective feature extractor, but we will see this aspect of it in one of the later recipes.

6. Draw the keypoints on top of the input image, as follows:

    ```
    img_sift = np.copy(img)
    cv2.drawKeypoints(img, keypoints, img_sift, flags=cv2.DRAW_
    MATCHES_FLAGS_DRAW_RICH_KEYPOINTS)
    ```

7. Display the input and output images:

    ```
    cv2.imshow('Input image', img)
    cv2.imshow('SIFT features', img_sift)
    cv2.waitKey()
    ```

8. The full code is given in the `feature_detector.py` file that is already provided to you. The input image is as follows:

9. The output image looks like the following:

Building a Star feature detector

SIFT feature detector is good in many cases. However, when we build object recognition systems, we may want to use a different feature detector before we extract features using SIFT. This will give us the flexibility to cascade different blocks to get the best possible performance. So, we will use the **Star feature detector** in this case to see how to do it.

How to do it...

1. Create a new Python file, and import the following packages:

```
import sys

import cv2
import numpy as np
```

2. Define a class to handle all the functions that are related to Star feature detection:

```
class StarFeatureDetector(object):
    def __init__(self):
        self.detector = cv2.xfeatures2d.StarDetector_create()
```

3. Define a function to run the detector on the input image:

```
    def detect(self, img):
        return self.detector.detect(img)
```

4. Load the input image in the `main` function. We will use `table.jpg`:

```
if __name__=='__main__':
    # Load input image -- 'table.jpg'
    input_file = sys.argv[1]
    input_img = cv2.imread(input_file)
```

5. Convert the image to grayscale:

```
    # Convert to grayscale
    img_gray = cv2.cvtColor(input_img, cv2.COLOR_BGR2GRAY)
```

6. Detect features using the Star feature detector:

```
    # Detect features using Star feature detector
    keypoints = StarFeatureDetector().detect(input_img)
```

7. Draw keypoints on top of the input image:

```
    cv2.drawKeypoints(input_img, keypoints, input_img,
            flags=cv2.DRAW_MATCHES_FLAGS_DRAW_RICH_KEYPOINTS)
```

8. Display the output image:

```
    cv2.imshow('Star features', input_img)
    cv2.waitKey()
```

9. The full code is given in the `star_detector.py` file that is already provided to you. The output image looks like the following:

Creating features using visual codebook and vector quantization

In order to build an object recognition system, we need to extract feature vectors from each image. Each image needs to have a signature that can be used for matching. We use a concept called **visual codebook** to build image signatures. This codebook is basically the dictionary that we will use to come up with a representation for the images in our training dataset. We use vector quantization to cluster many feature points and come up with centroids. These centroids will serve as the elements of our visual codebook. You can learn more about this at `http://mi.eng.cam.ac.uk/~cipolla/lectures/PartIB/old/IB-visualcodebook.pdf`.

Before you start, make sure that you have some training images. You were provided with a sample training dataset that contains three classes, where each class has 20 images. These images were downloaded from `http://www.vision.caltech.edu/html-files/archive.html`.

To build a robust object recognition system, you need tens of thousands of images. There is a dataset called `Caltech256` that's very popular in this field! It contains 256 classes of images, where each class contains thousands of samples. You can download this dataset at `http://www.vision.caltech.edu/Image_Datasets/Caltech256`.

How to do it...

1. This is a lengthy recipe, so we will only look at the important functions. The full code is given in the `build_features.py` file that is already provided to you. Let's look at the class defined to extract features:

```
class FeatureBuilder(object):
```

2. Define a method to extract features from the input image. We will use the Star detector to get the keypoints and then use SIFT to extract descriptors from these locations:

```
def extract_ features(self, img):
    keypoints = StarFeatureDetector().detect(img)
    keypoints, feature_vectors = compute_sift_features(img,
keypoints)
    return feature_vectors
```

3. We need to extract centroids from all the descriptors:

```
def get_codewords(self, input_map, scaling_size, max_
samples=12):
    keypoints_all = []

    count = 0
    cur_label = ''
```

4. Each image will give rise to a large number of descriptors. We will just use a small number of images because the centroids won't change much after this:

```
for item in input_map:
    if count >= max_samples:
        if cur_class != item['object_class']:
            count = 0
        else:
            continue

    count += 1
```

5. The print progress is as follows:

```
if count == max_samples:
    print "Built centroids for", item['object_class']
```

6. Extract the current label:

```
cur_class = item['object_class']
```

7. Read the image and resize it:

```
img = cv2.imread(item['image_path'])
img = resize_image(img, scaling_size)
```

8. Set the number of dimensions to 128 and extract the features:

```
num_dims = 128
feature_vectors = self.extract_image_features(img)
keypoints_all.extend(feature_vectors)
```

9. Use vector quantization to quantize the feature points. **Vector quantization** is the *N*-dimensional version of "rounding off". You can learn more about it at http://www.data-compression.com/vq.shtml.

```
kmeans, centroids = BagOfWords().cluster(keypoints_all)
return kmeans, centroids
```

10. Define the class to handle bag of words model and vector quantization:

```
class BagOfWords(object):
    def __init__(self, num_clusters=32):
        self.num_dims = 128
        self.num_clusters = num_clusters
        self.num_retries = 10
```

11. Define a method to quantize the datapoints. We will use **k-means clustering** to achieve this:

```
def cluster(self, datapoints):
    kmeans = KMeans(self.num_clusters,
        n_init=max(self.num_retries, 1),
        max_iter=10, tol=1.0)
```

12. Extract the centroids, as follows:

```
res = kmeans.fit(datapoints)
centroids = res.cluster_centers_
return kmeans, centroids
```

13. Define a method to normalize the data:

```
def normalize(self, input_data):
    sum_input = np.sum(input_data)

    if sum_input > 0:
        return input_data / sum_input
    else:
        return input_data
```

14. Define a method to get the feature vector:

```
def construct_feature(self, img, kmeans, centroids):
    keypoints = StarFeatureDetector().detect(img)
    keypoints, feature_vectors = compute_sift_features(img,
keypoints)
    labels = kmeans.predict(feature_vectors)
    feature_vector = np.zeros(self.num_clusters)
```

15. Build a histogram and normalize it:

```
for i, item in enumerate(feature_vectors):
    feature_vector[labels[i]] += 1

    feature_vector_img = np.reshape(feature_vector,
((1, feature_vector.shape[0])))
    return self.normalize(feature_vector_img)
```

16. Define a method the extract the SIFT features:

```
# Extract SIFT features
def compute_sift_features(img, keypoints):
    if img is None:
        raise TypeError('Invalid input image')

    img_gray = cv2.cvtColor(img, cv2.COLOR_BGR2GRAY)
    keypoints, descriptors = cv2.xfeatures2d.SIFT_create().
compute(img_gray, keypoints)
    return keypoints, descriptors
```

As mentioned earlier, please refer to build_features.py for the complete code. You should run the code in the following way:

```
$ python build_features.py --data-folder /path/to/training_images/
--codebook-file codebook.pkl --feature-map-file feature_map.pkl
```

This will generate two files called codebook.pkl and feature_map.pkl. We will use these files in the next recipe.

Training an image classifier using Extremely Random Forests

We will use **Extremely Random Forests** (**ERFs**) to train our image classifier. An object recognition system uses an image classifier to classify the images into known categories. ERFs are very popular in the field of machine learning because of their speed and accuracy. We basically construct a bunch of decision trees that are based on our image signatures, and then train the forest to make the right decision. You can learn more about random forests at https://www.stat.berkeley.edu/~breiman/RandomForests/cc_home.htm. You can learn about ERFs at http://www.montefiore.ulg.ac.be/~ernst/uploads/news/id63/extremely-randomized-trees.pdf.

How to do it...

1. Create a new Python file, and import the following packages:

```
import argparse
import cPickle as pickle

import numpy as np
from sklearn.ensemble import ExtraTreesClassifier
from sklearn import preprocessing
```

2. Define an argument parser:

```
def build_arg_parser():
    parser = argparse.ArgumentParser(description='Trains the
classifier')
    parser.add_argument("--feature-map-file", dest="feature_map_
file", required=True,
help="Input pickle file containing the feature map")
    parser.add_argument("--model-file", dest="model_file",
required=False,
help="Output file where the trained model will be stored")
    return parser
```

3. Define a class to handle ERF training. We will use a label encoder to encode our training labels:

```
class ERFTrainer(object):
    def __init__(self, X, label_words):
        self.le = preprocessing.LabelEncoder()
        self.clf = ExtraTreesClassifier(n_estimators=100, max_
depth=16, random_state=0)
```

4. Encode the labels and train the classifier:

```
        y = self.encode_labels(label_words)
        self.clf.fit(np.asarray(X), y)
```

5. Define a function to encode the labels:

```
def encode_labels(self, label_words):
    self.le.fit(label_words)
    return np.array(self.le.transform(label_words), dtype=np.
float32)
```

6. Define a function to classify an unknown datapoint:

```
def classify(self, X):
    label_nums = self.clf.predict(np.asarray(X))
```

```
        label_words = self.le.inverse_transform([int(x) for x in
label_nums])
        return label_words
```

7. Define the `main` function and parse the input arguments:

```
if __name__ =='__main__':
    args = build_arg_parser().parse_args()
    feature_map_file = args.feature_map_file
    model_file = args.model_file
```

8. Load the feature map that we created in the previous recipe:

```
    # Load the feature map
    with open(feature_map_file, 'r') as f:
        feature_map = pickle.load(f)
```

9. Extract the feature vectors:

```
    # Extract feature vectors and the labels
    label_words = [x['object_class'] for x in feature_map]
    dim_size = feature_map[0]['feature_vector'].shape[1]
    X = [np.reshape(x['feature_vector'], (dim_size,)) for x in
feature_map]
```

10. Train the ERF, which is based on the training data:

```
    # Train the Extremely Random Forests classifier
    erf = ERFTrainer(X, label_words)
```

11. Save the trained ERF model, as follows:

```
    if args.model_file:
        with open(args.model_file, 'w') as f:
            pickle.dump(erf, f)
```

12. The full code is given in the `trainer.py` file that is provided to you. You should run the code in the following way:

$ python trainer.py --feature-map-file feature_map.pkl --model-file erf.pkl

This will generate a file called `erf.pkl`. We will use this file in the next recipe.

Building an object recognizer

Now that we trained an ERF model, let's go ahead and build an object recognizer that can recognize the content of unknown images.

How to do it...

1. Create a new Python file, and import the following packages:

```
import argparse
import cPickle as pickle

import cv2
import numpy as np

import build_features as bf
from trainer import ERFTrainer
```

2. Define the argument parser:

```
def build_arg_parser():
    parser = argparse.ArgumentParser(description='Extracts \
features \
from each line and classifies the data')
    parser.add_argument("--input-image", dest="input_image",
required=True,
help="Input image to be classified")
    parser.add_argument("--model-file", dest="model_file",
required=True,
help="Input file containing the trained model")
    parser.add_argument("--codebook-file", dest="codebook_file",
required=True, help="Input file containing the codebook")
    return parser
```

3. Define a class to handle the image tag extraction functions:

```
class ImageTagExtractor(object):
    def __init__(self, model_file, codebook_file):
        with open(model_file, 'r') as f:
            self.erf = pickle.load(f)

        with open(codebook_file, 'r') as f:
            self.kmeans, self.centroids = pickle.load(f)
```

4. Define a function to predict the output using the trained ERF model:

```
def predict(self, img, scaling_size):
    img = bf.resize_image(img, scaling_size)
    feature_vector = bf.BagOfWords().construct_feature(
img, self.kmeans, self.centroids)
    image_tag = self.erf.classify(feature_vector)[0]
    return image_tag
```

5. Define the `main` function and load the input image:

```
if __name__=='__main__':
    args = build_arg_parser().parse_args()
    model_file = args.model_file
    codebook_file = args.codebook_file
    input_image = cv2.imread(args.input_image)
```

6. Scale the image appropriately, as follows:

```
scaling_size = 200
```

7. Print the output on the Terminal:

```
print "\nOutput:", ImageTagExtractor(model_file,
codebook_file).predict(input_image, scaling_size)
```

8. The full code is given in the `object_recognizer.py` file that is already provided to you. You should run the code in the following way:

```
$ python object_recognizer.py --input-image imagefile.jpg --model-
file erf.pkl --codebook-file codebook.pkl
```

You will see the output class printed on the Terminal.

10
Biometric Face Recognition

In this chapter, we will cover the following recipes:

- ▶ Capturing and processing video from a webcam
- ▶ Building a face detector using Haar cascades
- ▶ Building eye and nose detectors
- ▶ Performing Principal Components Analysis
- ▶ Performing Kernel Principal Components Analysis
- ▶ Performing blind source separation
- ▶ Building a face recognizer using Local Binary Patterns Histogram

Introduction

Face recognition refers to the task of identifying the person in a given image. This is different from face detection where we locate the face in a given image. During face detection, we don't care who the person is. We just identify the region of the image that contains the face. Therefore, in a typical biometric face-recognition system, we need to determine the location of the face before we can recognize it.

Face recognition is very easy for humans. We seem to do it effortlessly, and we do it all the time! How do we get a machine to do the same thing? We need to understand what parts of the face we can use to uniquely identify a person. Our brain has an internal structure that seems to respond to specific features, such as edges, corners, motion, and so on. The human visual cortex combines all these features into a single coherent inference. If we want our machine to recognize faces with accuracy, we need to formulate the problem in a similar way. We need to extract features from the input image and convert it into a meaningful representation.

Capturing and processing video from a webcam

We will use a webcam in this chapter to capture video data. Let's see how to capture the video from the webcam using OpenCV-Python.

How to do it...

1. Create a new Python file, and import the following packages:

```
import cv2
```

2. OpenCV provides a video capture object that we can use to capture images from the webcam. The 0 input argument specifies the ID of the webcam. If you connect a USB camera, then it will have a different ID:

```
# Initialize video capture object
cap = cv2.VideoCapture(0)
```

3. Define the scaling factor for the frames captured using the webcam:

```
# Define the image size scaling factor
scaling_factor = 0.5
```

4. Start an infinite loop and keep capturing frames until you press the *Esc* key. Read the frame from the webcam:

```
# Loop until you hit the Esc key
while True:
    # Capture the current frame
    ret, frame = cap.read()
```

5. Resizing the frame is optional but still a useful thing to have in your code:

```
    # Resize the frame
    frame = cv2.resize(frame, None, fx=scaling_factor, fy=scaling_
factor,
            interpolation=cv2.INTER_AREA)
```

6. Display the frame:

```
    # Display the image
    cv2.imshow('Webcam', frame)
```

7. Wait for 1 ms before capturing the next frame:

```
    # Detect if the Esc key has been pressed
    c = cv2.waitKey(1)
    if c == 27:
        break
```

8. Release the video capture object:

```
# Release the video capture object
cap.release()
```

9. Close all active windows before exiting the code:

```
# Close all active windows
cv2.destroyAllWindows()
```

10. The full code is given in the `video_capture.py` file that's already provided to you for reference. If you run this code, you will see the video from the webcam, similar to the following screenshot:

Building a face detector using Haar cascades

As we discussed earlier, face detection is the process of determining the location of the face in the input image. We will use **Haar cascades** for face detection. This works by extracting a large number of simple features from the image at multiple scales. The simple features are basically edge, line, and rectangle features that are very easy to compute. It is then trained by creating a cascade of simple classifiers. The **Adaptive Boosting** technique is used to make this process robust. You can learn more about it at `http://docs.opencv.org/3.1.0/d7/d8b/tutorial_py_face_detection.html#gsc.tab=0`. Let's take a look at how to determine the location of a face in the video frames captured from the webcam.

How to do it...

1. Create a new Python file, and import the following packages:

```
import cv2
import numpy as np
```

2. Load the face detector cascade file. This is a trained model that we can use as a detector:

```
# Load the face cascade file
face_cascade = cv2.CascadeClassifier('cascade_files/haarcascade_
frontalface_alt.xml')
```

3. Check whether the cascade file loaded properly:

```
# Check if the face cascade file has been loaded
if face_cascade.empty():
    raise IOError('Unable to load the face cascade classifier xml
file')
```

4. Create the video capture object:

```
# Initialize the video capture object
cap = cv2.VideoCapture(0)
```

5. Define the scaling factor for image downsampling:

```
# Define the scaling factor
scaling_factor = 0.5
```

6. Keep looping until you hit the *Esc* key:

```
# Loop until you hit the Esc key
while True:
    # Capture the current frame and resize it
    ret, frame = cap.read()
```

7. Resize the frame:

```
    frame = cv2.resize(frame, None, fx=scaling_factor, fy=scaling_
factor,
            interpolation=cv2.INTER_AREA)
```

8. Convert the image to grayscale. We need grayscale images to run the face detector:

```
    # Convert to grayscale
    gray = cv2.cvtColor(frame, cv2.COLOR_BGR2GRAY)
```

9. Run the face detector on the grayscale image. The 1.3 parameter refers to the scale multiplier for each stage. The 5 parameter refers to the minimum number of neighbors that each candidate rectangle should have so that we can retain it. This candidate rectangle is basically a potential region where there is a chance of a face being detected:

```
# Run the face detector on the grayscale image
face_rects = face_cascade.detectMultiScale(gray, 1.3, 5)
```

10. For each detected face region, draw a rectangle around it:

```
# Draw rectangles on the image
for (x,y,w,h) in face_rects:
    cv2.rectangle(frame, (x,y), (x+w,y+h), (0,255,0), 3)
```

11. Display the output image:

```
# Display the image
cv2.imshow('Face Detector', frame)
```

12. Wait for 1 ms before going to the next iteration. If the user presses the *Esc* key, break out of the loop:

```
# Check if Esc key has been pressed
c = cv2.waitKey(1)
if c == 27:
    break
```

13. Release and destroy the objects before exiting the code:

```
# Release the video capture object and close all windows
cap.release()
cv2.destroyAllWindows()
```

14. The full code is given in the `face_detector.py` file that's already provided to you for reference. If you run this code, you will see the face being detected in the webcam video:

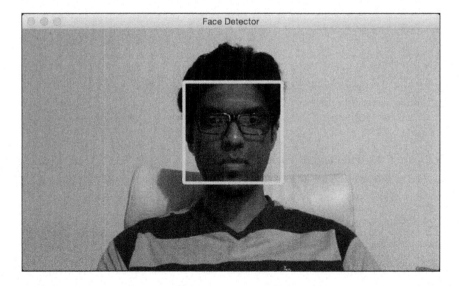

Building eye and nose detectors

The Haar cascades method can be extended to detect all types of objects. Let's see how to use it to detect the eyes and nose in the input video.

How to do it...

1. Create a new Python file, and import the following packages:

```
import cv2
import numpy as np
```

2. Load the face, eyes, and nose cascade files:

```
# Load face, eye, and nose cascade files
face_cascade = cv2.CascadeClassifier('cascade_files/haarcascade_
frontalface_alt.xml')
eye_cascade = cv2.CascadeClassifier('cascade_files/haarcascade_
eye.xml')
nose_cascade = cv2.CascadeClassifier('cascade_files/haarcascade_
mcs_nose.xml')
```

3. Check whether the files loaded correctly:

```
# Check if face cascade file has been loaded
if face_cascade.empty():
    raise IOError('Unable to load the face cascade classifier xml
file')

# Check if eye cascade file has been loaded
if eye_cascade.empty():
    raise IOError('Unable to load the eye cascade classifier xml
file')

# Check if nose cascade file has been loaded
if nose_cascade.empty():
    raise IOError('Unable to load the nose cascade classifier xml
file')
```

4. Initialize the video capture object:

```
# Initialize video capture object and define scaling factor
cap = cv2.VideoCapture(0)
```

5. Define the scaling factor:

```
scaling_factor = 0.5
```

6. Keep looping until the user presses the *Esc* key:

```
while True:
    # Read current frame, resize it, and convert it to grayscale
    ret, frame = cap.read()
```

7. Resize the frame:

```
    frame = cv2.resize(frame, None, fx=scaling_factor, fy=scaling_
factor,
            interpolation=cv2.INTER_AREA)
```

8. Convert the image to grayscale:

```
    gray = cv2.cvtColor(frame, cv2.COLOR_BGR2GRAY)
```

9. Run the face detector on the grayscale image:

```
    # Run face detector on the grayscale image
    faces = face_cascade.detectMultiScale(gray, 1.3, 5)
```

10. As we know that eyes and noses are always on faces, we can run these detectors only in the face region:

```
    # Run eye and nose detectors within each face rectangle
    for (x,y,w,h) in faces:
```

11. Extract the face ROI:

```
        # Grab the current ROI in both color and grayscale images
        roi_gray = gray[y:y+h, x:x+w]
        roi_color = frame[y:y+h, x:x+w]
```

12. Run the eye detector:

```
        # Run eye detector in the grayscale ROI
        eye_rects = eye_cascade.detectMultiScale(roi_gray)
```

13. Run the nose detector:

```
        # Run nose detector in the grayscale ROI
        nose_rects = nose_cascade.detectMultiScale(roi_gray, 1.3,
5)
```

14. Draw circles around the eyes:

```
        # Draw green circles around the eyes
        for (x_eye, y_eye, w_eye, h_eye) in eye_rects:
            center = (int(x_eye + 0.5*w_eye), int(y_eye + 0.5*h_
eye))
            radius = int(0.3 * (w_eye + h_eye))
            color = (0, 255, 0)
            thickness = 3
            cv2.circle(roi_color, center, radius, color,
thickness)
```

15. Draw a rectangle around the nose:

```
for (x_nose, y_nose, w_nose, h_nose) in nose_rects:
    cv2.rectangle(roi_color, (x_nose, y_nose), (x_nose+w_
nose,
        y_nose+h_nose), (0,255,0), 3)
    break
```

16. Display the image:

```
# Display the image
cv2.imshow('Eye and nose detector', frame)
```

17. Wait for 1 ms before going to the next iteration. If the user presses the *Esc* key, then break the loop.

```
# Check if Esc key has been pressed
c = cv2.waitKey(1)
if c == 27:
    break
```

18. Release and destroy the objects before exiting the code.

```
# Release video capture object and close all windows
cap.release()
cv2.destroyAllWindows()
```

19. The full code is given in the `eye_nose_detector.py` file that's already provided to you for reference. If you run this code, you will see the eyes and nose being detected in the webcam video:

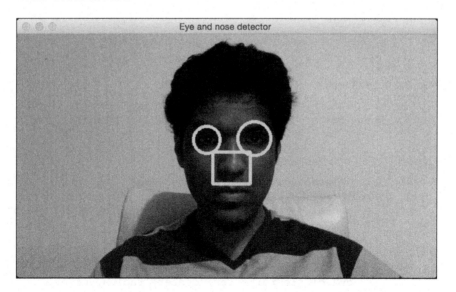

Performing Principal Components Analysis

Principal Components Analysis (PCA) is a dimensionality reduction technique that's used very frequently in computer vision and machine learning. When we deal with features with large dimensionalities, training a machine learning system becomes prohibitively expensive. Therefore, we need to reduce the dimensionality of the data before we can train a system. However, when we reduce the dimensionality, we don't want to lose the information present in the data. This is where PCA comes into the picture! PCA identifies the important components of the data and arranges them in the order of importance. You can learn more about it at http://dai.fmph.uniba.sk/courses/ml/sl/PCA.pdf. It is used a lot in face recognition systems. Let's see how to perform PCA on input data.

How to do it...

1. Create a new Python file, and import the following packages:

```
import numpy as np
from sklearn import decomposition
```

2. Let's define five dimensions for our input data. The first two dimensions will be independent, but the next three dimensions will be dependent on the first two dimensions. This basically means that we can live without the last three dimensions because they do not give us any new information:

```
# Define individual features
x1 = np.random.normal(size=250)
x2 = np.random.normal(size=250)
x3 = 2*x1 + 3*x2
x4 = 4*x1 - x2
x5 = x3 + 2*x4
```

3. Let's create a dataset with these features.

```
# Create dataset with the above features
X = np.c_[x1, x3, x2, x5, x4]
```

4. Create a PCA object:

```
# Perform Principal Components Analysis
pca = decomposition.PCA()
```

5. Fit a PCA model on the input data:

```
pca.fit(X)
```

6. Print the variances of the dimensions:

```
# Print variances
variances = pca.explained_variance_
print '\nVariances in decreasing order:\n', variances
```

7. If a particular dimension is useful, then it will have a meaningful value for the variance. Let's set a threshold and identify the important dimensions:

```
# Find the number of useful dimensions
thresh_variance = 0.8
num_useful_dims = len(np.where(variances > thresh_variance)[0])
print '\nNumber of useful dimensions:', num_useful_dims
```

8. Just like we discussed earlier, PCA identified that only two dimensions are important in this dataset:

```
# As we can see, only the 2 first components are useful
pca.n_components = num_useful_dims
```

9. Let's convert the dataset from a five-dimensional set to a two-dimensional set:

```
X_new = pca.fit_transform(X)
print '\nShape before:', X.shape
print 'Shape after:', X_new.shape
```

10. The full code is given in the pca.py file that's already provided to you for reference. If you run this code, you will see the following on your Terminal:

```
Variances in decreasing order:
[  1.13489352e+02   1.08125265e+01   3.34017371e-31   4.36320756e-32
   1.49223239e-32]

Number of useful dimensions: 2

Shape before: (250, 5)
Shape after: (250, 2)
```

Performing Kernel Principal Components Analysis

PCA is good at reducing the number of dimensions, but it works in a linear manner. If the data is not organized in a linear fashion, PCA fails to do the required job. This is where Kernel PCA comes into the picture. You can learn more about it at http://www.ics. uci.edu/~welling/classnotes/papers_class/Kernel-PCA.pdf. Let's see how to perform Kernel PCA on the input data and compare it to how PCA performs on the same data.

How to do it...

1. Create a new Python file, and import the following packages:

```
import numpy as np
import matplotlib.pyplot as plt
```

```
from sklearn.decomposition import PCA, KernelPCA
from sklearn.datasets import make_circles
```

2. Define the seed value for the random number generator. This is needed to generate the data samples for analysis:

```
# Set the seed for random number generator
np.random.seed(7)
```

3. Generate data that is distributed in concentric circles to demonstrate how PCA doesn't work in this case:

```
# Generate samples
X, y = make_circles(n_samples=500, factor=0.2, noise=0.04)
```

4. Perform PCA on this data:

```
# Perform PCA
pca = PCA()
X_pca = pca.fit_transform(X)
```

5. Perform Kernel PCA on this data:

```
# Perform Kernel PCA
kernel_pca = KernelPCA(kernel="rbf", fit_inverse_transform=True,
gamma=10)
X_kernel_pca = kernel_pca.fit_transform(X)
X_inverse = kernel_pca.inverse_transform(X_kernel_pca)
```

6. Plot the original input data:

```
# Plot original data
class_0 = np.where(y == 0)
class_1 = np.where(y == 1)
plt.figure()
plt.title("Original data")
plt.plot(X[class_0, 0], X[class_0, 1], "ko", mfc='none')
plt.plot(X[class_1, 0], X[class_1, 1], "kx")
plt.xlabel("1st dimension")
plt.ylabel("2nd dimension")
```

7. Plot the PCA-transformed data:

```
# Plot PCA projection of the data
plt.figure()
plt.plot(X_pca[class_0, 0], X_pca[class_0, 1], "ko", mfc='none')
plt.plot(X_pca[class_1, 0], X_pca[class_1, 1], "kx")
plt.title("Data transformed using PCA")
plt.xlabel("1st principal component")
plt.ylabel("2nd principal component")
```

8. Plot Kernel PCA-transformed data:

```
# Plot Kernel PCA projection of the data
plt.figure()
plt.plot(X_kernel_pca[class_0, 0], X_kernel_pca[class_0, 1], "ko",
mfc='none')
plt.plot(X_kernel_pca[class_1, 0], X_kernel_pca[class_1, 1], "kx")
plt.title("Data transformed using Kernel PCA")
plt.xlabel("1st principal component")
plt.ylabel("2nd principal component")
```

9. Transform the data back to the original space using the Kernel method to show that the inverse is maintained:

```
# Transform the data back to original space
plt.figure()
plt.plot(X_inverse[class_0, 0], X_inverse[class_0, 1], "ko",
mfc='none')
plt.plot(X_inverse[class_1, 0], X_inverse[class_1, 1], "kx")
plt.title("Inverse transform")
plt.xlabel("1st dimension")
plt.ylabel("2nd dimension")

plt.show()
```

10. The full code is given in the `kpca.py` file that's already provided to you for reference. If you run this code, you will see four figures. The first figure is the original data:

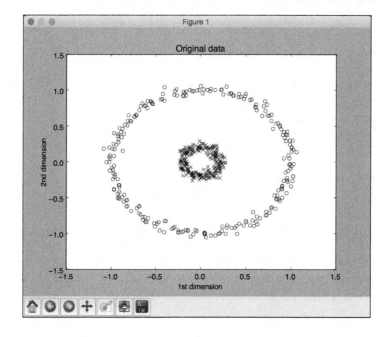

The second figure depicts the data transformed using PCA:

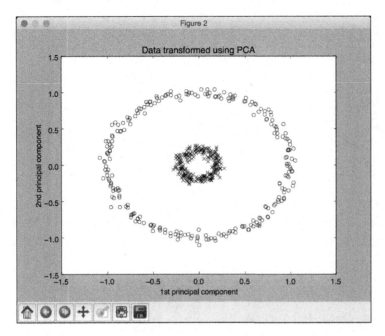

The third figure depicts the data transformed using Kernel PCA. Note how the points are clustered in the right part of the figure:

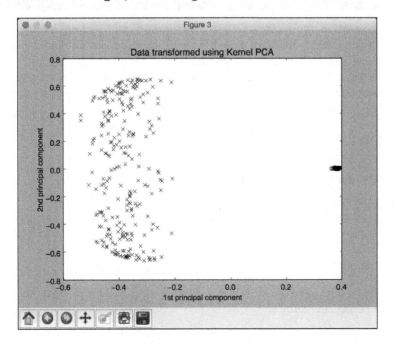

The fourth figure depicts the inverse transform of the data back to the original space:

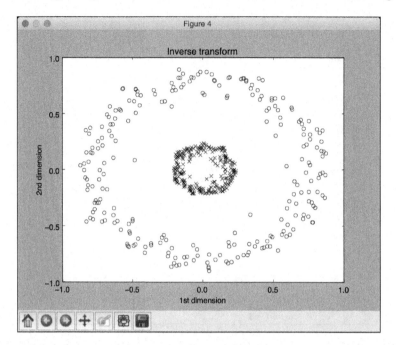

Performing blind source separation

Blind source separation refers to the process of separating signals from a mixture. Let's say a bunch of different signal generators generate signals and a common receiver receives all of these signals. Now, our job is to separate these signals from this mixture using the properties of these signals. We will use **Independent Components Analysis (ICA)** to achieve this. You can learn more about it at http://www.mit.edu/~gari/teaching/6.555/LECTURE_NOTES/ch15_bss.pdf. Let's see how to do it.

How to do it...

1. Create a new Python file, and import the following packages:

```
import numpy as np
import matplotlib.pyplot as plt
from scipy import signal

from sklearn.decomposition import PCA, FastICA
```

2. We will use data from the mixture_of_signals.txt file that's already provided to you. Let's load the data:

```
# Load data
input_file = 'mixture_of_signals.txt'
X = np.loadtxt(input_file)
```

3. Create the ICA object:

```
# Compute ICA
ica = FastICA(n_components=4)
```

4. Reconstruct the signals, based on ICA:

```
# Reconstruct the signals
signals_ica = ica.fit_transform(X)
```

5. Extract the mixing matrix:

```
# Get estimated mixing matrix
mixing_mat = ica.mixing_
```

6. Perform PCA for comparison:

```
# Perform PCA
pca = PCA(n_components=4)
signals_pca = pca.fit_transform(X)   # Reconstruct signals based on
orthogonal components
```

7. Define the list of signals to plot them:

```
# Specify parameters for output plots
models = [X, signals_ica, signals_pca]
```

8. Specify the colors of the plots:

```
colors = ['blue', 'red', 'black', 'green']
```

9. Plot the input signal:

```
# Plotting input signal
plt.figure()
plt.title('Input signal (mixture)')
for i, (sig, color) in enumerate(zip(X.T, colors), 1):
    plt.plot(sig, color=color)
```

10. Plot the ICA-separated signals:

```
# Plotting ICA signals
plt.figure()
plt.title('ICA separated signals')
plt.subplots_adjust(left=0.1, bottom=0.05, right=0.94,
        top=0.94, wspace=0.25, hspace=0.45)
```

11. Plot the subplots with different colors:

```
for i, (sig, color) in enumerate(zip(signals_ica.T, colors), 1):
    plt.subplot(4, 1, i)
```

```
        plt.title('Signal ' + str(i))
        plt.plot(sig, color=color)
```

12. Plot the PCA-separated signals:

```
# Plotting PCA signals
plt.figure()
plt.title('PCA separated signals')
plt.subplots_adjust(left=0.1, bottom=0.05, right=0.94,
        top=0.94, wspace=0.25, hspace=0.45)
```

13. Use a different color in each subplot:

```
for i, (sig, color) in enumerate(zip(signals_pca.T, colors), 1):
    plt.subplot(4, 1, i)
    plt.title('Signal ' + str(i))
    plt.plot(sig, color=color)

plt.show()
```

14. The full code is given in the `blind_source_separation.py` file that's already provided to you for reference. If you run this code, you will see three figures. The first figure depicts the input, which is a mixture of signals:

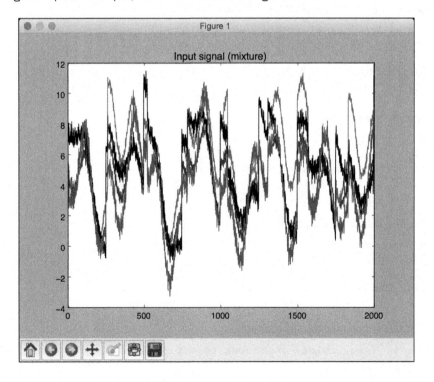

The second figure depicts the signals, separated using ICA:

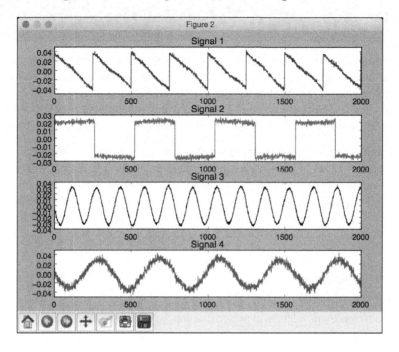

The third figure depicts the signals, separated using PCA:

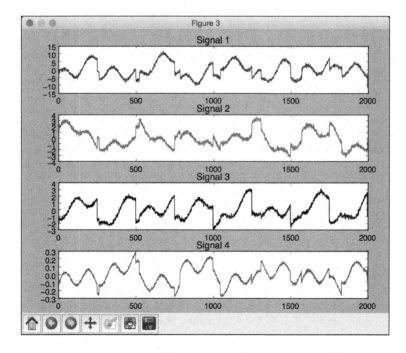

Building a face recognizer using Local Binary Patterns Histogram

We are now ready to build a face recognizer. We need a face dataset for training, so we've provided you a folder called `faces_dataset` that contains a small number of images sufficient for training. This dataset is a subset of the dataset that is available at `http://www.vision.caltech.edu/Image_Datasets/faces/faces.tar`. This dataset contains a good number of images that we can use to train a face-recognition system.

We will use **Local Binary Patterns Histograms** to build our face-recognition system. In our dataset, you will see different people. Our job is to build a system that can learn to separate these people from one another. When we see an unknown image, this system will assign it to one of the existing classes. You can learn more about Local Binary Patterns Histogram at `http://docs.opencv.org/2.4/modules/contrib/doc/facerec/facerec_tutorial.html#local-binary-patterns-histograms`. Let's see how to build a face recognizer.

How to do it...

1. Create a new Python file, and import the following packages:

    ```python
    import os

    import cv2
    import numpy as np
    from sklearn import preprocessing
    ```

2. Let's define a class to handle all the tasks that are related to label encoding for the classes:

    ```python
    # Class to handle tasks related to label encoding
    class LabelEncoder(object):
    ```

3. Define a method to encode the labels. In the input training data, labels are represented by words. However, we need numbers to train our system. This method will define a preprocessor object that can convert words to numbers in an organized fashion by maintaining the forward and backward mapping:

    ```python
    # Method to encode labels from words to numbers
    def encode_labels(self, label_words):
        self.le = preprocessing.LabelEncoder()
        self.le.fit(label_words)
    ```

4. Define a method to convert a word to a number:

    ```python
    # Convert input label from word to number
    def word_to_num(self, label_word):
        return int(self.le.transform([label_word])[0])
    ```

5. Define a method to convert the number back to the original word:

```
# Convert input label from number to word
def num_to_word(self, label_num):
    return self.le.inverse_transform([label_num])[0]
```

6. Define a method to extract images and labels from the input folder:

```
# Extract images and labels from input path
def get_images_and_labels(input_path):
    label_words = []
```

7. Recursively iterate through the input folder and extract all the image paths:

```
# Iterate through the input path and append files
for root, dirs, files in os.walk(input_path):
    for filename in (x for x in files if x.endswith('.jpg')):
        filepath = os.path.join(root, filename)
        label_words.append(filepath.split('/')[-2])
```

8. Initialize variables:

```
# Initialize variables
images = []
le = LabelEncoder()
le.encode_labels(label_words)
labels = []
```

9. Parse the input directory for training:

```
# Parse the input directory
for root, dirs, files in os.walk(input_path):
    for filename in (x for x in files if x.endswith('.jpg')):
        filepath = os.path.join(root, filename)
```

10. Read the current image in grayscale format:

```
# Read the image in grayscale format
image = cv2.imread(filepath, 0)
```

11. Extract the label from the folder path:

```
# Extract the label
name = filepath.split('/')[-2]
```

12. Perform face detection on this image:

```
# Perform face detection
faces = faceCascade.detectMultiScale(image, 1.1, 2,
minSize=(100,100))
```

13. Extract the ROIs and return them along with the label encoder:

```
# Iterate through face rectangles
for (x, y, w, h) in faces:
    images.append(image[y:y+h, x:x+w])
    labels.append(le.word_to_num(name))


return images, labels, le
```

14. Define the `main` function and define the path to the face cascade file:

```
if __name__=='__main__':
    cascade_path = "cascade_files/haarcascade_frontalface_alt.xml"
    path_train = 'faces_dataset/train'
    path_test = 'faces_dataset/test'
```

15. Load the face cascade file:

```
# Load face cascade file
faceCascade = cv2.CascadeClassifier(cascade_path)
```

16. Create Local Binary Patterns Histogram face recognizer objects:

```
# Initialize Local Binary Patterns Histogram face recognizer
recognizer = cv2.face.createLBPHFaceRecognizer()
```

17. Extract the images, labels, and label encoder for this input path:

```
# Extract images, labels, and label encoder from training
dataset
images, labels, le = get_images_and_labels(path_train)
```

18. Train the face recognizer using the data that we extracted:

```
# Train the face recognizer
print "\nTraining..."
recognizer.train(images, np.array(labels))
```

19. Test the face recognizer on unknown data:

```
# Test the recognizer on unknown images
print '\nPerforming prediction on test images...'
stop_flag = False
for root, dirs, files in os.walk(path_test):
    for filename in (x for x in files if x.endswith('.jpg')):
        filepath = os.path.join(root, filename)
```

20. Load the image:

```
# Read the image
predict_image = cv2.imread(filepath, 0)
```

21. Determine the location of the face using the face detector:

```
# Detect faces
faces = faceCascade.detectMultiScale(predict_image,
1.1,
            2, minSize=(100,100))
```

22. For each face ROI, run the face recognizer:

```
# Iterate through face rectangles
for (x, y, w, h) in faces:
    # Predict the output
    predicted_index, conf = recognizer.predict(
            predict_image[y:y+h, x:x+w])
```

23. Convert the label to word:

```
# Convert to word label
predicted_person = le.num_to_word(predicted_index)
```

24. Overlay the text on the output image and display it:

```
# Overlay text on the output image and display it
cv2.putText(predict_image, 'Prediction: ' +
predicted_person,
            (10,60), cv2.FONT_HERSHEY_SIMPLEX, 2,
(255,255,255), 6)
cv2.imshow("Recognizing face", predict_image)
```

25. Check whether the user pressed the *Esc* key. If so, break out of the loop:

```
c = cv2.waitKey(0)
if c == 27:
    stop_flag = True
    break

if stop_flag:
    break
```

26. The full code is in the `face_recognizer.py` file that's already provided to you for reference. If you run this code, you will get an output window, which displays the predicted outputs for test images. You can press the *Space* button to keep looping. There are three different people in the test images. The output for the first person looks like the following:

The output for the second person looks like the following:

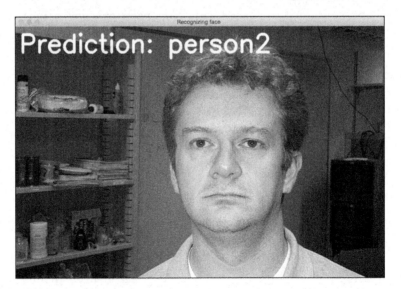

The output for the third person looks like the following:

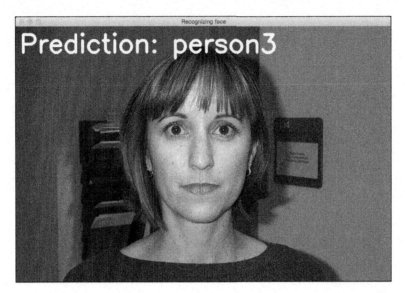

11
Deep Neural Networks

In this chapter, we will cover the following recipes:

- ▸ Building a perceptron
- ▸ Building a single layer neural network
- ▸ Building a deep neural network
- ▸ Creating a vector quantizer
- ▸ Building a recurrent neural network for sequential data analysis
- ▸ Visualizing the characters in an optical character recognition database
- ▸ Building an optical character recognizer using neural networks

Introduction

Our brain is really good at identifying and recognizing things. We want the machines to be able to do the same. A neural network is a framework that is modeled after the human brain to simulate our learning processes. Neural networks are designed to learn from data and recognize the underlying patterns. As with all learning algorithms, neural networks deal with numbers. Therefore, if we want to achieve any real world task involving images, text, sensors, and so on, we have to convert them into the numerical form before we feed them into a neural network. We can use a neural network for classification, clustering, generation, and many other related tasks.

A neural network consists of layers of **neurons**. These neurons are modeled after the biological neurons in the human brain. Each layer is basically a set of independent neurons that are connected to the neurons the adjacent layers. The input layer corresponds to the input data that we provide, and the output layer consists of the output that we desire. All the layers in between are called **hidden layers**. If we design a neural network with more hidden layers, then we give it more freedom to train itself with higher accuracy.

Let's say that we want the neural network to classify data, based on our needs. In order for a neural network to work accordingly, we need to provide labeled training data. The neural network will then train itself by optimizing the cost function. This cost function is the error between actual labels and the predicted labels from the neural network. We keep iterating until the error goes below a certain threshold.

What exactly are *deep* neural networks? Deep neural networks are neural networks that consist of many hidden layers. In general, this falls under the realm of deep learning. This is a field that is dedicated to the study of these neural networks, which are composed of multiple layers that are used across many verticals.

You can check out a tutorial on neural networks to learn more at `http://pages.cs.wisc.edu/~bolo/shipyard/neural/local.html`. We will use a library called **NeuroLab** throughout this chapter. Before you proceed, make sure that you install it. You can find the installation instructions at `https://pythonhosted.org/neurolab/install.html`. Let's go ahead and look at how to design and develop these neural networks.

Building a perceptron

Let's start our neural network adventure with a perceptron. A **perceptron** is a single neuron that performs all the computation. It is a very simple model, but it forms the basis of building up complex neural networks. Here is what it looks like:

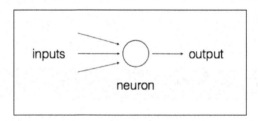

The neuron combines the inputs using different weights, and it then adds a bias value to compute the output. It's a simple linear equation relating input values with the output of the perceptron.

How to do it...

1. Create a new Python file, and import the following packages:

```
import numpy as np
import neurolab as nl
import matplotlib.pyplot as plt
```

2. Define some input data and their corresponding labels:

```
# Define input data
data = np.array([[0.3, 0.2], [0.1, 0.4], [0.4, 0.6], [0.9, 0.5]])
labels = np.array([[0], [0], [0], [1]])
```

3. Let's plot this data to see where the datapoints are located:

```
# Plot input data
plt.figure()
plt.scatter(data[:,0], data[:,1])
plt.xlabel('X-axis')
plt.ylabel('Y-axis')
plt.title('Input data')
```

4. Let's define a `perceptron` with two inputs. This function also needs us to specify the minimum and maximum values in the input data:

```
# Define a perceptron with 2 inputs;
# Each element of the list in the first argument
# specifies the min and max values of the inputs
perceptron = nl.net.newp([[0, 1],[0, 1]], 1)
```

5. Let's train the perceptron. The number of epochs specifies the number of complete passes through our training dataset. The `show` parameter specifies how frequently we want to display the progress. The `lr` parameter specifies the learning rate of the perceptron. It is the step size for the algorithm to search through the parameter space. If this is large, then the algorithm may move faster, but it might miss the optimum value. If this is small, then the algorithm will hit the optimum value, but it will be slow. So it's a trade-off; hence, we choose a value of `0.01`:

```
# Train the perceptron
error = perceptron.train(data, labels, epochs=50, show=15,
lr=0.01)
```

6. Let's plot the results, as follows:

```
# plot results
plt.figure()
plt.plot(error)
plt.xlabel('Number of epochs')
plt.ylabel('Training error')
plt.grid()
plt.title('Training error progress')

plt.show()
```

7. The full code is given in the `perceptron.py` file that's already provided to you. If you run this code, you will see two figures. The first figure displays the input data:

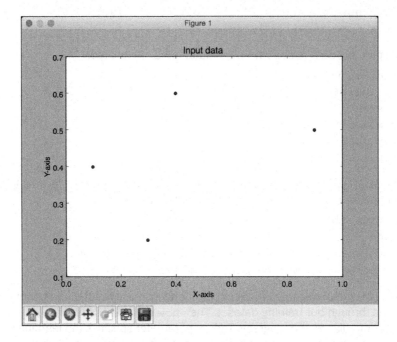

The second figure displays the training error progress:

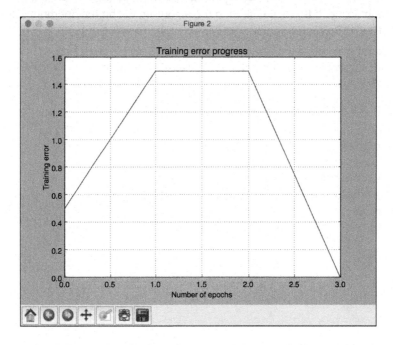

Building a single layer neural network

Now that we know how to create a perceptron, let's create a single layer neural network. A single layer neural network consists of multiple neurons in a single layer. Overall, we will have an input layer, a hidden layer, and an output layer.

How to do it...

1. Create a new Python file, and import the following packages:

```
import numpy as np
import matplotlib.pyplot as plt
import neurolab as nl
```

2. We will use the data in the `data_single_layer.txt` file. Let's load this:

```
# Define input data
input_file = 'data_single_layer.txt'
input_text = np.loadtxt(input_file)
data = input_text[:, 0:2]
labels = input_text[:, 2:]
```

3. Let's plot the input data:

```
# Plot input data
plt.figure()
plt.scatter(data[:,0], data[:,1])
plt.xlabel('X-axis')
plt.ylabel('Y-axis')
plt.title('Input data')
```

4. Let's extract the minimum and maximum values:

```
# Min and max values for each dimension
x_min, x_max = data[:,0].min(), data[:,0].max()
y_min, y_max = data[:,1].min(), data[:,1].max()
```

5. Let's define a single layer neural network with two neurons in the hidden layer:

```
# Define a single-layer neural network with 2 neurons;
# Each element in the list (first argument) specifies the
# min and max values of the inputs
single_layer_net = nl.net.newp([[x_min, x_max], [y_min, y_max]],
2)
```

6. Train the neural network until 50 epochs:

```
# Train the neural network
error = single_layer_net.train(data, labels, epochs=50, show=20,
lr=0.01)
```

7. Plot the results, as follows:

```
# Plot results
plt.figure()
plt.plot(error)
plt.xlabel('Number of epochs')
plt.ylabel('Training error')
plt.title('Training error progress')
plt.grid()

plt.show()
```

8. Let's test the neural network on new test data:

```
print single_layer_net.sim([[0.3, 4.5]])
print single_layer_net.sim([[4.5, 0.5]])
print single_layer_net.sim([[4.3, 8]])
```

9. The full code is in the `single_layer.py` file that's already provided to you. If you run this code, you will see two figures. The first figure displays the input data:

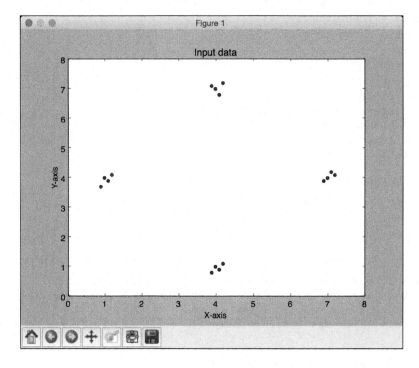

The second figure displays the training error progress:

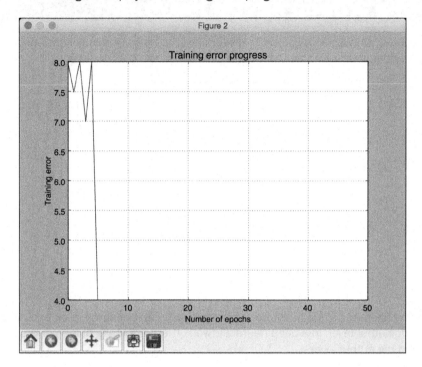

You will see the following printed on your Terminal, indicating where the input test points belong:

```
[[ 0.  0.]]
[[ 1.  0.]]
[[ 1.  1.]]
```

You can verify that the outputs are correct based on our labels.

Building a deep neural network

We are now ready to build a deep neural network. A deep neural network consists of an input layer, many hidden layers, and an output layer. This looks like the following:

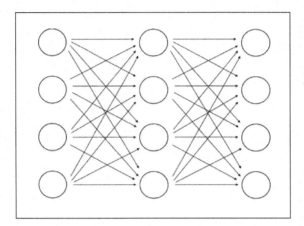

The preceding figure depicts a multilayer neural network with one input layer, one hidden layer, and one output layer. In a deep neural network, there are many hidden layers between the input and the output layers.

How to do it...

1. Create a new Python file, and import the following packages:

```
import neurolab as nl
import numpy as np
import matplotlib.pyplot as plt
```

2. Let's define parameters to generate some training data:

```
# Generate training data
min_value = -12
max_value = 12
num_datapoints = 90
```

3. This training data will consist of a function that we define that will transform the values. We expect the neural network to learn this on its own, based on the input and output values that we provide:

```
x = np.linspace(min_value, max_value, num_datapoints)
y = 2 * np.square(x) + 7
y /= np.linalg.norm(y)
```

4. Reshape the arrays:

```
data = x.reshape(num_datapoints, 1)
labels = y.reshape(num_datapoints, 1)
```

5. Plot input data:

```
# Plot input data
plt.figure()
plt.scatter(data, labels)
plt.xlabel('X-axis')
plt.ylabel('Y-axis')
plt.title('Input data')
```

6. Define a deep neural network with two hidden layers, where each hidden layer consists of 10 neurons:

```
# Define a multilayer neural network with 2 hidden layers;
# Each hidden layer consists of 10 neurons and the output layer
# consists of 1 neuron
multilayer_net = nl.net.newff([[min_value, max_value]], [10, 10,
1])
```

7. Set the training algorithm to **gradient descent** (you can learn more about it at `https://spin.atomicobject.com/2014/06/24/gradient-descent-linear-regression`):

```
# Change the training algorithm to gradient descent
multilayer_net.trainf = nl.train.train_gd
```

8. Train the network:

```
# Train the network
error = multilayer_net.train(data, labels, epochs=800, show=100,
goal=0.01)
```

9. Run the network on training data to see the performance:

```
# Predict the output for the training inputs
predicted_output = multilayer_net.sim(data)
```

10. Plot the training error:

```
# Plot training error
plt.figure()
plt.plot(error)
plt.xlabel('Number of epochs')
plt.ylabel('Error')
plt.title('Training error progress')
```

11. Let's create a set of new inputs and run the neural network on them to see how it performs:

```
# Plot predictions
x2 = np.linspace(min_value, max_value, num_datapoints * 2)
y2 = multilayer_net.sim(x2.reshape(x2.size,1)).reshape(x2.size)
y3 = predicted_output.reshape(num_datapoints)
```

12. Plot the outputs:

```
plt.figure()
plt.plot(x2, y2, '-', x, y, '.', x, y3, 'p')
plt.title('Ground truth vs predicted output')

plt.show()
```

13. The full code is in the `deep_neural_network.py` file that's already provided to you. If you run this code, you will see three figures. The first figure displays the input data:

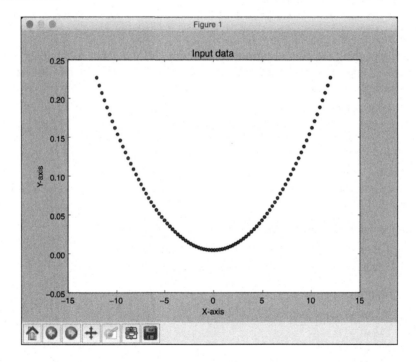

The second figure displays the training error progress:

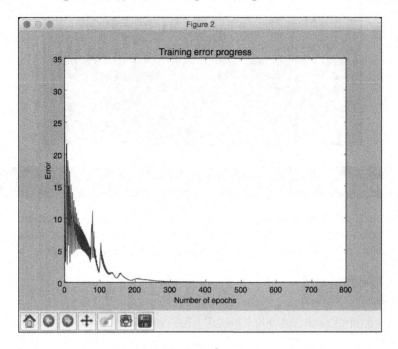

The third figure displays the output of the neural network:

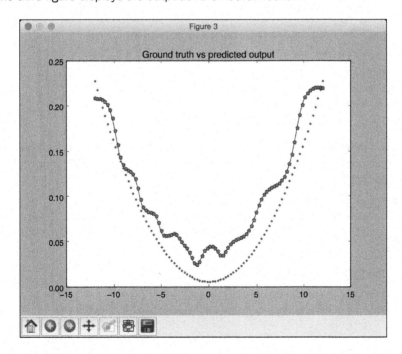

You will see the following on your Terminal:

```
Epoch: 100; Error: 1.64795788647;
Epoch: 200; Error: 0.517736068801;
Epoch: 300; Error: 0.13545620002;
Epoch: 400; Error: 0.0521272422892;
Epoch: 500; Error: 0.0465021594702;
Epoch: 600; Error: 0.0483261849312;
Epoch: 700; Error: 0.0431681554217;
Epoch: 800; Error: 0.0346446191022;
The maximum number of train epochs is reached
```

Creating a vector quantizer

You can use neural networks for vector quantization as well. **Vector quantization** is the *N*-dimensional version of "rounding off". This is very commonly used across multiple areas in computer vision, natural language processing, and machine learning in general.

How to do it...

1. Create a new Python file, and import the following packages:

    ```
    import numpy as np
    import matplotlib.pyplot as plt
    import neurolab as nl
    ```

2. Let's load the input data from the `data_vq.txt` file:

    ```
    # Define input data
    input_file = 'data_vq.txt'
    input_text = np.loadtxt(input_file)
    data = input_text[:, 0:2]
    labels = input_text[:, 2:]
    ```

3. Define a **learning vector quantization** (**LVQ**) neural network with two layers. The array in the last parameter specifies the percentage weightage to each output (they should sum up to 1):

    ```
    # Define a neural network with 2 layers:
    # 10 neurons in input layer and 4 neurons in output layer
    net = nl.net.newlvq(nl.tool.minmax(data), 10, [0.25, 0.25, 0.25,
    0.25])
    ```

4. Train the LVQ neural network:

    ```
    # Train the neural network
    error = net.train(data, labels, epochs=100, goal=-1)
    ```

5. Create a grid of values for testing and visualization:

```
# Create the input grid
xx, yy = np.meshgrid(np.arange(0, 8, 0.2), np.arange(0, 8, 0.2))
xx.shape = xx.size, 1
yy.shape = yy.size, 1
input_grid = np.concatenate((xx, yy), axis=1)
```

6. Evaluate the network on this grid:

```
# Evaluate the input grid of points
output_grid = net.sim(input_grid)
```

7. Define the four classes in our data:

```
# Define the 4 classes
class1 = data[labels[:,0] == 1]
class2 = data[labels[:,1] == 1]
class3 = data[labels[:,2] == 1]
class4 = data[labels[:,3] == 1]
```

8. Define the grids for all these classes:

```
# Define grids for all the 4 classes
grid1 = input_grid[output_grid[:,0] == 1]
grid2 = input_grid[output_grid[:,1] == 1]
grid3 = input_grid[output_grid[:,2] == 1]
grid4 = input_grid[output_grid[:,3] == 1]
```

9. Plot the outputs:

```
# Plot outputs
plt.plot(class1[:,0], class1[:,1], 'ko', class2[:,0], class2[:,1],
'ko',
                class3[:,0], class3[:,1], 'ko', class4[:,0],
class4[:,1], 'ko')
plt.plot(grid1[:,0], grid1[:,1], 'b.', grid2[:,0], grid2[:,1],
'gx',
                grid3[:,0], grid3[:,1], 'cs', grid4[:,0],
grid4[:,1], 'ro')
plt.axis([0, 8, 0, 8])
plt.xlabel('X-axis')
plt.ylabel('Y-axis')
plt.title('Vector quantization using neural networks')

plt.show()
```

10. The full code is in the `vector_quantization.py` file that's already provided to you. If you run this code, you will see the following figure where the space is divided into regions. Each region corresponds to a bucket in the list of vector-quantized regions in the space:

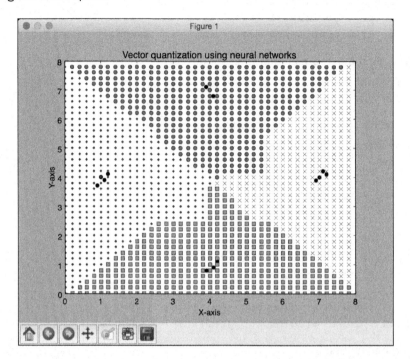

Building a recurrent neural network for sequential data analysis

Recurrent neural networks are really good at analyzing sequential and time-series data. You can learn more about them at `http://www.wildml.com/2015/09/recurrent-neural-networks-tutorial-part-1-introduction-to-rnns`. When we deal with sequential and time-series data, we cannot just extend generic models. The temporal dependencies in the data are really important, and we need to account for this in our models. Let's look at how to build them.

How to do it...

1. Create a new Python file, and import the following packages:

```
import numpy as np
import matplotlib.pyplot as plt
import neurolab as nl
```

2. Define a function to create a waveform, based on input parameters:

```
def create_waveform(num_points):
    # Create train samples
    data1 = 1 * np.cos(np.arange(0, num_points))
    data2 = 2 * np.cos(np.arange(0, num_points))
    data3 = 3 * np.cos(np.arange(0, num_points))
    data4 = 4 * np.cos(np.arange(0, num_points))
```

3. Create different amplitudes for each interval to create a random waveform:

```
    # Create varying amplitudes
    amp1 = np.ones(num_points)
    amp2 = 4 + np.zeros(num_points)
    amp3 = 2 * np.ones(num_points)
    amp4 = 0.5 + np.zeros(num_points)
```

4. Combine the arrays to create the output arrays. This data corresponds to the input and the amplitude corresponds to the labels:

```
    data = np.array([data1, data2, data3, data4]).reshape(num_
points * 4, 1)
    amplitude = np.array([[amp1, amp2, amp3, amp4]]).reshape(num_
points * 4, 1)

    return data, amplitude
```

5. Define a function to draw the output after passing the data through the trained neural network:

```
# Draw the output using the network
def draw_output(net, num_points_test):
    data_test, amplitude_test = create_waveform(num_points_test)
    output_test = net.sim(data_test)
    plt.plot(amplitude_test.reshape(num_points_test * 4))
    plt.plot(output_test.reshape(num_points_test * 4))
```

6. Define the `main` function and start by creating sample data:

```
if __name__=='__main__':
    # Get data
    num_points = 30
    data, amplitude = create_waveform(num_points)
```

7. Create a recurrent neural network with two layers:

```
    # Create network with 2 layers
    net = nl.net.newelm([[-2, 2]], [10, 1], [nl.trans.TanSig(),
nl.trans.PureLin()])
```

8. Set the initialized functions for each layer:

```
# Set initialized functions and init
net.layers[0].initf = nl.init.InitRand([-0.1, 0.1], 'wb')
net.layers[1].initf= nl.init.InitRand([-0.1, 0.1], 'wb')
net.init()
```

9. Train the recurrent neural network:

```
# Training the recurrent neural network
error = net.train(data, amplitude, epochs=1000, show=100,
goal=0.01)
```

10. Compute the output from the network for the training data:

```
# Compute output from network
output = net.sim(data)
```

11. Plot training error:

```
# Plot training results
plt.subplot(211)
plt.plot(error)
plt.xlabel('Number of epochs')
plt.ylabel('Error (MSE)')
```

12. Plot the results:

```
plt.subplot(212)
plt.plot(amplitude.reshape(num_points * 4))
plt.plot(output.reshape(num_points * 4))
plt.legend(['Ground truth', 'Predicted output'])
```

13. Create a waveform of random length and see whether the network can predict it:

```
# Testing on unknown data at multiple scales
plt.figure()

plt.subplot(211)
draw_output(net, 74)
plt.xlim([0, 300])
```

14. Create another waveform of a shorter length and see whether the network can predict it:

```
plt.subplot(212)
draw_output(net, 54)
plt.xlim([0, 300])

plt.show()
```

15. The full code is in the `recurrent_network.py` file that's already provided to you. If you run this code, you will see two figures. The first figure displays training errors and the performance on the training data:

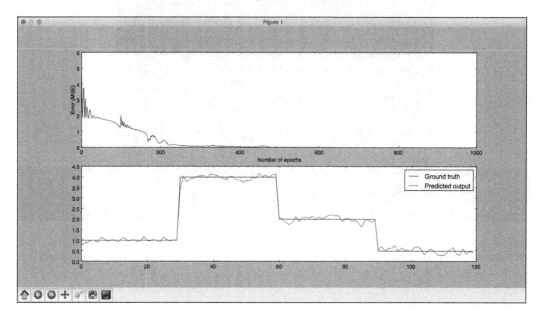

The second figure displays how a trained recurrent neural net performs on sequences of arbitrary lengths:

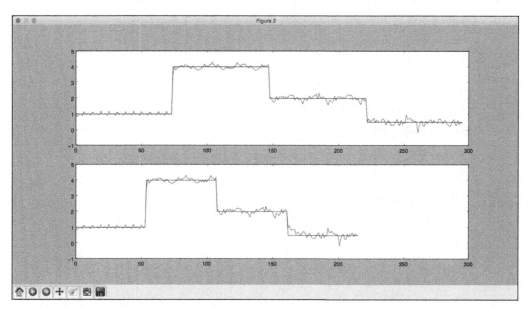

You will see the following on your Terminal:

```
Epoch: 100; Error: 2.0202165367;
Epoch: 200; Error: 0.276370891;
Epoch: 300; Error: 0.0902055024828;
Epoch: 400; Error: 0.0662254210369;
Epoch: 500; Error: 0.0291456739963;
Epoch: 600; Error: 0.0274479103273;
Epoch: 700; Error: 0.0221256973779;
Epoch: 800; Error: 0.0227723305931;
Epoch: 900; Error: 0.0207200477057;
Epoch: 1000; Error: 0.0159299080472;
The maximum number of train epochs is reached
```

Visualizing the characters in an optical character recognition database

We will now look at how to use neural networks to perform optical character recognition. This refers to the process of identifying handwritten characters in images. We will use the dataset available at `http://ai.stanford.edu/~btaskar/ocr`. The default file name after downloading is `letter.data`. To start with, let's see how to interact with the data and visualize it.

How to do it...

1. Create a new Python file, and import the following packages:

```python
import os
import sys

import cv2
import numpy as np
```

2. Define the input file name:

```python
# Load input data
input_file = 'letter.data'
```

3. Define visualization parameters:

```python
# Define visualization parameters
scaling_factor = 10
start_index = 6
end_index = -1
h, w = 16, 8
```

4. Keep looping through the file until the user presses the *Esc* key. Split the line into tab-separated characters:

```
# Loop until you encounter the Esc key
with open(input_file, 'r') as f:
    for line in f.readlines():
        data = np.array([255*float(x) for x in line.split('\t')
[start_index:end_index]])
```

5. Reshape the array into the required shape, resize it, and display it:

```
        img = np.reshape(data, (h,w))
        img_scaled = cv2.resize(img, None, fx=scaling_factor,
fy=scaling_factor)
        cv2.imshow('Image', img_scaled)
```

6. If the user presses *Esc*, break the loop:

```
        c = cv2.waitKey()
        if c == 27:
            break
```

7. The full code is in the `visualize_characters.py` file that's already provided to you. If you run this code, you will see a window displaying characters. For example, *o* looks like the following:

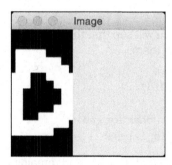

The character *i* looks like the following:

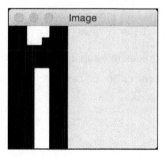

Building an optical character recognizer using neural networks

Now that we know how to interact with the data, let's build a neural network-based optical character-recognition system.

How to do it...

1. Create a new Python file, and import the following packages:

```
import numpy as np
import neurolab as nl
```

2. Define the input filename:

```
# Input file
input_file = 'letter.data'
```

3. When we work with neural networks that deal with large amounts of data, it takes a lot of time to train. To demonstrate how to build this system, we will take only 20 datapoints:

```
# Number of datapoints to load from the input file
num_datapoints = 20
```

4. If you look at the data, you will see that there are seven distinct characters in the first 20 lines. Let's define them:

```
# Distinct characters
orig_labels = 'omandig'

# Number of distinct characters
num_output = len(orig_labels)
```

5. We will use 90% of the data for training and remaining 10% for testing. Define the training and testing parameters:

```
# Training and testing parameters
num_train = int(0.9 * num_datapoints)
num_test = num_datapoints - num_train
```

6. The starting and ending indices in each line of the dataset file:

```
# Define dataset extraction parameters
start_index = 6
end_index = -1
```

7. Create the dataset:

```
# Creating the dataset
data = []
labels = []
with open(input_file, 'r') as f:
    for line in f.readlines():
        # Split the line tabwise
        list_vals = line.split('\t')
```

8. Add an error check to see whether the characters are in our list of labels:

```
# If the label is not in our ground truth labels, skip it
if list_vals[1] not in orig_labels:
    continue
```

9. Extract the label, and append it the main list:

```
# Extract the label and append it to the main list
label = np.zeros((num_output, 1))
label[orig_labels.index(list_vals[1])] = 1
labels.append(label)
```

10. Extract the character, and append it to the main list:

```
# Extract the character vector and append it to the main
list
cur_char = np.array([float(x) for x in list_vals[start_
index:end_index]])
data.append(cur_char)
```

11. Exit the loop once we have enough data:

```
# Exit the loop once the required dataset has been loaded
if len(data) >= num_datapoints:
    break
```

12. Convert this data into NumPy arrays:

```
# Convert data and labels to numpy arrays
data = np.asfarray(data)
labels = np.array(labels).reshape(num_datapoints, num_output)
```

13. Extract the number of dimensions in our data:

```
# Extract number of dimensions
num_dims = len(data[0])
```

14. Train the neural network until `10,000` epochs:

```
# Create and train neural network
net = nl.net.newff([[0, 1] for _ in range(len(data[0]))], [128,
16, num_output])
net.trainf = nl.train.train_gd
error = net.train(data[:num_train,:], labels[:num_train,:],
epochs=10000,
        show=100, goal=0.01)
```

15. Predict the output for test inputs:

```
# Predict the output for test inputs
predicted_output = net.sim(data[num_train:, :])
print "\nTesting on unknown data:"
for i in range(num_test):
    print "\nOriginal:", orig_labels[np.argmax(labels[i])]
    print "Predicted:", orig_labels[np.argmax(predicted_
output[i])]
```

16. The full code is in the `ocr.py` file that's already provided to you. If you run this code, you will see the following on your Terminal at the end of training:

```
Epoch: 8900; Error: 0.167967242056;
Epoch: 9000; Error: 0.141695146517;
Epoch: 9100; Error: 0.123315386106;
Epoch: 9200; Error: 0.123516370118;
Epoch: 9300; Error: 0.153659730139;
Epoch: 9400; Error: 0.106912207871;
Epoch: 9500; Error: 0.0833274962321;
Epoch: 9600; Error: 0.204787347758;
Epoch: 9700; Error: 0.208864612943;
Epoch: 9800; Error: 0.177338615833;
Epoch: 9900; Error: 0.152109654098;
Epoch: 10000; Error: 0.130557716464;
The maximum number of train epochs is reached
```

The output of the neural network is shown in the following screenshot:

```
Testing on unknown data:

Original: o
Predicted: o

Original: m
Predicted: m
```

12
Visualizing Data

In this chapter, we will cover the following recipes:

- ▸ Plotting 3D scatter plots
- ▸ Plotting bubble plots
- ▸ Animating bubble plots
- ▸ Drawing pie charts
- ▸ Plotting date-formatted time series data
- ▸ Plotting histograms
- ▸ Visualizing heat maps
- ▸ Animating dynamic signals

Introduction

Data visualization is an important pillar of machine learning. It helps us formulate the right strategies to understand data. Visual representation of data assists us in choosing the right algorithms. One of the main goals of data visualization is to communicate clearly using graphs and charts. These graphs help us communicate information clearly and efficiently.

We encounter numerical data all the time in the real world. We want to encode this numerical data using graphs, lines, dots, bars, and so on to visually display the information contained in those numbers. This makes complex distributions of data more understandable and usable. This process is used in a variety of situations, including comparative analysis, tracking growth, market distribution, public opinion polls, and many others.

We use different charts to show patterns or relationships between variables. We use histograms to display the distribution of data. We use tables when we want to look up a specific measurement. In this chapter, we will look at various scenarios and discuss what visualizations we can use in these situations.

Plotting 3D scatter plots

In this recipe, we will learn how to plot 3D scatterplots and visualize them in three dimensions.

How to do it...

1. Create a new Python file, and import the following packages:

```
import numpy as np
import matplotlib.pyplot as plt
from mpl_toolkits.mplot3d import Axes3D
```

2. Create the empty figure:

```
# Create the figure
fig = plt.figure()
ax = fig.add_subplot(111, projection='3d')
```

3. Define the number of values that we should generate:

```
# Define the number of values
n = 250
```

4. Create a `lambda` function to generate values in a given range:

```
# Create a lambda function to generate the random values in the
given range
f = lambda minval, maxval, n: minval + (maxval - minval) *
np.random.rand(n)
```

5. Generate X, Y, and Z values using this function:

```
# Generate the values
x_vals = f(15, 41, n)
y_vals = f(-10, 70, n)
z_vals = f(-52, -37, n)
```

6. Plot these values:

```
# Plot the values
ax.scatter(x_vals, y_vals, z_vals, c='k', marker='o')
ax.set_xlabel('X axis')
ax.set_ylabel('Y axis')
ax.set_zlabel('Z axis')

plt.show()
```

7. The full code is in the `scatter_3d.py` file that's already provided to you. If you run this code, you will see the following figure:

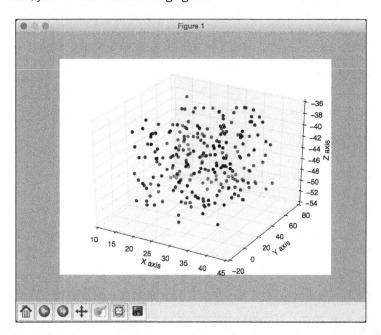

Plotting bubble plots

Let's see how to plot bubble plots. The size of each circle in a 2D bubble plot represents the amplitude of that particular point.

How to do it...

1. Create a new Python file, and import the following packages:

```
import numpy as np
import matplotlib.pyplot as plt
```

2. Define the number of values that we should generate:

```
# Define the number of values
num_vals = 40
```

3. Generate random values for x and y:

```
# Generate random values
x = np.random.rand(num_vals)
y = np.random.rand(num_vals)
```

4. Define the area value for each point in the bubble plot:

```
# Define area for each bubble
# Max radius is set to a specified value
max_radius = 25
area = np.pi * (max_radius * np.random.rand(num_vals)) ** 2
```

5. Define the colors:

```
# Generate colors
colors = np.random.rand(num_vals)
```

6. Plot these values:

```
# Plot the points
plt.scatter(x, y, s=area, c=colors, alpha=1.0)

plt.show()
```

7. The full code is in the `bubble_plot.py` file that's already provided to you. If you run this code, you will see the following figure:

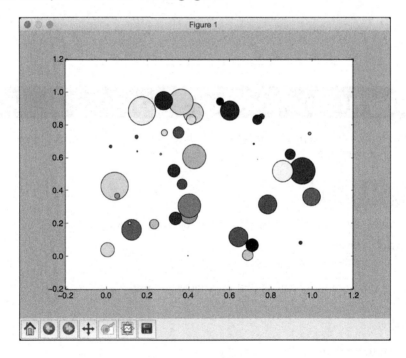

Animating bubble plots

Let's look at how to animate a bubble plot. This is useful when you want to visualize data that's transient and dynamic.

How to do it...

1. Create a new Python file, and import the following packages:

```
import numpy as np
import matplotlib.pyplot as plt
from matplotlib.animation import FuncAnimation
```

2. Let's define a `tracker` function that will dynamically update the bubble plot:

```
def tracker(cur_num):
    # Get the current index
    cur_index = cur_num % num_points
```

3. Define the color:

```
    # Set the color of the datapoints
    datapoints['color'][:, 3] = 1.0
```

4. Update the size of the circles:

```
    # Update the size of the circles
    datapoints['size'] += datapoints['growth']
```

5. Update the position of the oldest datapoint in the set:

```
    # Update the position of the oldest datapoint
    datapoints['position'][cur_index] = np.random.uniform(0, 1, 2)
    datapoints['size'][cur_index] = 7
    datapoints['color'][cur_index] = (0, 0, 0, 1)
    datapoints['growth'][cur_index] = np.random.uniform(40, 150)
```

6. Update the parameters of the scatterplot:

```
    # Update the parameters of the scatter plot
    scatter_plot.set_edgecolors(datapoints['color'])
    scatter_plot.set_sizes(datapoints['size'])
    scatter_plot.set_offsets(datapoints['position'])
```

7. Define the `main` function and create an empty figure:

```
if __name__=='__main__':
    # Create a figure
    fig = plt.figure(figsize=(9, 7), facecolor=(0,0.9,0.9))
    ax = fig.add_axes([0, 0, 1, 1], frameon=False)
    ax.set_xlim(0, 1), ax.set_xticks([])
    ax.set_ylim(0, 1), ax.set_yticks([])
```

8. Define the number of points that will be on the plot at any given point of time:

```
# Create and initialize the datapoints in random positions
# and with random growth rates.
num_points = 20
```

9. Define the datapoints using random values:

```
datapoints = np.zeros(num_points, dtype=[('position', float,
2),
            ('size', float, 1), ('growth', float, 1), ('color',
float, 4)])
    datapoints['position'] = np.random.uniform(0, 1, (num_points,
2))
    datapoints['growth'] = np.random.uniform(40, 150, num_points)
```

10. Create the scatterplot that will be updated every frame:

```
# Construct the scatter plot that will be updated every frame
scatter_plot = ax.scatter(datapoints['position'][:, 0],
datapoints['position'][:, 1],
                    s=datapoints['size'], lw=0.7,
edgecolors=datapoints['color'],
                    facecolors='none')
```

11. Start the animation using the `tracker` function:

```
# Start the animation using the 'tracker' function
animation = FuncAnimation(fig, tracker, interval=10)

plt.show()
```

12. The full code is in the `dynamic_bubble_plot.py` file that's already provided to you. If you run this code, you will see the following figure:

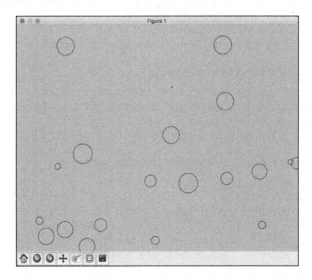

Drawing pie charts

Let's see how to plot pie charts. This is useful when you want to visualize the percentages of a set of labels in a group.

How to do it...

1. Create a new Python file, and import the following packages:

```
import numpy as np
import matplotlib.pyplot as plt
```

2. Define the labels and values:

```
# Labels and corresponding values in counter clockwise direction
data = {'Apple': 26,
        'Mango': 17,
        'Pineapple': 21,
        'Banana': 29,
        'Strawberry': 11}
```

3. Define the colors for visualization:

```
# List of corresponding colors
colors = ['orange', 'lightgreen', 'lightblue', 'gold', 'cyan']
```

4. Define a variable to highlight a section of the pie chart by separating it from the rest. If you don't want to highlight any section, set all the values to 0:

```
# Needed if we want to highlight a section
explode = (0, 0, 0, 0, 0)
```

5. Plot the pie chart. Note that if you use Python 3, you should use `list(data.values())` in the following function call:

```
# Plot the pie chart
plt.pie(data.values(), explode=explode, labels=data.keys(),
        colors=colors, autopct='%1.1f%%', shadow=False,
startangle=90)

# Aspect ratio of the pie chart, 'equal' indicates tht we
# want it to be a circle
plt.axis('equal')

plt.show()
```

6. The full code is in the `pie_chart.py` file that's already provided to you. If you run this code, you will see the following figure:

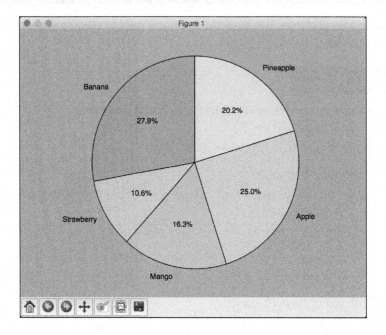

If you change the explode array to (0, 0.2, 0, 0, 0), then it will highlight the **Strawberry** section. You will see the following figure:

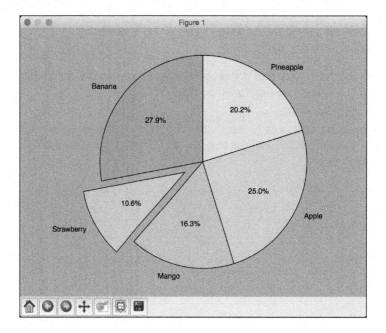

Plotting date-formatted time series data

Let's look at how to plot time series data using date formatting. This is useful in visualizing stock data over time.

How to do it...

1. Create a new Python file, and import the following packages:

```
import numpy
import matplotlib.pyplot as plt
from matplotlib.mlab import csv2rec
import matplotlib.cbook as cbook
from matplotlib.ticker import Formatter
```

2. Define a function to format the dates. The __init__ function sets the class variables:

```
# Define a class for formatting
class DataFormatter(Formatter):
    def __init__(self, dates, date_format='%Y-%m-%d'):
        self.dates = dates
        self.date_format = date_format
```

3. Extract the value at any given time and return it in the following format:

```
# Extact the value at time t at position 'position'
def __call__(self, t, position=0):
    index = int(round(t))
    if index >= len(self.dates) or index < 0:
        return ''

    return self.dates[index].strftime(self.date_format)
```

4. Define the main function. We'll use the Apple stock quotes CSV file that is available in matplotlib:

```
if __name__=='__main__':
    # CSV file containing the stock quotes
    input_file = cbook.get_sample_data('aapl.csv',
asfileobj=False)
```

5. Load the CSV file:

```
# Load csv file into numpy record array
data = csv2rec(input_file)
```

6. Extract a subset of these values to plot them:

```
# Take a subset for plotting
data = data[-70:]
```

7. Create the formatter object and initialize it with the dates:

```
# Create the date formatter object
formatter = DataFormatter(data.date)
```

8. Define the X and Y axes:

```
# X axis
x_vals = numpy.arange(len(data))

# Y axis values are the closing stock quotes
y_vals = data.close
```

9. Plot the data:

```
# Plot data
fig, ax = plt.subplots()
ax.xaxis.set_major_formatter(formatter)
ax.plot(x_vals, y_vals, 'o-')
fig.autofmt_xdate()
plt.show()
```

10. The full code is in the `time_series.py` file that's already provided to you. If you run this code, you will see the following figure:

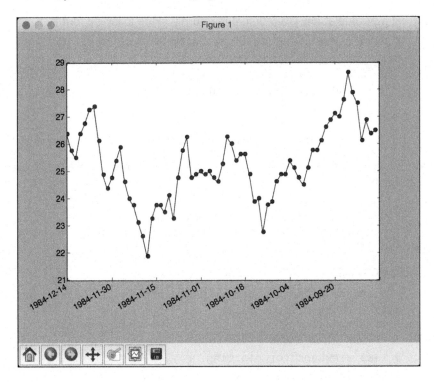

Plotting histograms

Let's see how to plot histograms in this recipe. We'll compare two sets of data and build a comparative histogram.

How to do it...

1. Create a new Python file, and import the following packages:

    ```
    import numpy as np
    import matplotlib.pyplot as plt
    ```

2. We'll compare the production quantity of apples and oranges in this recipe. Let's define some values:

    ```
    # Input data
    apples = [30, 25, 22, 36, 21, 29]
    oranges = [24, 33, 19, 27, 35, 20]

    # Number of groups
    num_groups = len(apples)
    ```

3. Create the figure and define its parameters:

    ```
    # Create the figure
    fig, ax = plt.subplots()

    # Define the X axis
    indices = np.arange(num_groups)

    # Width and opacity of histogram bars
    bar_width = 0.4
    opacity = 0.6
    ```

4. Plot the histogram:

    ```
    # Plot the values
    hist_apples = plt.bar(indices, apples, bar_width,
            alpha=opacity, color='g', label='Apples')

    hist_oranges = plt.bar(indices + bar_width, oranges, bar_width,
            alpha=opacity, color='b', label='Oranges')
    ```

5. Set the parameters of the plot:

    ```
    plt.xlabel('Month')
    plt.ylabel('Production quantity')
    plt.title('Comparing apples and oranges')
    ```

```
plt.xticks(indices + bar_width, ('Jan', 'Feb', 'Mar', 'Apr',
'May', 'Jun'))
plt.ylim([0, 45])
plt.legend()
plt.tight_layout()

plt.show()
```

6. The full code is in the `histogram.py` file that's already provided to you. If you run this code, you will see the following figure:

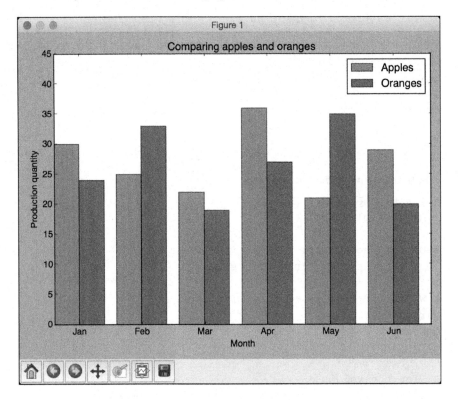

Visualizing heat maps

Let's look at how to visualize heat maps in this recipe. This is a pictorial representation of data where two groups are associated point by point. The individual values that are contained in a matrix are represented as color values in the plot.

How to do it...

1. Create a new Python file, and import the following packages:

    ```
    import numpy as np
    import matplotlib.pyplot as plt
    ```

2. Define the two groups:

    ```
    # Define the two groups
    group1 = ['France', 'Italy', 'Spain', 'Portugal', 'Germany']
    group2 = ['Japan', 'China', 'Brazil', 'Russia', 'Australia']
    ```

3. Generate a random 2D matrix:

    ```
    # Generate some random values
    data = np.random.rand(5, 5)
    ```

4. Create a figure:

    ```
    # Create a figure
    fig, ax = plt.subplots()
    ```

5. Create the heat map:

    ```
    # Create the heat map
    heatmap = ax.pcolor(data, cmap=plt.cm.gray)
    ```

6. Plot these values:

    ```
    # Add major ticks at the middle of each cell
    ax.set_xticks(np.arange(data.shape[0]) + 0.5, minor=False)
    ax.set_yticks(np.arange(data.shape[1]) + 0.5, minor=False)

    # Make it look like a table
    ax.invert_yaxis()
    ax.xaxis.tick_top()

    # Add tick labels
    ax.set_xticklabels(group2, minor=False)
    ax.set_yticklabels(group1, minor=False)

    plt.show()
    ```

7. The full code is in the `heatmap.py` file that's provided to you. If you run this code, you will see the following figure:

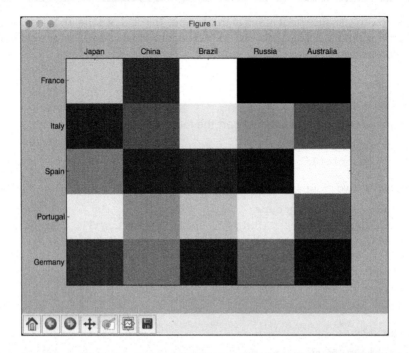

Animating dynamic signals

When we visualize real-time signals, it's nice to look at how the waveform builds up. In this recipe, we will see how to animate dynamic signals and visualize them as they are encountered in real time.

How to do it...

1. Create a new Python file, and import the following packages:

```
import numpy as np
import matplotlib.pyplot as plt
import matplotlib.animation as animation
```

2. Create a function to generate a damping sinusoid signal:

```
# Generate the signal
def generate_data(length=2500, t=0, step_size=0.05):
    for count in range(length):
        t += step_size
        signal = np.sin(2*np.pi*t)
```

```
    damper = np.exp(-t/8.0)
    yield t, signal * damper
```

3. Define an `initializer` function to initialize parameters of the plot:

```
# Initializer function
def initializer():
    peak_val = 1.0
    buffer_val = 0.1
```

4. Set these parameters:

```
    ax.set_ylim(-peak_val * (1 + buffer_val), peak_val * (1 +
buffer_val))
    ax.set_xlim(0, 10)
    del x_vals[:]
    del y_vals[:]
    line.set_data(x_vals, y_vals)
    return line
```

5. Define a function to draw the values:

```
def draw(data):
    # update the data
    t, signal = data
    x_vals.append(t)
    y_vals.append(signal)
    x_min, x_max = ax.get_xlim()
```

6. If the values go past the current X axis limits, then update and extend the graph:

```
    if t >= x_max:
        ax.set_xlim(x_min, 2 * x_max)
        ax.figure.canvas.draw()

    line.set_data(x_vals, y_vals)

    return line
```

7. Define the `main` function:

```
if __name__=='__main__':
    # Create the figure
    fig, ax = plt.subplots()
    ax.grid()
```

8. Extract the line:

```
    # Extract the line
    line, = ax.plot([], [], lw=1.5)
```

9. Create variables and initialize them to empty lists:

```
# Create the variables
x_vals, y_vals = [], []
```

10. Define and start the animation using the animator object:

```
# Define the animator object
animator = animation.FuncAnimation(fig, draw, generate_data,
        blit=False, interval=10, repeat=False, init_
func=initializer)

plt.show()
```

11. The full code is in the `moving_wave_variable.py` file that's already provided to you. If you run this code, you will see the following figure:

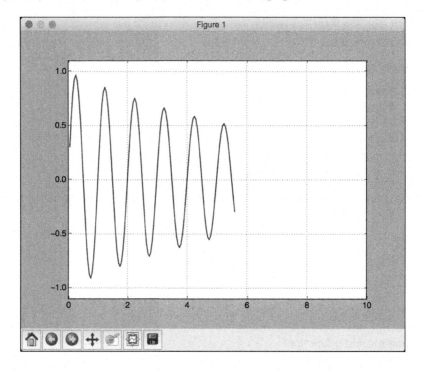

Index

Symbols

3D scatter plots
plotting 266

A

accuracy
evaluating, with cross-validation 38
AdaBoost 17
Adaptive Boosting technique
reference 221
Affinity Propagation 99
agglomerative clustering
about 88
reference 88
used, for grouping data 88-91
audio data
plotting 156, 157
reading 156, 157
audio signal
generating, custom parameters
used 160-162
transforming, into frequency
domain 158, 159

B

bag-of-words model
building 138-141
bicycle demand distribution
estimating 22-26
blind source separation
about 232
performing 232-235
reference 232

bubble plots
animating 269, 270
plotting 267, 268

C

canny edge detector
about 201
URL 201
cars
evaluating, based on characteristics 43-45
characters
visualizing, in optical character recognition
database 260, 261
chunking
about 137
used, for dividing text 137, 138
classifier
constructing 27, 28
class imbalance
tackling 64-66
clustering 77
clustering algorithms
performance, evaluating 91-95
color scheme options
reference 32
Computer Vision 195, 196
Conditional Random Fields (CRFs)
about 189
building, for sequential text data 189-191
confidence measurements
extracting 67, 68
confusion matrix
about 40
visualizing 40-42
corner detection 206, 207

cross-validation
  about 38
  used, for evaluating accuracy 38
customer segmentation model
  building 102-104
custom parameters
  used, for generating audio signals 160-162

D

data
  clustering, k-means algorithm used 78-80
  grouping, agglomerative clustering
      used 88-91
  preprocessing, different techniques used 2, 3
  preprocessing, tokenization used 132, 133
  preprocessing ways 3
  transforming, into time series
      format 174, 175
data preprocessing ways
  binarization 4
  mean removal 3
  normalization 4
  One Hot Encoding 5
  scaling 3
dataset
  similar users, finding 125-127
  splitting, for training and testing 36
dataset attributes
  buying 43
  doors 43
  lug_boot 43
  maint 43
  persons 43
  safety 43
data visualization 265
date-formatted time series data
  plotting 273, 274
DBSCAN algorithm
  about 95
  reference 95
  used, for estimating number of
      clusters 95-99
decision tree regressor 17
deep neural network
  building 250-254

Density-Based Spatial Clustering
      of Applications with Noise.
      See **DBSCAN algorithm**
dynamic signals
  animating 278-280

E

edge detection
  about 200
  performing 200-203
empty squares 58
epsilon 95
Euclidean distance score
  computing 122, 123
event predictor
  building 71-73
exemplars
  reference 99
Extremely Random Forests (ERFs)
  about 214
  reference 214
  used, for training image classifier 214-216
eye and nose detectors
  building 224, 225

F

face detector
  building, Haar cascades used 221-223
face recognition 219
face recognizer
  building, Local Binary Patterns Histograms
      used 236-241
features
  creating, visual codebook and vector
      quantization used 211-213
Fourier transforms
  URL 158
frequency domain
  audio signal, transforming 158, 159
  features, extracting 164-167
function compositions
  building, for data processing 106, 107

G

gender
identifying 144, 145
gradient descent
reference 251

H

Haar cascades
about 221
used, for face detection 221-223
Harris corner detector function
reference 206
heat maps
visualizing 277
hidden layers 243
Hidden Markov Models (HMMs)
about 185
building 167, 168
building, for sequential data 185-189
URL 167
used, for analyzing stock market
data 192, 193
hierarchical clustering 88
histogram equalization 204, 205
histograms
plotting 275
housing prices
estimating 17-19
hyperparameters 46
hypotrochoid 89

I

image classifier
training, Extremely Random Forests
used 214-216
images
compressing, vector quantization
used 81-85
operating, OpenCV-Python used 196-199
income bracket
estimating 52-54
inverse document frequency (IDF) 141, 144

K

Kernel Principal Components Analysis
performing 228-232
reference 228
k-means algorithm
about 78
reference 78
used, for clustering data 78-80
k-means clustering 213
k-nearest neighbors 113
k-nearest neighbors classifier
constructing 113-118
k-nearest neighbors regressor
constructing 119-121

L

label encoding 5, 6
Laplacian edge detector
about 200
URL 200
Latent Dirichlet Allocation (LDA)
about 152
reference 153
learning curves
about 50
extracting 50, 51
learning vector quantization (LVQ) neural
network 254
lemmatization
used, for converting text to base
form 135, 136
linear classifier
building, Support Vector Machine (SVMs)
used 56-61
linear regressor
building 7-10
Local Binary Patterns Histograms
about 236
reference 236
used, for building face recognizer 236-241
logistic regression classifier
building 30-34

M

machine learning pipelines
building 108-110
matplotlib
URL 2
Mean Shift
about 85
reference 85
Mean Shift clustering model
building 85-87
Mel Frequency Cepstral Coefficients (MFCC)
about 164
URL 164
model persistence
achieving 12
movie recommendations
generating 127-129
music
synthesizing 162-164
URL 162

N

Naïve Bayes classifier
about 35
building 35, 36
natural language processing (NLP) 131
Natural Language Toolkit (NLTK)
about 132
references 132
nearest neighbors
about 110
finding 110-112
neural networks
reference, for tutorial 244
used, for building optical character 262-264
NeuroLab
reference 244
neurons 243
nonlinear classifier
building, SVMs used 61-63
number of clusters
estimating automatically, DBSCAN algorithm
used 95-99
NumPy
URL 2

O

object recognizer
building 217, 218
OpenCV
about 196
URL 196
OpenCV-Python
used, for operating on images 196-199
optical character recognizer
building, neural networks used 262-264
optimal hyperparameters
searching 69, 70
Ordinary Least Squares 8

P

pandas
URL 174
patterns
finding, in stock market data 99-101
Pearson correlation score
computing 123-125
perceptron
about 244
building 244-246
performance report
extracting 42
pie charts
drawing 271, 272
Platt scaling
about 67
reference 67
polynomial regressor
building 15-17
predictive modeling 55, 56
Principal Components Analysis (PCA)
performing 227
reference 227
pystruct
reference 189
Python packages
matplotlib 2
NumPy 2
scikit-learn 2
SciPy 2

R

random forest regressor 22
recommendation engine 106
recurrent neural network
  building, for sequential data
        analysis 256-260
  reference 256
regression 7
regression accuracy
  computing 11, 12
  explained variance score 12
  mean absolute error 11
  mean squared error 11
  median absolute error 12
  R2 score 12
regularization 14
relative importance of features
  computing 20-22
Ridge Regression 14
ridge regressor
  building 13-15

S

Scale Invariant Feature Transform (SIFT) 208
SciPy
  URL 2
sentiment analysis
  about 146
  performing 146-149
SIFT feature points
  detecting 208, 209
Silhouette Coefficient score 91
simple classifier
  building 28-30
single layer neural network
  building 247, 249
sobel filter
  about 200
  URL 200
solid squares 58
speech recognizer
  about 155
  building 168-171

Star feature detector
  building 210, 211
statistics
  extracting, from time series data 182-185
stock market data
  analyzing, Hidden Markov Models
        used 192, 193
  patterns, finding in 99-101
Support Vector Machine (SVMs)
  references, for tutorials 56
  used, for building linear classifier 56-61
  used, for building nonlinear classifier 61-63

T

term frequency (TF) 141, 144
text
  converting, to base form with
        lemmatization 135, 136
  dividing, chunking used 137
  patterns, identifying with topic
        modeling 150-153
text analysis 131, 132
text classifier
  building 141-143
text data
  stemming 134, 135
tf-idf
  about 141
  URL 141
time series data
  about 173
  operating on 179-181
  slicing 176-178
  statistics, extracting from 182-185
time series format
  data, transforming into 174, 175
tokenization
  about 132
  used, for preprocessing data 132, 133
topic modeling
  about 150
  used, for identifying patterns in text 150-153
traffic
  estimating 74, 75

U

unsupervised learning 77

V

validation curves
extracting 46-49
vector quantization
about 81, 213, 254
reference 81, 213
used, for compressing image 81-85
used, for creating features 211-213
vector quantizer
creating 254, 255

video
capturing, from webcam 220, 221
processing, from webcam 220, 221
visual codebook
about 211
references 211
used, for creating features 211-214

W

weak learners 18
wholesale vendor and customers
reference 102

CPSIA information can be obtained
at www.ICGtesting.com
Printed in the USA
LVOW04s0041080517

33653LV00003B/23/P